DS 779.26

China's new democracy

DATE DUE

AUG 3 0 1991		
JUL 1 8 1993		

DEMCO 38-297

CHINA'S NEW DEMOCRACY
— with full texts of the three constitutions of the People's Republic of China

Qi Xin and others
Cosmos Books

Cosmos Books Ltd.
30 Johnston Road
Basement
HONG KONG

Copyright © Qi Xin, 1979
All Rights Reserved

Printed by:
Sun Fung Printing Co.
Block C, 14th Floor
Melbourne Industrial Building
16 Westlands Road
Quarry Bay
HONG KONG

North American Agent:
Chinese Periodical Distribution
716 N. Figueroa
Los Angeles, Ca. 90012
U.S.A.
Tel. (213)628-6858

FOREWORD

This book contains a selection of articles translated from *The Seventies Monthly (Qishi niandai yuekan)*, a Hong Kong based Chinese periodical that gives analysis of China, Taiwan and the international scene. The majority of the articles herein are written by the research group — Qi Xin. This group of journalists and scholars is already widely known to English readers through the books, *The Case of the Gang of Four* and *Teng Hsiao-ping: A Political Biography*, which contain articles on recent Chinese political events and important Chinese political figures.

The aim of this collection is to introduce western readers to some of the issues and arguments surrounding China's recent attempts to encourage democracy and legality. Traditionally lacking in a democratic background, following the feudal-fascist rule of Lin Biao and the Gang of Four during the Cultural Revolution, people throughout China, whether they be Communist Party leaders, workers or peasants, are now demanding a more democratic government and the protection of their constitutional rights. The first part of this book, entitled 'Democracy and Legality in the new New China', concentrates on the discussion of the socialist form of democracy (or 'democratic centralism'), the growth of an awareness for the need of democracy during the thirty years of the People's Republic and the present (1978) Constitution of China.

Many people associate the extremism and dogmatism of China in the past years with the Cultural Revolution (1966-76). However, the origins of such extreme 'leftism' are to be found rather in the nature of the Communist Party of China and the years of the Great Leap Forward (1957-9).

The second part of this book consists of articles by Qi Xin which attempt to analyze the major political trends in China from 1949—1978, the origins of extreme 'leftism' in the CPC and the reasons for the failures of the Cultural Revolution. The last article, 'China 1978 – from a new power struggle to the end of class struggle?', gives a detailed study of political developments in China during 1978 and the all-important events of the Third Plenum of the Eleventh Congress of the CPC at the end of 1978. Appendices include the three constitutions of the People's Republic, the CPC Party Constitution (1977) and Mao's *Talk to the 7,000*.

The Translators,
March 1979
Hong Kong

CONTENTS

Forward

Part I Democracy and Legality in the new New China

A Political Blueprint . . . . *Liu Chengyun*	1
Democracy and Democratic Centralism. . . . . *Liu Chengyun*	7
Democracy and the Legal System in Communist China . . . . *Jin Huang*	11
Towards Rule by Law— Comments on the Characteristics of the 1978 Constitution. . . . . *He Ming*	39
Democracy, Government by Law and the New Chinese Constitution. . *Zhu Yangmin*	51
Respect for Law —Reflections on a Small Incident at the Customs . . . . *Wu Qing*	71

Part II The Chinese Communist Party and the New Democracy

Proceeding from Reality . . . . *Qi Xin*	75
Demolishing the Myth of the Infallibility of Mao Zedong. . . . . *Qi Xin*	81
The 'Leftist' Ideological Trend in China . . . . *Qi Xin*	99
'Leftism' and the Cultural Revolution . . . . *Qi Xin*	127
China 1978—from a new power struggle to the end of class struggle? . . . . *Qi Xin*	137

Appendices:
- i) 1954 Constitution of the People's Republic of China 151
- ii) 1975 Constitution of the People's Republic of China 185
- iii) 1978 Constitution of the People's Republic of China 201
- iv) 1977 Constitution of the Communist Party of China 230
- v) Mao Zedong's Talk at an Enlarged Working Conference Convened by the Central Committee of the Communist Party of China (January 30, 1962) (The Talk to the 7000) 247
- vi) Comminique of the Third Plenary Session of the 11th Central Committee of the Communist Party of China (December 22, 1978) 279

PART ONE

Democracy and Legality

in

the new New China

A Political Blueprint

Liu Chengyun

Ever since the sixties the Chinese regime has been claiming to work for a political situation in which there will be "both centralism and democracy, both discipline and freedom, both unity of will and personal ease of mind and liveliness."

This situation is both an end in itself and a means to another end. The end is "to promote socialist revolution and socialist construction, make it easier to overcome difficulties, build a modern industry and modern agriculture more rapidly and make the Party and State more secure and better able to weather storm and stress."

The quotes are from Mao Zedong. He first put forth the idea of such a political situation in a speech made on February 27, 1957 entitled *On the Correct Handling of Contradictions Among the People*.[1]

"Our Constitution," he said, "lays it down that citizens of the People's Republic of China enjoy freedom of speech, the press, assembly, association, procession, demonstration, religious belief and so on. Our Constitution also provides that the organs of state must practice democratic centralism, that they must rely on the masses and that their personnel must serve the people. Our socialist democracy is the broadest kind of democracy, such as is not to be found

---

[1] see *Selected Works of Mao Tsetung Vol. V*, Foreign Languages Press, Peking, pp. 384–421.

2 *China's New Democracy*

in any bourgeois state. . . . But this freedom is freedom under leadership and this democracy is democracy under centralized guidance, not anarchy. . . . Both democracy and freedom are relative, not absolute, and they come into being and develop in specific historical conditions. Within the ranks of the people, democracy is correlative with centralism and freedom with discipline. . . . This unity of democracy and centralism, of freedom and discipline, constitutes our democratic centralism. Under this system, the people enjoy broad democracy and freedom, but at the same time they have to keep within the bounds of socialist discipline."

The words were probably directed at some people who wanted China to adopt western democracy. For in an earlier speech made on November 15, 1956 he said, "A few cadres with an intellectual background at the level of department or bureau head advocated great democracy. . . Their 'great democracy' means the adoption of the bourgeois parliamentary system of the West and the imitation of such western stuff as 'parliamentary democracy' and 'freedom of the press' and 'freedom of speech.' "

Eight months later on July 9, 1957, in a speech entitled *Beat Back the Attacks of the Bourgeois Rightists*,[2] Mao said, "I believe most of our people are fine people and the Chinese nation is a fine nation. Ours is a nation which is very sensible, warm-hearted, intelligent and courageous. I hope a situation will be created in which we have both unity of will and liveliness, that is, both centralism and democracy, both discipline and freedom."

He could have envisaged such a political situation to suit the needs of the anti-Rightist campaign then under way. But the idea did not vanish with the conclusion of the campaign. At an Enlarged Working Conference of the Communist Party Central Committee in 1962 he elucidated the idea further, "I said in 1957 that we should create 'a political situation in which we have both centralism and democracy, both discipline and freedom, both unity of will and personal ease of mind and liveliness.' We should create such

---

2 Ibid., pp. 457–72.

A Political Blueprint   3

a political situation both inside and outside the Party. Otherwise it will be impossible to arouse the enthusiasm of the masses. . . . Without democracy there can't be correct centralism because centralism can't be established when people have divergent views and don't have unity of understanding. What is meant by centralism? First, there must be concentration of correct ideas. Unity of understanding, of policy, plan, command and action is attained on the basis of concentrating correct ideas. This is unity through centralism. . . . Without democracy, without ideas coming from the masses, it is impossible to formulate good lines, principles, policies or methods. As far as the formulation of lines, principles, policies and methods is concerned, our leading organs merely play the role of a processing plant. . . . Unless we fully promote people's democracy and inner-Party democracy and unless we fully implement proletarian democracy, it will be impossible for China to have true proletarian centralism. Without a high degree of democracy it is impossible to have a high degree of centralism, and without a high degree of centralism it is impossible to establish a socialist economy."

I have quoted Mao Zedong at length because the Chinese leaders seem to regard such a situation, which embodies three sets of paradoxical phenomena, as a political blueprint. Since 1962 the "six phenomena" have frequently appeared in *People's Daily* editorials and other important documents. They appeared in Hua Guofeng's *Political Report* at the 11th Party Congress,[3] Ye Jianying's *Report on the Revision of the Party Constitution*,[4] in the revised Party Constitution, in the most recently revised Constitution of the People's Republic of China and Ye Jianying's report on the revision of that Constitution. Clearly the present Communist leadership has not given up the political blueprint set forth

[3] See *The Eleventh National Congress of The Communist Party of China (Documents)*, Foreign Languages Press, Peking 1977, pp. 1–113.

[4] See *Documents of the First Session of the Fifth National People's Congress of the People's Republic of China*, Foreign Languages Press, Peking 1978.

by Mao in 1957. It therefore merits our attention.

We who have never lived in a socialist society find it hard to imagine such a situation. Taken as a whole it seems to represent an ideal collective life in which everyone contributes his share selflessly for the good of the whole. The people present their ideas and suggestions to the leaders, the leaders put the ideas and suggestions together and work out certain policies from them. Then everyone gives up his own ideas and interests and works together with others to carry out these policies. Since no one harbors selfish ideas and all understand and help one another, work is carried out not only with unity of will but in a lively atmosphere. Such a political situation is far superior to the democratic system in the capitalist society in which every person works for his private interests. It is infinitely superior to the political systems of feudalism, autocracy or dictatorship.

The "six phenomena" situation is no doubt an ideal blueprint. But in analyzing it we must examine the component parts and see if, put together, they can achieve the desired effect.

Take democracy. The meaning of the term as used by Mao Zedong is quite different from that used in the West. It is the same with the term freedom. What Mao meant by freedom was only the freedom to express different opinions. As for the other freedoms mentioned in the Constitution — freedom of the press, assembly, association, procession, demonstrtation and religion — to attain them the people must have the right to incorporate their different ideas in different organizations, whether short term ones or long term ones. Once there are such organizations then the ideas represented by one organization will not be easily incorporated in another organization holding different ideas. In the West freedom of association results in party politics. In China most of the political parties are left from pre-liberation days. Does dictatorship of the proletariat permit the formation of new political parties, allow them to take in new members and run newspapers propagating their ideas? If this is permitted, does it run counter to the principles of discipline, centralism, unity of will?

A Political Blueprint 5

Questions like these show that the task to find definitions for the six terms, examine the conditions needed to satisfy the definitions, and then study how to create the conditions, is an arduous but meaningful task.

It is not the purpose of this article to attempt such a study here. Here I only wish to point out the contradiction between the "six phenomena" and struggle.

Let us take a count of the large-scale struggles the Chinese Communist Party has carried out since 1949 in order to rapidly transform an essentially feudal society into a socialist society, to rectify the Party's work style and keep to a correct political line. They are:

1950 — Land reform
1951—1952— The "Three Anti" and "Five Anti" Movements
1955 — Gao-Rao Incident
1957 — Anti Rightist Campaign
1959 — Peng Dehuai Incident
1965 — Criticism of Luo Ruiqing and Wu Han
1966 — Cultural Revolution begins
1971 — Lin Biao Incident
1974 — Criticism of Lin Biao and Confucius
1976 — Criticism of Deng Xiaoping
   Criticism of the Gang of Four

The above shows that in nearly 30 years there had been an average of one important struggle every three years, the longest being the Cultural Revolution. Whether the struggles were power struggles as some people claim or two-line struggles as the Chinese Party calls them, whether the struggles were between two antagonistic forces or were contradictions among the people, the fact remains that a characteristic of the Chinese political scene since liberation has been ceaseless struggle. A political situation of struggle is incompatible with the "six phenomena" situation.

Why? The very existence of struggle proves that ideas have not been centralized and that views have remained disunified. A great many acts in violation of the law and the Party Constitution during the struggles shows that discipline has been destroyed. Since there has been no unity of will, there couldn't have been personal ease of mind and liveliness. A lot of the changes made during the struggles shows that many people have been extremely selfish. In a word, the very occurrence of struggle has destroyed the "six phenomena" situation.

This contradiction between the "six phenomena" situation and struggle is primarily a political problem that China has yet to solve. The most recently revised Constitution of the Chinese Communist Party continues to stress the existence of class contradiction and class struggle in the long historical period of socialist society and holds that the contradiction "can only be solved by the theory and practice of continuing the revolution under the dictatorship of the proletariat." In other words, the Chinese Communist Party has not given up struggles as a means of ruling. Yet the same Constitution calls for an effort to create a "six phenomena" political situation. Since the two are mutually contradictory the Chinese Communist Party must make its choice — either to create a "six phenomena" situation or solve problems through struggle.

Democracy and Democratic Centralism

Liu Chengyun

At discussions comparing western democracy and socialist democracy one often hears the argument that the western democratic system, which is characterized mainly by general elections held regularly to decide which candidates and parties shall form government, is bourgeois in character and is therefore fake democracy; and that democratic centralism as practiced under socialism is real democracy. This argument regards both popular elections and democratic centralism as methods or processes for realizing democracy, except that the former is not effective while the latter is. Actually the western system of democracy based on general elections and the principles of democratic centralism have entirely different purposes. Many people mistakenly believe the two are the same.

Some people may argue that the Constitution of the People's Republic of China clearly states: "The People's Congresses at all levels and all other organs of state practice democratic centralism," that the Constitution of the Communist Party of China also states explicitly: "The Party is organized on the principles of democratic centralism." Since China regards democratic centralism as a method for practicing socialist democracy, their argument goes on, it can certainly be equated with the western democratic system. Some may even say it is superior to the western system.

I would like to offer some different views.

The purpose of periodic general elections is to ensure

that the people of a country will have a certain power of control over the persons and party in power. This power of control consists at least of the following: (1) The candidates and parties running for election must present a program which would appeal to the voters in order to get their votes. (2) When the people or parties in power fail to satisfy the voters, after a few years the voters can elect some other people or parties. Under conditions of freedom of speech a politician or party cannot cheat the voters for a long time or get re-elected after having disappointed the voters. Thus periodic general elections give the people a certain degree of control over those in power provided the latter do not resort to forcible repression. If democracy means the people have the final say and can control the persons and parties in power, then periodic general elections are a means toward achieving democracy.

The aim of democratic centralism is not to give the people control over persons or parties in power. It is to enable an organization to function effectively. In his report on revising the Party's Constitution at the 11th Party Congress held in August 1977, Ye Jianying said: "It is imperative to strengthen Party discipline in order to ensure our Party's unity of action." In the chapter on the Organizational System of the Party, the draft stresses, "The whole Party must observe democratic centralism discipline: The individual is subordinate to the organization, the minority is subordinate to the majority, the lower level is subordinate to the higher level, and the entire Party is subordinate to the Central Committee." He could not have put it more clearly "democratic centralism is Party discipline, the aim of which is to ensure the Party's unity of action." Ye also explained what is meant by "democracy" in "democratic centralism": ". . . we should settle controversial issues among the people by the democratic method, that is, by the method of discussion, criticism, persuasion and education and not by the method of coercion or repression." Democracy here clearly does not mean that the people should have the final say but that those in power should take an enlightened attitude and refrain from using

Democracy and Democratic Centralism 9

coercion.

To sum up, the aim of periodic general elections is democracy — people having control over those in power. The aim of democratic centralism is unity of action, and democracy — an enlightened attitude — is a means to that unity. Hence, while we assert that the class character of western periodic general elections prevents them from achieving the goal of democracy — the people having the final say — we cannot prove thereby that democratic centralism is superior, because the aim of democratic centralism has never been democracy, whether in the sense that the people have the final say or in the sense of an enlightened attitude.

Although the aims of periodic general elections and democratic centralism are quite different, as methods they are not entirely different. Elections are an indispensable step in practicing democratic centralism. Elections determine both the different levels of authority and the majority-minority relationship. Both the Constitution of the People's Republic and the Constitution of the Chinese Communist Party have provided for periodic congresses which require the election of delegates to attend them. Thus, periodic elections are a necessary part of the process of democratic centralism. The difference between this periodic election and the periodic elections in the West, apart from aims, also lies in election procedures such as the way candidates are nominated, the difference between the number of candidates and the number of those elected, election campaign activities, the difference between direct election (as in the west) and indirect election (as on the Chinese mainland). The difference in election procedures may well stem from the different aims of elections.

Just as the practice of democratic centralism includes periodic general elections, the periodic general elections of the west also include elements of democratic centralism, such as majority rule, free discussion and criticism, and the principle that the whole Party must obey the executive Central Committee. But as discipline in western political parties is usually lax, votes are often cast across party lines and candidates sometimes withdraw from their parties to enter an election independently.

Because elements of the two systems often overlap, we should not regard them as two entirely different systems and try to decide which is better. If we reject periodic general elections, we are not only rejecting the western system of election but also parts of the system of democratic centralism. If we regard democratic centralism as a perfect system, then we must admit that the western system of periodic general elections has merits too.

In conclusion then, democratic centralism is not superior to periodic general elections, nor vice versa. The aims of the two systems are totally different. If a regime wishes to practice western democracy it should adopt the system of periodic general elections and all the democratic measures arising from them. If a regime's aim is as Mao Zedong said,". . . to create a political situation in which we have both centralism and democracy, both discipline and freedom, both unity of will and personal ease of mind and liveliness, and thus to promote our socialist revolution and socialist construction, make it easier to overcome difficulties, build a modern industry and modern agriculture more rapidly and make our Party and state more secure and better able to weather storm and stress," then, Ye Jianying said, "so long as we earnestly practice democratic centralism, give full scope to democracy and exercise centralism on the basis of extensive democracy, we can certainly create the political situation Chairman Mao spoke of."

We who live overseas should understand the difference between the two systems and should not, because of our own preference for the western type of democracy, impose the aims of western society on the Chinese mainland, and insist that democratic centralism is a means to achieve these aims. For in so doing we will be overrating the western system of democracy and underrating democratic centralism.

Democracy and the Legal System in Communist China

Jin Huang

A focus of attention inside and outside China after the Cultural Revolution started has been democracy and the legal system. And from the many depressing disclosures which have been made public since the Gang of Four's ouster detailing how they had dumped democracy, stamped out liberty and wrecked the legal system, the whole system of laws in Communist China is now being seriously questioned. Several crucial questions are being asked, such as:

How much democracy is there for the people inside China? How can the people exercise effective supervision over officials whom they have not directly elected? What is the position of the law under the dictatorship of the proletariat? And as everything is under Communist Party leadership, what guarantees are there that everything the Communist Party decides on conforms to the interests of the vast majority of people? What happens when the situation becomes abnormal inside the Communist Party, such as when the Gang of Four was in power? Had the people in that case handed over their destiny to an errant political party?

I am not a political commentator and I too am assailed by many doubts. I have no satisfactory answer, but from what I saw and heard in my 24 years living in Hunan Province, I have got a few ideas.

Democracy in the Army

There never has been full democracy in any army,

12 China's New Democracy

neither in China nor anywhere else. Nor is there much freedom. Everyone knows that. In an army orders have to be obeyed, on pain of death. But in the Chinese Communist army, ever since its founding, there has been what is known as the "Three Democracies", that is, economic democracy, political democracy and military democracy. In the winter-spring of 1946–47 the Chinese Communist Party Central Committee issued a proclamation to the whole army to use the time it was not fighting to consolidate its ranks through a movement to implement the "Three Democracies." Then after the People's Republic was established in 1949 the Chinese Communists applied their experience in implementing the "Three Democracies" to all departments throughout the country.

The content of the "Three Democracies" is: economic democracy, in which the rank-and-file elect representatives who are empowered to assist the company leadership in managing the company's supplies and mess; political democracy, this means the right of the rank-and-file soldiers to expose and criticise the errors and misdeeds of officers, violations of "The Three Main Rules of Discipline and the Eight Points for Attention."[1]

The rank-and-file communist soldier has always had the right to speak out freely and criticise mistakes of their officers during army rectification meetings, and even have serious offenders removed from their posts. Occasional cases of beatings and forcing soldiers to knee[1] on bricks for hours on end and other forms of physical punishment have been reported. But after the offending commanders have made sincere self-criticisms they are forgiven by the men and unity is achieved

---

[1] The Three Main Rules of Discipline are: Obey orders in all your actions; don't take a single needle or piece of thread from the masses; turn in everything captured. *The Eight Points of Attention* are: Speak politely; pay fairly for what you buy; return everything you borrow; pay for anything you damage; don't hit people or swear at people; don't damage crops; don't take liberties with women; and don't ill-treat captives.

Democracy and the Legal System in Communist China 13

between officers and men and the combat effectiveness of the army is increased. After the "Three Democracies" movement commanders were said to "love their men as sons" and to have taken good care of their men. These officers, after mending their ways, were always the first in assault parties and the last to leave in rearguard actions. During the rectification, the rank and file make criticisms, but they also make self-criticisms in which they examine their own actions and thinking. This has led to better discipline and higher morale.

With regard to military democracy, it has two aspects: One, there is mutual instruction between officers and soldiers during military training; two, meetings of the rank and file are called before an imminent action to discuss ways and means to ensure its success. After discussions have hardened into a plan everyone of the combatants then knows what he is expected to do and how to do it. This was responsible for the success of many operations. The soldiers called these meetings "Zhuge Liang sessions". [2]

In an article entitled *Chinese Communist Law during the Land Reform Movement*[3], I dealt briefly with the leadership role of the Chinese Communists in the land reform movement which took place right after the defeat of the Guomindang armies. Through the land reform the peasants were taught what was democracy and what was freedom and how to use democracy for their ends. The peasants also learned to "speak bitterness" (recall the sufferings they had been made to endure in the past) and through study sessions and taking part in "struggle meetings" (mass meetings for recounting the crimes of their former oppressors and exploiters) the peasants came to understand why and how to fight the landlords. In this way people's power was established in the rural areas. Democracy and freedom were not abstract terms. They were very real. The peasants could then speak and decide what they wanted from life, while the counter-

---

[2] Zhuge Liang was a statesman and strategist in the period of the Three Kingdoms (221-265), who has become a symbol of resourcefulness and wisdom in Chinese folklore.

[3] See *The Seventies* (Chinese), August 1977.

revolutionaries and other bad elements were deprived of this freedom. For them, it was not democracy, but the dictatorship of the proletariat.

Four "Unfree's"

During the land reform even the poor and lower-middle peasants did not enjoy unlimited freedom. Imagine what would have happened if there was no discipline and every poor and lower-middle peasant took it into his head to walk into a landlord's house and take what he liked and "freely" shared the landlord's land. That would have led to confused squabbling and fighting among the peasants. They would not have been able to crush the landlord class's resistance. To this end, the peasants had to have a common understanding, a common policy and work together in harmony under the leadership of their Peasants' Association and, in accordance with the land reform policy of the Communists, expropriate landlord property in an orderly fashion and share the land and property among themselves. And to safeguard the longterm interests of the people, the property and interests of the industrialists, businessmen and professionals such as doctors and teachers and other non-supporters of the feudal system were protected. This was one "non-freedom" or restraint which was placed on the people.

During the time when mutual-aid teams and agricultural co-operatives were being set up sections of the peasantry, particularly the middle peasants, (mainly the well-off middle peasants) did not feel very "free." They could see that pooling manpower and resources brought higher yields and if they did not join then they would miss out. If they joined, however, they were afraid the poor and lower-middle peasants would encroach upon their interests. They were also afraid that production would suffer through too many people getting together. They also did not like the discipline they would have to submit to once they joined a group. Nor did they like being prevented from getting something from the collective for nothing. They felt that their acquisitiveness, their wanting to make good at the expense of others, was being restricted. They were not accustomed to owning things collectively. Somehow or other, they felt that their "freedom" was being curtailed and thus they did not feel "free." This was another "non-freedom".

I want to go on to write about the situation when I myself did not feel "free."

I am a Hakka man and have an ingrained aversion to physical labour of any kind. It so happened that in 1957 when I went back to work after recovering from TB the cadres were all asked to take part in physical labour. I was only a minor administration clerk in the Health Bureau of Changsha, but I was very afraid of being asked to go and work, doing physical labour somewhere. At that time everyone was saying at study sessions how much they would like to remould their ideology through physical labour in the countryside. Liu Zhengjie, the head of our Health Bureau, started the ball rolling. He collected night-soil in the neighbourhood, cleaned out the public lavatories and swept the streets. The press, radio, and public address system of the Bureau were daily and hourly commending such cadres and also criticising those who were reluctant to do physical labour. I felt the pressure strongly. I could not bring myself to say that I hated physical exertion. I felt as though I was being "forced." I was being pressured to do physical labour. I really felt I had "no freedom."

Then the Communists wanted cadres to go down to the countryside to become peasants. The Health Bureau approved two Communist Party members' application and then called on for others to follow suit. The walls of our bureau were soon covered with applications and expressions of determination written in bold characters. I was very uneasy. I wondered if I too should put in an application asking the Party branch to approve of my going to the countryside. I was very troubled. It was a most trying time. If I applied and was accepted, I was afraid for my health. If I did not "express willingness" to go, I was afraid the others would look down on me. I was also afraid of giving my leadership a bad impression. I wrote and scrapped several applications before I finally mustered up enough courage to write one and take it to the office of the Party branch. When I got to the door I hesitated for a long while. I did not feel at all "free." Finally I mustered some courage and walked in with the application. The Bureau Head Liu read it and said he approved of my action. But then he went on to point out that it took time to get used to working with one's hands and that one should not be over-zealous and that one must also consider the individual's state of health. He turned down my application. I felt a big burden lifted off me. But at the same time I made up my mind to get myself into good physical shape. When, later, I got over my fears, I felt quite "free." Anyway, that was a third form of "non-freedom."

The fourth instance concerns a very highly qualified doctor in the infectious diseases hospital in Changsha. He knew several languages and he worked hard to make a name and fortune. When he felt he could handle most types of diseases met with in the hospital he demanded to be sent to the Hunan Provincial Medical School to do research. He was not given permission. The hospital wanted him to stay and help them find better ways to cure some of the diseases. He was terribly disappointed. He felt there were no spectacular successes to be had working in the hospital. He grew slack in his work and buried himself in his books. Colleagues pointed out to him that that was not the way to behave and patients and their immediate relatives grew dissatisfied with his work. The doctor felt there was "no freedom." After a while, through help from colleagues and through political study sessions, he slowly came to see that he was not desirous of really serving the people but was out to make a name for himself. He also saw that the work he was asked to do directly benefited the people. With this realisation he grew happier and took a more responsible attitude towards his work and then he felt much "freer."

The above four instances of persons feeling that they were "not free" have almost been experienced by nearly

Democracy and the Legal System in Communist China 17

everyone on the mainland at one time or another. They are the result of the Chinese Communists curbing backward tendencies and establishing a new ethic among the people. In doing so tremendous social pressure is brought to bear on people to see that serving the people, regardless of the work one is called upon to do, is an honourable and proper way of life. In China no one dares say publicly that he refuses to serve the people or will not take part in physical labour or take the socialist path, because it has been established in people's minds that not to do so is anti-social. It is an enormous strain for people unwilling to serve the people to live in such an environment because even the merest sign of this anti-social thinking revealed in an unguarded moment invites immediate censure or a swift rebuke. If someone who has been heard uttering such unthinkable things does something wrong, then when a mass movement comes along that person can expect others to suspect him of purposely making that mistake. He will be investigated, people will put up big character posters about him. He might even be hauled before a mass meeting and criticised. Even his immediate relatives will criticise him. He will find no sympathy anywhere. There simply is no room for anyone unwilling to follow the revolution and wants to remain "free" to be backward. There is no freedom in China for holding back social progress.

The above has nothing in common with infringement of civil rights or violating the law because the Chinese Constitution of 1954 stipulates that capitalist enterprises and commercial undertakings and individuals farming for themselves and handicraftsmen working on their own all have to be reformed. This of course includes reforming their incorrect ways of thinking as well as emancipating them from their backward ideological heritage. This is enforcing, not violating, socialist laws.

The Chinese Constitution clearly lays down that there are no civil liberties for landlords, rich peasants, counter-revolutionaries and other bad elements, only the dictatorship of the proletariat. These people are not free to say or do what they like.

The Gang of Four exploited the "Big Democracy," that is, the right to air one's views freely, put up big character posters, hold big debates and so on, of the Cultural Revolution to create counter-revolutionary opinion. The Gang charged everyone from Premier Zhou Enlai down to the lowest echelon cadres in communes as "capitalist-roaders" in an attempt to take in the masses and overthrow the cadres so as to seize Party and state power. The Gang was a bunch of new and old counter-revolutionaries. So, of course, they have now been deprived of their freedom. People have tried to exploit the arrest of Yang Xiguang[4] of Hunan Province to claim that the Chinese Communists hold human rights in contempt. Yang was responsible for drafting the *Declaration of the Hunan Provincial Great Alliance Proletarian Revolutionary Committee* which claimed that upwards of 90 per cent of the Communist cadres were "Red capitalists," the C. P. C. was a "new bureaucracy," "a new exploiting, oppressing class," and so on. These absurd charges are exactly the charges which Wang Hongwen, Zhang Chunqiao, Jiang Qing and Yao Wenyuan made when this gang claimed that the majority of leading cadres were "capitalist-roaders." I worked in Hunan for twenty-four years and though I was only a very minor clerk I did have opportunities

---

[4] I was in Changsha when Yang Xiguang was apprehended and I know something about this case. Yang was formerly a pupil of the No. 1 Middle School in Changsha and had spearheaded the attack against Premier Zhou Enlai in the early days of the Cultural Revolution. His mother was a deputy chairman of the Hunan Trades Union and had been a secretary of Zhou Enlai's in Yenan. After Yang was arrested, his mother Chen Su committed suicide. Yang's father was Yang Dipu, formerly Secretary General of the Hunan Party Committee. He was demoted for opposing the Great Leap Forward, the General Line and People's Communes and posted to head the province's agricultural development bureau. He had meticulously implemented Liu Shaoqi's line during the "Four Clean-up" movement and had made himself extremely unpopular for attacking many cadres, workers and students harshly. He was also born of an exploiting family. I think Yang Xiguang should have been arrested for anarchist activities but whether the sentence is too heavy for someone of his age is debatable.

to visit a lot of places and to meet cadres of many ranks. I don't think one can accuse Party cadres of being exploiters and oppressors of the people. Most of them really worked hard and did their best to serve the people, but then again, they were not all angels, and they had their faults. But to condemn all merely because they had some faults or shortcomings is not quite fair.

Violations of the Legal System

According to my own experience the Chinese Communists do take a serious view of socialist democracy and the law. But it cannot be denied that their legal system is far from perfect. There are many instances when the legal system is not enforced. This generally happens in the following four circumstances:

First, due to bureaucratic style of some leading cadres. Between the autumn of 1964 and the spring of 1965, Tao X, a woman deputy head of Changsha County, selected Meihua Brigade of the Meihua People's Commune to *dundian* (to live, direct work and gather experience at a grassroots unit.) The Hunan Provincial Party Committee had been asked by the Central Committee of the C. P. C. to get Changsha County to turn a part of its paddy acreage into double-cropping ricefields and popularize an improved rice strain. This was quite revolutionary, for never had Hunan grown two crops of rice in one year, so naturally some of the peasants were hesitant when they were asked to grow two crops. According to the mass line customarily practiced by the Chinese Communists, painstaking work should have been carried out first to persuade the peasants to accept this novel idea. This generally involved setting up trial or demonstration plots to enable people to see for themselves the advantages of the new system. But Tao simply ordered the production brigades to set aside a part of their land for growing two rice crops that year. This meant doubling the rice acreage and hence using much more manure. Tao thereupon ordered last year's rice stalks chopped up and ploughed into the mud to form the extra manure. She did not take into account the fact that stalks in central Hunan were used as cooking fuel. Without these stalks the peasants would have no fuel to cook their meals, let alone fuel to keep warm in winter. This caused much hardship for the members of the brigades.

The Changsha Party Committee ordered the rice sown earlier than usual, well before the date for sowing indicated by the ancient agricultural calender. As luck would have it, it began to rain. It rained for several days on and there was even some hail. This threatened to hold up the sowing. But Tao ordered the sowing to be done within the time planned. The result was that 70 per cent of the seeds rotted in the fields. With no more of the improved rice strain left in the county, the best grain from the granaries was commandeered for seed. That year, the average yield per *mu* was 580 catties, 80 more than normal. Tao was delighted. "If we're to revolutionize farming," she said, "we've got to apply some pressure."

Tao's high-handedness and despotic method of work made her highly unpopular among cadres and peasants alike. She was behaving like a boss of the old days. She simply tossed aside socialist, comradely equality in work. Her behaviour was unpardonable because the production brigades and production teams are collectively owned, so the state has no right to issue orders to them. This is clearly laid down in the *Sixty Points* the Communist Party had worked out for the rural areas. This, however, is how the peasants look at it: (a) It was right for the county leadership to popularize the improved rice and introduce double-cropping to get higher yields. It could help the county get in 800 catties per *mu* and thus better the figure set down in the National Programme[5] and, (b) If the commune members had farmed more meticulously and not negligently added to by all the labour and manure they had put into the two crops,

---

[5] The *National Programme for Agricultural Development* set grain yield targets for different areas of the country, as:- 200 kilogrammes per *mu* for areas north of the Yellow River; 250 kilogrammes

Democracy and the Legal System in Communist China 21

there should have been a return of at least 150 catties more rice per *mu*. The commune members conceded that Tao worked hard, running here and there, rain or shine, driving herself 14 to 15 hours a day. She had even loaned a part of her salary to some brigades to buy manure, and although she was in her thirties and a mother she seldom found time to go home. In Xintian County and in my own home of Jiaoling County in Guangdong Province there are many cadres like Tao. During the Cultural Revolution the peasants criticised cadres like Tao for violating democracy and the law and depriving them of democratic rights.

Second, people in power usurping the name of the Central Committee and issuing orders which were undemocratic and violated the legal system. I shall give two instances to illustrate this point.

(a) When the Chinese Communists began their socialist education movement in the rural areas in 1963 (also known as the "Four Clean"), Mao Zedong drew up a Ten Point policy (the so-called *Early Ten Points*) which clearly stated that the target of the movement were those in authority in the Party taking the capitalist road (capitalist-roaders) and that most of the cadres were good and only a small number were bad. Liu Shaoqi, however, without the knowledge of the Central Committee drew up another Ten Point policy (*Later Ten Points*) which claimed that most of the rural cadres were bad and should be severely worked over and the experience of the work team at Taoyuan[6] should be taken as the model. This "Taoyuan Model" advocated ruthless struggle

---

per *mu* for areas south of the Yellow River and north of the Huai River; 400 kilogrammes per *mu* for areas south of the Huai River and the Jinjing Mountains and the Bailong River. To surpass the 200 kg. target is described as "crossing the Yellow River" and to exceed the 400-kg. target as "crossing the Yangtze River."

[6] The *Taoyuan Experience*. In 1963, when Mao called on the whole nation to start the socialist education movement in both town and countryside, Liu Shaoqi sent a work team with his wife as the leader to Hobei Province's Taoyuan Brigade. Her experience there was summed up for all work teams to follow.

against rural cadres. Many provinces then sent out work teams to conduct the movement according to Liu's *Ten Points*. In the name of the Central Committee they mobilised the masses and gave the rural cadres hell. Those who had no stomach for this had grave charges levelled at them. Quite a few rural cadres were driven to take their own lives. In counties which closely followed Liu's *Ten Points* large numbers of cadres, particularly those from exploiting class families, or who had worked in pre-liberation days, or who had made mistakes at work, and even high school and primary school teachers were ruthlessly purged. When Mao Zedong found out, Liu Shaoqi was severely criticised inside the Central Committee and it was reaffirmed that the majority of the rural cadres were either good or relatively good. Those who had made grave mistakes should be taught to see their errors and the method used with these people should be the method of "curing the disease to save the patient." They should be given help to see where and why they went wrong and given a chance to change. As for those who were incorrigible, they were only a "tiny handful." Mao then helped draw up the *Resolution on Some Questions Related to the Socialist Revolution in the Rural Areas* (the *Twenty Points*). In the counties where the *"Four Clean"* was heavily influenced by the Liu Shaoqi line quite a number of cadres and teachers lost their jobs and their posts were taken by others. They received no compensation for their lost jobs and salaries, although according to the spirit of the Constitution these people should have been compensated.

(b) Lin Biao and the Gang of Four also exploited the prestige of and upsurped the name of the Central Committee during the Cultural Revolution for their own nefarious purposes. For example, Lin Biao promulgated *Six Points for Public Security Work* to boost his image and wreck the guidelines for public security work. People who had worked in the old society, or who had been pressganged into the Guomindang (KMT) armies, as well as intellectuals were all treated as "bad elements." People who came from exploiting class families were all classified as hostile elements and dictatorship was exercised on them. Even veteran Communist cadres who had once been imprisoned by their Guomindang enemies were branded "traitors", "turncoats" and "enemy agents" and made the targets of the dictatorship of the proletariat. These were serious violations of the Constitution. Those over whom the dictatorship should be exercised are clearly stated in the Constitution. They are very few, only landlords, rich peasants, counter-revolutionaries and other bad elements. But the *Six Points* of Lin Biao listed no less than 21 categories of people subject to the dictatorship.

Third, the narrow class outlook of those unable to take into consideration the longer-term interests of the working people and the demands of social progress also contributed largely to wrecking the socialist legal system.

Take the way intellectuals were treated. The intellectuals from the old society have their ideological shortcomings, but the Communists' policy of "uniting, educating and remoulding" their world outlook has been effective to varying degrees. Intellectuals have done many good things for the people. They have made contributions in science, technology and culture. But a lot of the working people recall with bitterness how many intellectuals in the old days had taken part in exploiting them and they resented the intellectuals born of exploiting families and former members of the Guomindang enjoying a higher standard of living than they. This is an expression of egalitarianism current in the thinking of many who ignore present economic realities. Unfortunately, this way of looking at things is rather widespread and deeply ingrained. During the Cultural Revolution Lin Biao and the Gang of Four made out that they were very, very revolutionary and fuelled this narrow class bigotry and exploited it for their own ends and caused enormous harm.

Complexity of Mass Movements

I know from personal experience that every time the Chinese Communists start a nationwide mass movement there are invevitably excesses at first. The Communists know this themselves and do not immediately try to curb it. During the preliminary stages they want to build up the momentum for the movement, not to dampen the ardour of the masses. For instance, at the start of the land reform landlords were sometimes beaten and abused. It happened during the start of the Three Anti and the Five Anti[7] movements in the early 1950s. Confessions were extorted and believed, and also during the Three Anti movement (to weed out counter-revolutionaries), suspects were hauled before mass meetings and charged with this and that and put into solitary confinement, and suffered cruel and harsh treatment. But in the second stage of every movement, when the masses are more or less fully aroused, the Communists then organise group studies of their policies to teach the masses to understand the aim of the current movement and how to correctly apply these policies and differentiate between the true and false, the worse offenders and the lesser offenders, the chief culprit and the accomplices, and so on. At this stage the masses begin to feel not so "free." But they quickly adjust themselves to the new demands and the movement moves into the third and final stage. At this stage policies are strictly adhered to, each case is calmly and objectively appraised and carefully studied and a verdict arrived at on the basis of established facts and valid evidence. The time, the place and other evidence have to be corroborated by at least two people before a case is established against the defendant. People who should not have been charged or "struggled" against in the first place are exonerated and given a public apology. Cao Ying,

---

[7] *Three Anti* and *Five Anti*. In 1952 there were two movements, the first was the *Three Anti*, which was directed against corruption, waste and bureaucracy in Communist Party and government organisations and state enterprises. This was followed by the *Five Anti* movement against bribery of state officials, tax evasion, theft of state property, cheating on government contracts and stealing economic information for speculation which were quite widespread among private industrial and commercial enterprises at that time.

first secretary of the Party Committee of Changsha during the Five-Anti movement publicly apologised to capitalists who had erroneously been "struggled" against. The apologies were made in city hall. Of course there were a few lower echelon cadres who, like the Party branch secretary of the school where I took part in the Anti-Counterrevolutionary movement, apologised most grudgingly and with the greatest reluctance.

So it is understandable why even veteran Communists like Deng Xiaoping were attacked at the start of the Cultural Revolution. People like Deng are old hands at mass movements and they knew what to expect. By all precedents in the long history of political movements carried out by the Chinese Communists all excesses should have been quickly righted by the second stage of the movement. But Lin Biao and the Gang of Four exploited the spontaneous, biased actions of the masses and exacerbated them. They whipped up this incipient adverse current into a huge tidal wave so as to topple large numbers of central and local leading cadres. In 1970, Lin Biao's thug Pu Zhanya, former leading member of the Guangzhou Military Region, made use of Mao's directive that cadres should go down to the countryside and temper themselves through working and living with the peasants to send more than 3,000 cadres out of Changsha (including the writer) to Xintian and other counties to do manual labour. Later we were told to "resign" and become full-fledged peasants. It was said that this was "demanded by the revolution." Actually, it was to make room for some 3,000 of Lin Biao's men to step in. Luckily this little stratagem of theirs fell through and was never carried out.

At that time, like everyone else, I could not understand why no attempt was made to redress the excesses. I was forced to the conclusion that it was better to leave the country. It was not until after the Gang of Four were overthrown that I like everyone else realised why things had been as they were.

In the various mass movements launched by the Chinese Communists I remember there were always a few individuals who tried to make themselves out to be extremely revolutionary so as to exploit the feelings of the masses and to sabotage the movement. During the land reforms some landlords guilty of minor crimes were inhumanly abused by these self-appointed "activists", so that they could win popular support and seize the leadership. The Chinese Communists kept this sort of activist at a distance and some of the more opportunistic elements were coldly asked what they were up to and told to desist for their own good. But the more power-hungry opportunists ignored the warning and later at the final stage of the movement they found themselves in serious trouble. A similar thing happened in the state organs of Changsha during the Three Anti movement. I was in a Changsha home for tubercular patients and I heard the head of the hospital Zhang Shaodi relay a directive of Wang Shoudao, then chairman of the provincial government, and now a leader in the Central Committee, which said that no leader of a state organ can be dismissed from office without his personal approval. But on the pretext that certain leaders had committed serious bureaucratic errors some people beat them up during a mass criticism meeting in a bid to put them out of the way and so take over their office. During the Anti-Counterrevolutionary movement too, there were people who acted very revolutionarily and tried to use the opportunity afforded by the many mass meetings to kill and silence those who knew too much about their crimes. The would-be murderers were, however, frustrated in time. But during the Cultural Revolution similar excesses went on and on unchecked to everyone's bewilderment and dismay.

The *Decision of the C. C. of the C. P. C. Concerning the Great Proletarian Cultural Revolution* (the *Sixteen Points*) that Mao Zedong had drawn up as the guideline for the Cultural Revolution in August 1966 pointed out that various ideological trends including reactionary trends were bound to appear in the course of the movement. This was not to be feared, it said. They could serve as "teachers by negative example." Even certain crimes and criminals could be left to be dealt with at the last stage of the movement. Reading

Democracy and the Legal System in Communist China 27

the *16 Points* again and reviewing what Lin Biao and the Gang of Four did and the many weird things which cropped up in the course of the Cultural Revolution, one should not have been unduly surprised and puzzled.

Along with their disclosures about the Gang of Four the Chinese Communists are putting a lot of effort into re-establishing the legal system. Boosters, smash-and-grabbers, people guilty of assault and battery and other criminal activities are now being rounded up and punished according to law. I have every reason to believe that "County Head Yin"[8] with whom Chen Ruoxi has such profound sympathies will be exonerated and rehabilitated and that the bloodthirsty young "Red Guards" killer will be apprehended and duly punished.

Fourth, the force of habit.

The deep-rooted feudal ideas in China came in for a severe pounding after the Communists came into power, particularly in the mammoth propaganda campaign mounted against the feudal marriage system and later in publicizing the Constitution of 1954. Equality of the sexes and marrying a partner of one's own free choice became more or less an accepted thing. But 2,000 years of feudalism is quite a force to reckon with. The feudal traditions are still very much in evidence today. In Xintian County, Sanyuantou Brigade, poor peasants still frequently bash their wives. One old poor peasant was notorious for wife-beating but no one interfered because they held that it was not their business to interfere with someone else's "private affairs." But one day he locked the door and beat her so badly that the brigade Party secretary had to interfere. He was afraid he would soon be dealing

---

[8] *Mayor Yin* is a collection of short stories written by Chen Ruoxi and put out by a publisher in Taibei. One of the stories is about a Guomindang officer who surrendered to the Chinese Communists and later was made head of a county. He was purported to have been shot by Red Guards during the Cultural Revolution. Another story concerned an intellectual who returned to China after the Communist takeover and how he was frustrated in marrying a girl. It is also available in English.

with a case of manslaughter. He broke down the door and entered and found the woman unconscious. The woman was rushed to hospital which probably saved her life. In another brigade a mother-in-law beat and drove her daughter-in-law to her death. Of course, many brigade members were against such a practice, but nothing much was done about it, law or no law. If anyone was criticised it was done half-heartedly. I reported these two cases to the commune hoping something would be done about it, but I got a cold reception and nothing ever came of my interference.

Even in state organs and industrial enterprises young people are often obstructed by leading cadres or their parents from marrying someone they chose, despite the Constitution and the Marriage Law. It was quite correct and proper during the war years to demand that Party members intending to marry should submit details of their future wife or husband for Party approval. Consent was given by the organisation only after a close examination of the social background and birth to prevent class enemies making use of marriages to obtain classified information and so forth. But that was during the war. It is definitely not so today. No one should have to obtain the consent of their organisation to get married. The Marriage Law makes no provision for this. But this is still the rule today rather than the exception.

I had a neighbour whose daughter worked in a factory and was being groomed for admission into the Communist Party by her factory. She fell in love with a technician from Guangdong who was not from worker or peasant parents. On top of this he had some relative or other living overseas. This last item was enough to put anyone off in Hunan from marrying that man. The girl's father withheld his permission, afraid that the marriage would "complicate" his "family and social relations" and his daughter would find it very hard to get into the Party. And as the factory had a "Party admission quota" to fulfil the factory leadership also refused to give the girl permission to marry this young technician. The girl's father who was a Party member did it out of his "concern" for his daughter's "welfare" and was fearful of hurting his own prospects. Thus the father and the factory leadership were in actual fact latter-day "Lady Dowager Jia's" after the domineering character in the classical novel *A Dream of Red Mansions*, and unconsciously supporters of feudalism. Luckily, the girl had plenty of pluck and brushing aside these obstacles went to the Public Security Department and registered her marriage with the technician. She was duly issued with a marriage certificate according to the Marriage Law and in spring last year my son and daughter returned to Guangzhou to congratulate the young couple.

The girl's father was concerned about his daughter because it could adversely affect him. It in no way differs from the marriages of convenience so common in capitalist societies. The factory leadership may not have started out being feudal, but it was putting exclusive emphasis on social status, on birth. It did not take into account the political stand and performance of the young man as it should have done, and so it was distorting Party policy concerning the appraisal of people's class origin and playing the role of Lady Dowager Jia and upholding feudal traditions.

Before the young Australian woman Ms. Susan Day and the Chinese man Mr. Song could marry, Hua Guofeng and Deng Xiaoping had to intervene, which shows how the minds of the people in China including some very high-ranking Communist cadres are still very much fettered by feudal ideas, as in this case, in matrimonial matters. The Gang of Four had fully exploited this force of habit to wreck foreign policy. Mao Zedong knew what he was talking about when he called for a revolution in the superstructure, and in the sphere of ideology.

When people talk about democracy and the legal system of Communist China they point out that the Communist leadership is not directly elected by the people. The state is one huge political body and no electoral system can enable each citizen to keep a personal check on the leaders elected. In China supervision of the leaders can only be left to their colleagues and people close to them, including those in direct contact with them, such as security agents and so on. Much depends on the degree of political responsibility of these people and their ability to detect revisionism. Liu Shaoqi who claimed he was a "Chinese Marx" during the *"Four Clean"* duped many leading central and provincial cadres into carrying out his line which struck directly at a large number of people. So it is very necessary to get the public to take a greater interest in state affairs and upgrade their grasp of Marxism-Leninism. Prior to the Cultural Revolution most people like myself did not pay any particular attention to state affairs but put our trust blindly in the leading Communist cadres.

What the Cultural Revolution Did to People's Thinking

Let me relate two stories about the way people thought during the Cultural Revolution. One is about a family who lived next door to me in Changsha. The husband was a cadre and the wife a textile worker. The father-in-law who was in his seventies, and the mother-in-law both lived with the couple. At that time people were divided into "rebels" and "conservatives." The husband and father-in-law were "rebels" and the womenfolk "conservatives." They fought like cats and dogs, each accusing the other of being "revisionist." One day the quarrel grew very heated and they came to blows. They smashed whatever they laid hands on. Although husbands and wives did fight like this because of opposing views during the Cultural Revolution it was not a common sight. But it was very common for members of the same family to quarrel because of contending factional views. It is indicative of how people felt about state affairs then and also of the fact that they are rather intolerant and not very democratic and could resort to violence in an attempt to resolve differences of view. But when the Gang of Four was ousted there was nationwide rejoicing and this contrasted sharply with the way people reacted when, before the Cultural Revolution, they heard about Gao Gang and Rao Shushi trying to seize Party and state power in 1954. To them, it was merely a piece of news.

Democracy and the Legal System in Communist China 31

My other story is about something which took place in the 4th production team of the Sanyuantou Brigade in Xintian County. In the winter of 1969, Liu, the head of the Jantou People's Commune, came in person to the 4th production team to decide where and how to build a retention pond to solve the team's irrigation problem. He selected a spot in a hollow up in the hills behind the village. The production team members wanted it built on a slope east of the village even though it meant more labour, because they said the hollow Liu had selected leaked. Liu insisted on his site. A Communist Party member and cadre of the team announced:"If you're going to dig in the eastern slope, don't come crying to me for grain when you're short." Liu turned up the next day to supervise. When the whistle blew everyone in the village set off for the eastern slope and with an old peasant they had confidence in, to guide them, set to work. Liu declared that someone was "sabotaging" his scheme and threatened he would "root out" this "hostile element" and deal with him. No one took any notice of him. So Liu departed with the technician he had brought with him from the county. It later turned out that the 4th production team members were right.

Xintian County in Hunan Province is an out-of-the-way hill county. In the old days before the country's liberation every time a petty official turned up he had to be dined and wined lavishly. After liberation in 1949 the people of this impoverished, backward county were still living in awe and dread of officials because their lives depended on the state diverting relief grain each year to keep them from starving. They could not grow enough to last them the whole year as the soil was very lean and production in the early years after liberation was pretty backward. The peasants' fear of offending cadres was very understandable. When the Cultural Revolution broke out, however, the peasants of the 4th production team dared to criticise the commune cadres and the Party committee of the county for cutting back the number of agricultural co-operatives in the midfifties. They wrote and put up many big-character posters against commune and county cadres and even sent a young high school graduate to criticise these cadres before a mass meeting. Through meetings and writing big-character posters and reading them the peasants learnt more about the policies of the Chinese Communist Party. They also saw that they had the backing of Mao Zedong so they were no longer in awe of cadres. That was why they also dared to go against Liu and build the retention pond where they thought was best. They knew their democratic rights and dared to exercise them. The retention pond they built worked and their grain problem was solved and they did not have to rely on relief any more. In 1970 they brought in a huge harvest and got rid of their label as a "beggarly lot." That year their grain averaged per person was 450 catties.

The above shows the breadth and depth the masses were mobilised and involved in the Cultural Revolution. The rise and fall of the Gang of Four sharpened further the people's power of discernment and this will improve understanding and implementation of socialist laws and bring about wider democracy.

Party Traditions

Of course it is also extremely important to improve the social system to enhance socialist democracy and the legal system so that the people have more effective control and supervision of the leaders. The Chinese Communists in their 11th National Party Congress called for implementing Mao Zedong's revolutionary line in an all-round and correct way, restoring and carrying forward the fine traditions and style of work of the Party. A new Party Constitution was also promulgated. This will be very important towards improving the legal system, mass supervision of leaders and mutual checks among leaders themselves. I would like to say something of what I know personally about the traditions and style of work of leading Communist cadres.

a) All members of the Communist Party in China are required to attend a branch meeting once a week. At these meetings self-criticism and criticism are carried out, mainly the former, with the members measuring themselves against Party standards. They examine how they have carried out Party tasks and policies, their work style and how close their ties with the masses are and so on.

The Party branch is not organised along professions or trades, but consists of all comrades working in the same unit. The branch Mao Zedong belonged to was made up of members of his staff, including his secretaries, attendants, guards, cooks and drivers. It is said that Mao had to seek permission from the leader of his branch, who was a cook, when he could not attend branch meetings. It is also claimed that Mao had frequently, like the others, reported to the branch what was going on in his mind. The Party branch in the bureau of health at Changsha was also organised along these lines.

b) The Chinese Communists have regular "rectifications" inside the Party to which non-Party members are invited. During these rectifications Party members holding leading posts are asked to give a strict accounting of their actions. Party members who have a lot of faults are severely criticised by Party and non-Party colleagues alike. Sometimes, the worst ones are selected for special criticism sessions. Every time a rectification occurs the Party members are understandably tense and nervous.

Rationally, they welcome criticisms from the masses, knowing that it keeps them up to the mark. But at the same time, emotionally, they would rather there be no criticisms. Should any Party member try to suppress criticism, fly into a rage or seek vengeance, he can expect being severely disciplined by his superiors and his punishment made public. Since the Gang of Four was thrown out the Chinese Communists have started another inner-Party rectification.

Apart from the regular big rectifications, there are end-of-year and end-of-task appraisals. Every time a job is completed the participants have to sum up. For example, a mobile medical unit at the end of its tour of duty in the countryside and before returning to town has to sum up its work in a report. There are mini-rectifications and they are very helpful in keeping Party members on their toes, and their ties with masses close.

c) All leading organs of the Chinese Communist Party are run on the system of Party committee leadership with the leader assuming personal responsibility. Major decisions are made only after full discussions, then tasks delegated to individual members. Decisions cannot be made by any one individual. Such a system effectively prevents any military *coup d'etat*. Lin Biao could not arbitrarily use his post as Minister of Defence to deploy troops. Such a decision had to be decided by the Military Commission under the Central Committee of the Communist Party. Neither could Lin Biao's trusties move troops under their charge without first getting the units' Party committee's approval. This way of doing things is firmly fixed. So when Lin Biao broke security procedure in his dash for the airport after his attempted coup d'etat and was discovered, his son Lin Liguo had to shoot and kill his body-guard before they could get to the airport to their getaway plane.[9]

d) Directives brought down to lower levels of command have to be carried out by cadres at the lower level no matter how high ranking the bearer of the directive is. The bearer has no powers to bypass his subordinates. When Vice-Chairman of the provincial Party committee of Hunan, Shang Zijian came down to Jiantou Commune to oversee spring ploughing and farming, the lowest rank of the four cadres he brought down was at least two rungs higher than the

---

[9] Lin Biao from his den in Beidaiho directed his men in Shanghai to murder Mao Zedong. When the assassination attempt fell through Lin Biao tried to escape to the Soviet Union in a Trident jet. According to security procedures, Lin's car had an escort in front and behind and had to travel at a certain speed. When Lin tried to make his driver overtake the car in front to make his getaway in the waiting plane his bodyguard refused and Lin's son shot him and took over. The plane was scheduled to take off the following day as ordered, but Lin's accomplice took over the plane and tried to get away. When the plane was over Mongolian airspace it ran out of fuel and the pilot, not familiar with the plane, tried to land. The fatal crash killed Lin and his accomplices.

commune head, but the Vice-Chairman and his aides all went and worked at the brigade that the commune Party secretary had arranged for them while they were in the commune. Before Shang Zijian and his aides left they too had to sum up and write in a report to the commune leadership. Of course, I have also seen some overbearing types, leaders who arrogantly issued orders right and left "like imperial magistrates" as Mao had so aptly described them in an article which has since become required study for all cadres.

e) Every so often leading cadres of the Communist Party have to go down to the countryside or to the factories and work as ordinary peasants and workers. This ensures their ties with the working people are not weakened and it also allows the working people to see what sort of leaders they have and allows the working people to exercise some sort of supervision over the leading cadres. High-ranking officers of the armed forces also have to serve as soldiers at the company every so often. It is routine for cadres to go down to grassroots units and work and live with the working people. In Daqing Oilfield the Party committee members even ask dependents of employes to exercise supervision over them.

Socialist Democracy and the Legal System

Below are some views I have of socialist democracy and the legal system.

a) In China only the people have freedom. Those who are against socialism have no freedom.

b) Socialist democracy serves socialism, by uniting the people, coordinating the will of the people, unifying policy and action, consolidating and enchancing people's power. It serves the task of building up the country and repulsing foreign aggression and bullying.

c) Democracy and freedom in socialist China is a method for the masses to educate themselves. It helps the people rid themselves of their faults and shortcomings and is conducive to socialism and the people. Consequently, democracy and freedom in socialist China is an excellent method for mobilizing the enthusiasm of the people for building socialism. Democracy in production which enabled the outstanding units of Daqing and Dazhai to overcome unimaginable difficulties in production are eminent examples of socialist freedom and democracy.

d) Although there are guarantees today in China which allow people to air their views freely, hold great debates and write and put up big-character posters, socialist democracy and socialist legality are far from perfect. Cadres and the masses have not completely got rid of all sorts of erroneous ideas and bad habits, and there is also a lot of bureaucracy. All these impair the functioning of the socialist legal system.

Narrow class sentiments, old ideas and old habits, people's inability to see and understand from the social development point of view the difference and contradiction between intellectuals and peasants and workers can be and has been exploited by unscrupulous people such as Lin Biao and the Gang of Four to whip up extremely destructive anarchist sentiments which wreck the socialist legal system.

e) Socialist democracy can effectively ensure the supervisory role of the masses over state leaders. However, there is still much to be desired in this respect.

f) There are limits to both bourgeois democracy and socialist democracy. There is no such thing as absolute, abstract democracy and freedom.

g) Ideas of absolute equality, anarchist, undemocratic ways, intolerance and suppression of differing views are still widespread; cadres making arbitrary decisions and working in a bureaucratic way are still very much in evidence. These and other shortcomings and faults are left-overs from the old society and the Chinese Communists have always worked energetically to stamp them out. However, these vestiges will be long in eliminating. They can be got rid of only step by step. During the Cultural Revolution however Lin Biao and the Gang of Four encouraged and promoted the growth of these vestiges and for some time they were quite virulent and caused enormous harm. But the reactionary excesses which had occurred cannot be attributed to the Chinese Com-

Democracy and the Legal System in Communist China 37

munists. It would be unfair. If they had not exposed and criticised the Gang of Four after these three men and a woman were thrown out of power and had not carried out a "sterilizing" campaign to eliminate the Gang's influence, then the blame could be laid at their doorstep.

Toward Rule by Law — Comments on the Characteristics of the 1978 Constitution[1]

He Ming

Since the founding of the People's Republic under the Chinese Communist Party, a total of three constitutions have been promulgated. The first Constitution, adopted in 1954 by the First National People's Congress, contained 106 articles. The second Constitution, enacted by the Fourth NPC in 1975 during the Cultural Revolution, was reduced to 30 articles. The latest Constitution, proclaimed by the Fifth NPC in March 1978, has 60 articles.

A preliminary comparision of the three texts shows that the first and the last are similar in many respects, while both are quite different from the second with regard to such ideas as democracy, socialist law, citizens' rights and the powers of the state. The general impression is: the second Constitution stressed class struggle, while the new Constitution stresses unity and progress. The second Constitution was a constitution of the Party, while the new Constitution is a constitution of the people. The second Constitution stressed dictatorship, while the new Constitution stresses democracy, law and human rights. Below is a brief comparative analysis.

Emphasis on Unity and Progress

Article 1 in the first Constitution stated: "The People's

---

[1] See Appendix, The Constitution of the People's Republic of China, March 5, 1978.

Republic of China is a people's democratic state led by the working class and based on the alliance of workers and peasants." The second Constitution changed it to: "The People's Republic of China is a socialist state of the dictatorship of the proletariat led by the working class and based on the alliance of workers and peasants." The new Constitution, while retaining the second version, treats the concept of the socialist state in a somewhat different way, as can be seen in both the Preamble and the articles.

The Preamble of the second Constitution laid stress on class struggle, the struggle between political lines, and the danger of capitalist restoration in the socialist period. The emphasis was on continuing the revolution and persisting in the Marxist-Leninist-Maoist orientation. The Preamble of the new Constitution, while adhering to these main elements of the "basic line," puts greater emphasis on the general task for the new period formulated under this line: "To persevere in continuing the revolution under the dictatorship of the proletariat, carry forward the three great revolutionary movements of class struggle, the struggle for production and scientific experiment and make China a great and powerful socialist country with modern agriculture, industry, national defense and science and technology by the end of the century." The former contained only fervid slogans about class struggles while the latter gives greater attention to concrete targets of this basic line and measures for carrying them out. As Ye Jianying explained in his *Report on the Revision of the Constitution*: "Unless we bring the superiority of the socialist system into full play and speedily develop the productive forces so as to secure, step by step, a powerful material base of modern large-scale production for our socialist system, we shall be unable to check the growth of the forces of capitalism effectively and, in the event of aggression by social-imperialism and imperialism, to avoid being at the receiving end of their attacks." The Gang of Four were great ones for sloganizing. But under their misrule the economy was so disrupted that capitalism ran rampant in many cities and rural areas and black markets boomed. In places such as Wenzhou County in Jiangsu, even the land was parceled out and peasants went back to individual farming. This shows that principles unsupported by concrete targets and measures for developing the economy are useless.

Article 7 of the new Constitution provides for three-level ownership in the rural economy with the production team as the basic accounting unit. It adds: "A production brigade may become the basic accounting unit when its conditions are ripe." "Conditions are ripe" means that a brigade had built a fairly strong economy (such as having developed its own factories and other undertakings) and the teams making up the brigade have achieved approximately the same level in economic development and income. This is an indication of the belief that promotion of economic growth through the development of production is an indispensable material condition for expanding collective ownership and gradually changing over to ownership by the whole people.

As to the enforcement of proletariat dictatorship, the second Constitution calls on the state to "punish all traitors and counter-revolutionaries" and "deprive the landlords, rich peasants, reactionary capitalists and other bad elements of political rights . . ." The new Constitution, while retaining "all traitors and counter-revolutionaries" has added "new-born bourgeois elements and other bad elements." This has been dictated by developments on the Chinese mainland in recent years. Many of those guilty of crimes and offenses no longer came from landlord, rich peasant or bourgeois families. An arch example was Wang Hongwen, one of the Gang of Four. The landlords, rich peasants and reactionary capitalists, being deprived of political rights and the resources for doing evil and being afraid of punishment, as a rule tend to behave themselves. In his *Report on the Revision of the Constitution*, Ye Jianying pointed out that there have been changes over the years among landlords, rich peasants, reactionary capitalists and elements guilty of counter-revolutionary or other crimes in the past. The

Constitution stipulates that the state provides these people with the opportunity to earn a living "so that they may be reformed through labor and become law-abiding citizens supporting themselves by their own labor." With regard to those who after remolding and education have really behaved well, "we should remove their labels as landlords, rich peasants, counter-revolutionaries or bad elements and give them citizenship rights." This work must be done systematically and in accordance with specific policies. This provision fits in with the actual conditions of Chinese society on the mainland after 29 years of proletarian dictatorship.

Although the Preamble of the second Constitution stated: "We should consolidate the great unity of the people of all nationalities" and "develop the revolutionary united front" it said nothing about the objects and content of the united front. The Preamble of the new Constitution is quite concrete: "We should consolidate and expand the revolutionary united front which is led by the working class and based on the worker-peasant alliance, and which unites the large numbers of intellectuals and other working people, patriotic democratic parties, patriotic personages, our compatriots in Taiwan, Hongkong and Macao, and our countrymen residing abroad." Even more significant is the revision of Article 3. In the second Constitution Article 3 said, "All power in the People's Republic of China belongs to the people. The organs through which the people exercise power are the People's Congresses at all levels, with deputies of workers, peasants and soldiers as their main body." Article 3 of the new Constitution has deleted "with deputies of workers, peasants and soldiers and soldiers as their main body" and rephrased the sentence as: "The organs through which the people exercise state power are the National People's Congress and the local People's Congress at various levels." This deletion does not mean that henceforth workers, peasants and soldiers will not make up the main body. In fact, Article 1 of the new Constitution has already included the phrases "led by the working class" and "based on the alliance of workers and peasants." At the Fifth NPC workers and peasants continued to account for the great majority of deputies. The deletion of the phrase is clearly intended to avoid the impression that people of other strata are neglected or excluded. The change contributes to promoting unity of all strata of the people.

In foreign policy, the new Constitution has laid down the theory of the three worlds and the policies of the Chinese Communist Party, adding also the phrase "against a new world war." This is a reflection of the Chinese Communists' desire to secure a peaceful environment to build up the country.

Constitution of the People, Not the Party

The new Constitution like the previous two stresses the Chinese Communist Party's leadership over the state, as can be seen in the Preamble and the chapter on General Principles. Article 2 in General Principles states: "The Communist Party of China is the core of leadership of the whole Chinese people." Article 19 : "The Chairman of the Central Committee of the Communist Party of China commands the armed forces of the People's Republic of China." But the Party's power is vested by the people and the new Constitution has given concrete expression to this. So viewed as a whole, it is a Constitution of the people, not a constitution of the Party, as was the case with the second Constitution in which the Party's leadership and power, not the power of the people, was stressed throughout.

Article 20 of the new Constitution states: "The National People's Congress is the highest organ of state power." In the second Constitution it read: "The National People's Congress is the highest organ of state power under the leadership of the Communist Party of China." The new Constitution has deleted the phrase "under the leadership of the Communist Party of China."

Regarding the election of the deputies to the NPC, the second Constitution only mentioned that they were to be "elected by the provinces, autonomous regions, municipalities directly under the Central Government, and the People's Liberation Army." It didn't explain how they should be elected, whether by selection or popular voting. The new Constitution specifies: "The deputies should be elected by secret ballot after democratic consultation."

The new Constitution also endows the NPC with much greater functions and powers than the second Constitution. It cites ten functions and powers for the NPC as compared with six in the second Constitution. The greatest difference is in the way the members of the State Council are appointed and removed from office. The second Constitution stipulated that the NPC shall "appoint and remove the Premier of the State Council and the members of the State Council on the proposal of the Central Committee of the Communist Party of China." In other words, the NPC could appoint or remove the Premier, Vice-Premier and ministers only on the recommendation of the Communist Party; it had no power to do so on its own initiative and could only rubberstamp the recommendations of the Chinese Communist Party. In the new Constitution the NPC has the power "to decide on the choice of the Premier of the State Council upon the recommendation of the Central Committee of the Communist Party of China. . . to decide on the choice of other members of the State Council upon the recommendation of the Premier of the State Council, and. . . to remove from office the members of the State Council, the President of the Supreme People's Court and the Chief Procurator of the Supreme People's Procuratorate." This is to say, the Chinese Communist Party can only recommend the candidate for the post of Premier, while the candidates for vice-premiers and ministers are to be recommended by the Premier. The Party has no right to remove from office members of the State Council; only the NPC has the power to appoint them or remove them from office.

The functions and powers of the NPC Standing Committee have been increased from seven in the second Constitution to thirteen in the new one. Seven functions and powers are provided for the Chairman of the NPC

Standing Committee in the new Constitution whereas none were stated in the second Constitution. The functions and powers of the State Council have been increased from five in the second Constitution to nine in the new.

The substantially increased functions and powers of the NPC, its Standing Committee and the Chairman of the Standing Committee mean that all affairs of the state are to be decided and carried out by the organs of state and not the Party. While presently Hua Guo-feng is both Chairman of the Party and Premier of the State Council, it is only a reflection of leadership by the Party, not the substitution of state organs by Party organs as was the case in the past.

The new Constitution has also added the provision that deputies to the NPC have the right to address inquiries to the State Council, the Supreme People's Court and the Supreme People's Procuratorate, "which are all under obligation to answer." For their part, deputies to the NPC "are subject to supervision by the units which elect them." "These electoral units have the power to replace at any time the deputies they elect, as prescribed by law." All this has the effect of creating mutual checks and balances which help prevent the NPC deputies and government officials from abusing their power.

All the above are concrete embodiments of the principle laid down in Article 17 under General Principles of the New Constitution: "The state adheres to the principle of socialist democracy, and ensures to the people the right to participate in the management of state affairs and of all economic and cultural undertakings, and the right to supervise the organs of state and their personnel." This principle was not stated in the second Constitution.

Citizens' Rights Broadened

The fundamental rights and duties of citizens are dealt with in Chapter Three in all three Constitutions. Revisions and provisions in this chapter of the new Constitution merit special attention. This is because ever since the Cultural Revolution began, especially during the period when Lin Biao and the Gang of Four held enormous power, the people's rights were largely ignored. For quite a long time the people were only enjoined to fulfil their duties but not allowed to enjoy their rights. People could be put under arrest at will and held incommunicado for investigation. During the wildest days of the Cultural Revolution, even physical tortures were used. Recent Chinese Communist reports on the rehabilitation of tens of thousands of people persecuted with trumped-up charges indicate to what extent human rights had been trampled on during the Cultural Revolution.

It is in this chapter, The Fundamental Rights and Duties of Citizens, that the new Constitution has made the greatest number of additions. The second Constitution contained only four articles. The new Constitution has sixteen, a fourfold increase.

The order in which rights and duties are set forth is also different. The second Constitution placed citizens' duties before their rights; the new Constitution cites 12 provisions on citizens' rights first, followed by four on their duties. This difference in order also shows which Constitution attaches more importance to citizens' rights.

The most important citizens' right, one on which the Chinese Communist Party was most criticized in the past, is the citizens' freedom of person. The new Constitution stipulates, "The citizens' freedom of person and their homes shall be inviolable. No citizen may be arrested except by decision of a people's court or with the sanction of a people's procuratorate, and the arrest must be made by a public security organ." This is a restraint on public security organs. They can carry out arrests but cannot issue warrants or sanction them; and no other organs except the public security organs are allowed to carry out arrests. When one recalls how, during the Cultural Revolution, Jiang Qing called for "smashing of the public security organs, procuratorial organs and people's courts" and replace them with "dictatorship by the masses" under which the "masses" could arrest and imprison people at will in total defiance of the courts, procuratorates and public security organs, one realizes why this provision of the new Constitution merits special attention.

Article 41 in Chapter Two, The Structure of the State, of the new Constitution states: "All cases in the people's courts are heard in public" and "the accused has the right to defense." This provision designed to protect human rights was also not found in the second Constitution.

The new Constitution is also more specific about other fundamental rights of citizens, including: "Citizens have the freedom to engage in scientific research, literary and artistic creation and other cultural activities." This may be considered a drastic change from the provision in the second Constitution that "the proletariat must exercise all-round distatorship over the bourgeoisie in the superstructure, including all spheres of culture." The new Constitution makes no mention of the term "all-round dictatorship." Instead it states in General Principles: "The state upholds the leading position of Marxism-Leninism-Mao Zedong Thought in all spheres of ideology and culture." Also: "The state applies the policy of 'letting a hundred flowers blossom and a hundred schools of thought contend' so as to promote the development of the arts and sciences and bring about a flourishing socialist culture." This is because all-round dictatorship has been proved impossible in the field of ideology. People may be put under a dictatorial rule but not their minds. Correct ideas can develop only when pitted against erroneous ideas.

How to Ensure Enforcement

More important than properly defining citizens' rights, the system of democracy and law and order, and the limits of the powers of government cadres, is to ensure that these provisions are carried out. The second Constitution did provide, though briefly, that "Citizens have the right to lodge to organs of state at any level written or oral complaints of transgression of law or neglect of duty on the part of any person working in an organ of state. No one shall attempt to hinder or obstruct the making of such complaints or retaliate." "Citizens enjoy freedom of speech, correspondence, the press, assembly, association, procession, demonstration and the freedom to strike." Why then, after this Constitution was proclaimed in 1975, did the Gang of Four still dare to abuse their power and cause countless shocking incidents? Why did Jiang Qing still feel free to harass and vilify Zhang Tianmin, writer of the screenplay *The Pioneers* accusing him of "lodging a vicious complaint" against her? Why were millions of people who went to Tian An Men Square during Qing Ming in April, 1976 to mourn Zhou En-lai and express their political wishes suppressed and attacked, and why was the incident branded as "counter-revolutionary"? And why, after the incident, were people still forced to march in processions, their faces expressionless, to show support for the April 7 Resolutions? All this made a mockery of the provisions in the second Constitution that citizens have the right to lodge complaints against state personnel and the freedom to hold demonstrations and processions.

Article 43 of the new Constitution provides that the people's procuratorates should exercise procuratorial authority to ensure observance of the Constitution and the law by all cadres and citizens. Article 22 provides for the NPC "to supervise the enforcement of the Constitution and the law." Article 36 provides for local people's congresses at various levels to "ensure the observance and enforcement of the Constitution, laws and decrees."

In his *Report on the Revision of the Constitution*, Ye Jianying devotes a whole section of the "Enforcement of the Constitution." He points out emphatically that, "after the Constitution is adopted, we must make sure that it is fully observed in letter and spirit. No one will be allowed to violate the Constitution. . . . We should now launch a nationwide campaign to publicize the Constitution and educate the people. . . Strengthen the socialist legal system. . . see to it that all who support socialism feel that their freedom of person, democratic rights, and legitimate economic interests as prescribed by the Constitution are solidly assured."

The provisions of the Constitution and Ye Jian-ying's report all show that the Chinese Communist leadership is deeply aware of the harm done by the disruption of law and order in the past and is determined to see to it that everything is done in conformity with law from now on. But determination alone is not enough, concrete measures are needed to strengthen the system of rule by law.

The March 16, 1978 *People's Daily* published an article by Han Youtong, a Vice-President of the Chinese Academy of Social Sciences and a specialist on jurisprudence, "To do things according to law," she said, "we must have laws to go by, and we must strictly observe laws." She suggests that "first, besides adopting the Constitution as the basic law, there is a great amount of other legislative work to be done, including the enactment of a criminal code and criminal laws of procedure, a civil code and civil laws of procedure, the compiling of trial cases, the enactment of laws on economic construction, and the revision of laws currently in effect. Secondly, the judiciary should be strengthened to strictly enforce the law. Thirdly, leading organs and leading cadres should be models of the enforcement of the Constitution and observance of law. Fourthly, there should be a mass education, conducted through the media and school textbooks, to establish firmly in the people's minds the concept of law."

If these can be put into effect, it will show the Chinese Communist Party is determined to establish a rule by law. This should be a good beginning. Let us hope that in this new period of development, the vestiges of the system of rule by man will be gradually replaced by a more thoroughgoing rule by law.

Democracy, Government by Law and the New Chinese Constitution

Zhu Yangmin

(1) Promised the People in lieu of a preface

The fifth National People's Congress (NPC) and the Fifth National Committee of the Chinese People's Political Consultative Conference (CPPCC) and the National Science Conference were held in early 1978, all within days of each other. The foundations for longterm stability and order were laid down at these meetings. China now has a new constitution and responsible leaders. The CPPCC has a new constitution and Chinese science and technology have been given a new orientation. The new leaders have categorically announced their determination to modernize China's agriculture, industry, national defence and science and technology (the "four modernizations") by the end of this century. They have written their determination into the preamble of their constitution and they frankly acknowledge the country's present backwardness. Deng Xiaoping said at the National Science Conference: "How do things stand with the technical level of our production? Several hundred million people are busy producing food. We still have not really solved the grain problem. Average annual output of grain per farm worker is about 1,000 kilogrammes in China, whereas in the United States the figure is over 50,000 kilogrammes, a disparity of several dozen times." This is boldly facing up to realities.

See Appendix, The Constitution of the People's Republic of China, March 5, 1978.

The leaders have also stopped isolating themselves from the rest of the world. This is evinced by the stream of people they are sending abroad to observe and study and by the droves of visitors invited to China in 1978-9 to see things for themselves. They are now paying attention to the time factor and making themselves get things done within a set time. For example, they have promised to achieve "initial results in one year, marked results in three" and the economy to reach a new level within eight years, science and technology to be up to a certain level by a certain date and so on. All these are demonstrative of the realistic, down-to-earth attitude of the new leaders, which is a sharp contrast to that of the Gang of Four, who kicked up a deafening din about leaving Britain behind and overtaking the United States at some nebulous date by some equally nebulous means. The new leaders of today are practical men, they say what they mean. They have given their word to the people and will stand or fall by it. It is an expression of confidence and of their determination. At the same time it is a measure to restore to the Communist Party the prestige it once had enjoyed among the people before the Gang of Four shattered it during their several years in power. This is a good beginning towards bringing about great order in China. But a good beginning is not necessarily something already half done. Every minute of the next 22 years must be used to the maximum to get the whole nation to pull its weight to bring about the four modernizations within that time. To this end a pressing problem confronting the Communist Party today is to bring about political modernization so as to create a political environment in which every citizen can work with his mind at ease. The catalyst to modernizing politics to bring about the four modernizations is the institution of socialist democracy and government by law.

The four modernizations are splendid goals to strive for. In the next 22 years China not only has to work energetically to close the gap between the economically advanced countries but must cover the distance transversed in these 22 years by the advanced countries as well. This is not going to be easy. Communist China today is like a student sitting an examination. She knows that when the year 2001 turns up she must hand in her papers, and the answers returned must be good enough for an A grade pass from the world. But can she do it? She must do what has been written into the Constitution if the Party, draws the right lesson from the devastation caused by the Gang of Four's arbitrary rule and provides a reasonable and modern political environment for the people.

Apart from commenting on the new constitution I want to give my views and suggestions on how to use the Standing Committee of the NPC and the CPPCC to establish socialist democracy and rule by law.

(II) On the Constitution from the Angle of Party Leadership and Popular Decision

Since the Constitution was adopted in March by the Fifth NPC many articles have appeared about this new constitution, mainly dwelling on the subject of the monopoly of power in a single political party – the dictatorship of the proletariat. They are making a mountain out of a molehill. They are overlooking China's historical background and the recent revolution. In my view the right approach to take in regard to the new constitution should be one of taking into account the political realities and making sincere criticisms which will be of help to the Chinese nation. In previous articles I have pointed out :

The people's right to elect their own representatives must be guaranteed; the National People's Congress should in name and in fact be the supreme organ of state power; the President of the Supreme People's Court and the Chief Procurator must be elected by the NPC so that the judiciary and the procuratorate are independent; there must be freedom of speech and the press there must be an article preventing the government by law becoming government by a person; there must be a stipulation guaranteeing that every citizen is equal before the law; and there must be no more classifying intellectuals under a separate category and other discriminatory practices based on social position. The reasons why I pointed out only these opinions which concerned political democracy and the government by law were: first, I had not a copy on hand of the draft of the constitution which should have been distributed to the people to discuss, and secondly, if the points I made were amended and genuinely carried out then China would move a step towards democracy and government by law. I am going to make three points concerning the constitution from the point of "leadership by the Party and decision by the people."

A. Commendable Points

Compared with the 1975 Constitution the draftees of the new constitution have omitted passages inserted by the Gang of Four. This is to be commended. For example:

(i) the right to elect deputies by the people. Article 3 of the 1975 constitution said: "Deputies are elected through democratic consultation." Not a word is mentioned about how they are to be elected. Article 21 of the new constitution stipulates: "Deputies should be elected by secret ballot after democratic consultation." This is much better. If the new constitution is really enforced, "democratic consultation" should be a method for nominating the candidates and "secret ballot" should be the guarantee that it is the people who will make the decision. Then the candidates decided upon through democratic consultation will then not be necessarily elected. Those who are elected by secret ballot are, of course, deputies the people have confidence in;

(ii) as to the powers and functions of the National People's Congress, article 16 of the old constitution has this to say: "The National People's Congress is the highest organ of state power under the leadership of the Communist Party of China." According to this definition the Party is the leader and the one who makes the decisions. This puts the Party above the people of the country. The National People's

Congress thus, in fact, is really what is ironically referred to by people as "a rubber stamp" of the Party. Article 20 of the new constitution reads: "The national People's Congress is the highest organ of state power." The words "under the leadership of the Communist Party of China" in the 1975 constitution have been deleted. The Communist Party with 35 million members is the single largest political party in China, but against the country's 900 million it is only a tiny 4 per cent of the population. To let a dedicated minority of Communists lead the revolution and national construction is one thing, but if they are made the masters of the people, then it is going against the founding tenets of the Communist Party of China and against Mao Zedong Thought. The Gang of Four's riding roughshod over the people is definitely something not to be emulated;

(iii) On the question of the independence of the judicature and the procuratorate, the Gang of Four and their followers had the Presidents of the People's Courts appointed by the permanent organs of the People's Congresses at the corresponding levels and the functions and powers of procuratorial organs were exercised by the organs of public security by administrative organs. The Gang of Four did this to "legalize" their "government without law" and had these provisions written into the Constitution in 1975. The new constitution has corrected this fault. According to article 22 of the new constitution the NPC elects the President of the Supreme People's Court and the Chief Procurator of the Supreme People's Procuratorate. According to articles 41, 42 and 43 cases are heard in public, in the presence of "representatives of the masses participating as assessors" and the accused has the right to defense. Another point is that of restoring the Supreme People's Procuratorate. Party members who are personnel of state organs, besides having to observe Party discipline, are now also made responsible to the law of the land. In contrast to the past, citizens now have a place to lodge complaints concerning the transgression of the law or negligence of duty by persons working in a state organ;

(iv) Concerning the rights and duties of citizens, the

1975 Constitution only had four vaguely worded articles, whereas the new constitution has expanded these to 16 articles and their content is quite specific, particularly article 52 which not only stipulates that citizens have the freedom to engage in scientific research, literary and artistic creation and other cultural activities, but also that the state encourages and assists the creative endeavours of citizens engaged in science, education, public health, sports and other cultural work. This means above all a great step towards freedom of thought. When the Gang of Four dominated the ideological scene it seemed that everyone's mind had become a copying machine, faithfully duplicating some model or another. No one seemed capable of original thought or creative work. Of course, in those witch-hunting days when labels were freely slapped on people, who in the world dared be original or creative?

The new constitution has also taken into account the rights and interests of returned overseas Chinese and their relatives. This is another slap at the Gang of Four who treated returned overseas Chinese and their relatives as no better than enemies.

B. Inadequacies

In regard to "decision by the people", amendments made to the old constitution have done much to effect a balance between "leaders" and "deciders." But compared with the 1954 Constitution one is left with the impression that the ideal of the people making the decisions is outweighed by the reality of the authoritarianism of the leadership. I was disappointed in not being able to find in the new constitution the stipulation in the 1954 constitution which reads "Citizens of the People's Republic of China are equal before the law." Everyone knows that the Gang of Four were proponents of lawlessness, so, of course, one cannot expect any mention of equality before the law from them. Besides, the Gang had carefully bred a small ruling elite which hounded and harassed the people during their years in power, so there

The New Chinese Constitution 57

was no equality for the people before the law. But in leaving out this provision the new constitution leads the world to assume that in socialist China there is a great majority who must obey the law and a particular class of people who enjoy special "intra-territorial rights." This is inconsistent with the declared revolutionary principle of earlier years to abolish all classes. Another serious defect is the practice of discriminating against intellectuals by putting them in a social category by themselves. This must be done away with. I pointed out in an earlier article the revision of article 86 which in the 1953 constitution reads "Citizens. . . whatever their nationality, race. . . social origin, religious belief, education. . . have the right to vote and stand for election" in the hope that the draftees of the new constitution would include it, as the social origin doctrine advocated by the Gang of Four was in reality an attempt to establish a new feudal system. Their "studying to make trouble so as to become officials", "people must marry people of their own class" and "superiors and inferiors" and so forth are unmitigated feudal rubbish, expressions of the feudal doctrine of social position. Revolution should wipe these out, not refurbish and revive them. In socialist China the interests of the workers and peasants must be guarded and respected. This is plain common sense and indisputable. But if the very fact that people who are engaged in mental labour, or because of their social relations to others is considered cause for discrimination and all opportunity is denied them then excesses are bound to occur. For many years the victims of this widespread, deeply-ingrained but unwritten doctrine of social position have led a life of hopeless despair. The deep-rooted nature and the extreme difficulty in eradicating this influence of the doctrine of social position can be observed in the official daily press calling again and again to refute and criticise this doctrine. To get these hapless people to lift up their heads again and become an active force needs more than exhortations by the press. There must be legal guarantees. If abolition of the doctrine of social position written into the constitution, it would be an effective antidote to this poisonous influence as well as a reassertion of the equality of all citizens before the law.

C. Puzzling Places

Finally, there are aspects of the new constitution which are quite puzzling. One is the length of term of office of the NPC. Article 24 of the 1975 constitution states "The National People's Congress is elected for a term of four years." It is explicitly stated that the NPC and its deputies are elected for a term of four years. Article 21 of the new constitution only states that the NPC is elected for a term of five years and the term of office for deputies is undefined. In the 1954 constitution there are explicit stipulations on the terms of office as well as the arrest and trial of state leaders elected or appointed by the NPC. In the new constitution the office of Chairman of the Standing Committee of the NPC and the Premier of the State Council and other state leaders seems to be "for life." In my view, determining how long state leaders can remain in office is conducive to smooth transference of power. Another puzzling aspect is that in the 1954 Constitution it says "Citizens of the People's Republic of China are equal before law" (article 85) and "Whatever their social origin." (article 86). There, the terms "citizen" and "people" are interchangeable. There is no similar declaration in the new constitution to this effect. In other articles the term "citizen" is used. Does this imply that "citizen" and "people" are two distinct social categories? For example, if article 3, "All power in the People's Republic of China belongs to the people" is a fact and if "people and citizen" are analogous then the "must" in article 56 "citizens must support the leadership of the Communist Party of China" is superfluous, because if *all* power belongs to the people, then the right to support the leadership of the Communist Party of China also belongs to the people, who, after weighing up what sort of "leadership" is being offered, will or will not give their support. Otherwise, "all power belongs to the people" amounts to nothing. The third point I want to deal with is the question of who commands the country's armed forces. In the 1954 Constitution it is explicitly stated that the armed forces of the country belong to the people and is under the state organ elected by the people. This is reasonable. Article 19 of the new constitution hands the command of the armed forces of the country to the Chairman of the Communist Party of China. This calls for reconsideration. It would be more consonant with the new constitution to place armed forces under the command of the Chairman of the Standing Committee of the NPC which is empowered to declare war and make peace.

Anyway, this article is not meant to be a commentary on the constitution. It merely presents some personal opinions from the point of view of "leadership from the Party" and "decision making by the people." The new constitution is far more democratic than the 1975 Constitution, but compared with the 1954 Constitution, there is still room for improvement. However, good laws improve with usage and what matters now is enforcing the constitution.

(III) The NPC Standing Committee and Limiting Party Leadership

Although today's constitution to some extent takes into consideration "decision by the people" there is still too much stress placed on the Party's role when compared with the 1954 Constitution. However fondly people may still think of that constitution it is merely a well-drawn up document in the history of Chinese constitutions because it was never really enforced. The crucial thing is whether or not the party in power will genuinely carry it out. If the party now leading the work of building up the country clearly sees that "decision-making by the people" is a trend as irresistible as socialism itself and in practice expedites the four modernizations within this century, then in implementing the new constitution it will be in the process of paving the way towards a state where "decision is made by the people." Below are some suggestions for using the Standing Committee of the NPC to attain the ideal of "decision by the people."

The new constitution does not employ the traditional three-legged or tripartite power structure, and there is no evidence of a system of mutual checks and restraints. It employs another form of tripartite power structure, that is, party power, popular power and state power. The preamble and articles 1 and 2 of the new constitution clearly state that "leadership by the Party" and article 3 that "all power in the People's Republic of China belongs to the people" can be taken to mean "decision-making by the people" and the NPC as exercising state power on behalf of the people, while the stipulation that "the State Council or the Central People's Government is the executive organ of the highest organ of state power; it is the highest organ of state administration," makes the State Council the equivalent to an organ exercising state power. In this tripartite power structure "leadership of the Party" seems dominant because the Premier of the State Council is appointed by the Central Committee of the CPC and will of course carry out the decisions made by the Party in the interests of the CPC. However, as the Standing Committee of the NPC occupies a pivotal place in this tripartite power structure it is not impossible for it, while upholding the principle of "decision making by the people" according to the Constitution, to devolve into an organ that makes the decisions for the people. All that it requires is for the Standing Committee of the NPC to firmly insist on being an organ representing the people in exercising state power and refuse to be a docile rubber stamp.

Has the Standing Committee of the NPC the power to uphold "decision-making by the people"? Yes, but only if everyone in China faithfully observes the constitution. We all know that the NPC is "the highest organ of state power" (article 20), but because it is not always in session its functions and powers are deputed to the Standing Committee of about 2,000 or so members. Consequently, it is the Standing Committee of the NPC which is the regular organ exercising state power on behalf of the people. If it regularly uses the power given it by articles 24 to 26 of the Constitution, sets up its own offices parallel with the Political Bureau of the Central Committee of the CPC and the State Council and asks all its members to report to work each day to exercise power on behalf of the people, it can legally:

a) fully exercise its functions and powers and gradually recover the right of the people to decide for themselves. For instance, according to article 25 paragraph 3, it exercises functions and powers which include, "to interpret the constitution and laws and to enact decrees" and, like parliaments of many countries, passes decrees which the majority support and which do not contravene socialist principles, and sends them to the State Council to be carried out. The State Council apparently cannot legally refuse. According to the same articles paragraphs 6, 7 and 8, when the Premier of the State Council and other leading state officials decided or elected by the NPC submits a list of members' names for the NPC to review, the Constitution does not stipulate that the Standing Committee of the NPC has to "rubber stamp" its approval, so why cannot it exercise its functions and powers and demand that these leaders submit a few more names for it to "decide on"? Or ask for more evidence and reasons for "removing" the person concerned?

b) The Standing Committee of the NPC in addition to taking positive action to recover the right of the people to decide for themselves, can also negatively act as the mediator between the interests of the Party and the people. In principle, most of the policies and plans initiated on the principle of "leadership by the Party" are, it is hoped, policies and plans the people endorse. But if policies desired by the Party are not what the people desire, what happens? In such a case the Standing Committee of the NPC, according to law, can act as the mediator between the two. As the NPC has the power to "examine and approve the national economic plan, the state budget and the final state accounts," and the power to interpret the constitution and laws, why cannot the Standing Committee enlarge the scope of its examination and approval in accordance with article 25 paragraph 13, and 'exercise such other functions and powers as are invested in it by the National People's Congress" and take over this power to "examine and approve"? It then can with great ease amend whatever the people are willing to accept in the policies and plans. The State Council which draws up the plans and makes proposals according to the wishes of the Party, on finding that it has to have the approval of someone else would be forced to take into consideration the wishes of the people when it is drawing up a plan or making a proposal. If the Standing Committee uses the above two methods frequently enough until it becomes an accepted practice, then the effect would be "decision-making by the people." The Standing Committee would then function as a counterbalancing force between "leadership by the Party" in the form of the Political Bureau of the CPC and the executive power of the State Council.

Going on past political experience in China I would like to point out that whether or not an organ with the powers invested in it by the constitution can perform its functions effectively depends all too frequently on the prestige of the head of the organ concerned. The person at the head of the Standing Committee today is Ye Jianying, Vice-Chairman of the Central Committee of the CPC and a man of great prestige and standing among the people. As a Party member, he will naturally take into consideration the principle of "leadership by the Party." But on the other hand, he is also the Chairman of the highest organ of state power, an organ which exercises political power on behalf of the people. In addition, members of the Standing Committee of the NPC are deputies elected by the people's congresses representing various democratic political parties, democratic personages and the various nationalities of China. So if he uses the constitution to lay down the foundation for realizing the ideal of the people deciding for themselves as Mao Zedong has proposed, would he not be doing something in the interest of the country, the people and the Chinese

Communist Party? In his report on the revision of the articles of the constitution, Ye Jianying said at the start that "in striving for the fulfilment of the general task for the new period, it is imperative to give full play to socialist democracy. Under our socialist system, the people are the masters of the country. Our socialist democracy truly ensures that the people run state affairs." This shows although he is Vice-Chairman of the Communist Party he is in fact making the realization of a socialist democracy which truly ensures that the people run state affairs his primary task. In speaking about the enforcement of the Constitution, he said, "One of the significant functions and powers of the National People's Congress as prescribed by the new constitution is to 'supervise the enforcement of the Constitution and the law.'" This clearly shows that if the NPC's Standing Committee genuinely enforces the Constitution it can influence the power of the Party to uphold the right of the people to run state affairs.

(IV) The CPPCC's Role

The Fifth National Committee of the Chinese People's Political Consultative Conference was held from February 24 to March 8, at the same time as the Fifth National People's Congress was in session. The CPPCC had once played a major role in the political life of New China. It was this body which in 1949 had drawn up and adopted a Common Program equivalent to a Constitution, which in turn gave birth to the People's Government. The First National People's Congress called in 1954 by the Chinese Communist Party, after amendments, turned this Common Program into a Constitution and produced the Standing Committee of the NPC, decided on the Chairman of the State and set up the State Council. After which, the CPPCC was put into cold storage and many of its members branded as Rightists or counter-revolutionaries and persecuted. Now, the CPPCC is again given great prominence. Its membership has been raised to nearly 2,000, almost twice the size of the NPC, and it has also been provided with a Constitution and a Chairman, another prestigious member of the CPC, Vice-Chairman Deng Xiaoping. What role has the CPPCC in this new period of building the country? What sort of political environment will enable it to become a viable force promoting the development of socialist democracy and legal government? What sort of relationship should there be between the ruling party and the CPPCC in actual political life?

A reading of the Constitution of the CPPCC shows that this conference will no longer sit side by side to "discuss" state affairs with the Communist Party as it did during the early years of the People's Republic. It has become an organ set up to assist the Party in its work of building up the country. Although there are four articles in Chapter 2 under "General Working Principles" of its Constitution defining its work, its main function appears confined to "collecting, collating and editing materials for the writing of books on such subjects as modern Chinese history of the Chinese revolution" and "treating seriously the letters the people send in and the complaints they make when they call." The CPPCC which at one time had sat as an equal with the ruling party to "discuss" state affairs has today been relegated to handling correspondence and collecting material to write history books. Rather a pity. I believe that if the ruling party really does carry out its policy of longterm coexistence and mutual supervision between the CPC and the various democratic parties and really lets the CPPCC members to say all they know and say it without reserve, and "blame not the speaker but be warned by his words", then the CPPCC in the new period can very well become "unofficial state censor and historian" and perform these functions well.

From recent disclosures in connection with the crimes of the Gang of Four, letters from the public have generally been from people who have been grievously wronged and are seeking redress. While the people are still acquainting themselves with democracy, and the Constitution provides guarantees for people to "bring a case against an official," most people would still rather bring their case to an unofficial "censor" or "magistrate" than to a court official's notice. Only through receiving visitors and letters from the people can members of the CPPCC get first-hand material, really get to know how the people feel and about their demands and so be able to "give advisory opinions and suggestions" to the CPC.

Heavy responsibility rests with the unofficial state historian. It can tip the scales either way by a mere brush stroke. It must go on facts so as to leave a credible record for posterity. As most people tend to put more confidence in what is written down by an unofficial historian, the National Committee of the CPPCC can very well make use of this "writing brush" to exert a "supervisory influence" over those holding power. As it will help build a new China, old patriots should willingly accept this role of being "unofficial state historian."

Now the question is, what political environment will enable members of the CPPCC to really be "imperial advisors" and "imperial historians"? The mere fact that the NPC and the CPPCC were convened at the same time shows how much value the Communist Party attaches to the latter. This being the case, the ruling party should consider the question of the legal status of this body and provide its members with various legal guarantees. From the Constitution of the CPPCC it apparently is only a "political headquarters" of the various democratic parties and democratic personages and not a political party out of power.

Although it has political status, it has no legal guarantees whatsoever. In general, legal status is more enduring than political status. Only when it acquires legal status will there be legal guarantees, and only then will people join this "potential party" to coexist with the CPC. Otherwise, when the older generation passes on, this conference will pass away with them. Again, when the Gang of Four was in power, was it not because there were no legal status and legal guarantees that the CPPCC was allowed to disappear without a sound and its members made to suffer prolonged insults, persecution and humiliation? Another thing, as it is written in its constitution, members of the CPPCC are charged with "saying all they know and saying it without reserve and blaming not the speaker" and with handling letters from the public and supplying information on the actual situation and getting people to speak out freely in the interests of the country, ought the Communist Party not allow the CPPCC as an organ representing public opinion to run a newspaper? In other articles I have repeatedly pointed out that the people of socialist China should have a newspaper of their own. Since the CPPCC is again being held in respect by the ruling political party it should be given the task of producing such a newspaper, starting with Peking and followed by the other major cities and provincial capitals, each putting out a daily *People's Voice* . Editors and contributors should use the freedom stipulated in article 45 of the Constitution granting freedom of speech, the press and the right to "speak out freely, air their views" and invoke article 52 "the state encourages and assists" creative endeavours of those engaged in journalism and publishing to publicly discuss matters, debate current policies and so on and become a partner in co-existence? Would not this set an example of freedom of speech in a socialist country? There are three positive aspects besides this one to the CPPCC putting out a daily *People's Voice*.

a) Respecting the Constitution of the country and its own constitution and not abusing freedom, the CPPCC would be "assisting" in the task of building up the country.

b) It will be getting a true picture of public opinion and so be able to analyse and work out appropriate measures to submit to the CPC for consideration.

c) there will be no lack of contributors and there will be a ready readership. The paper's accounts books will be open to the public and the profits earned will go to swell the state treasury and also help enrich the cultural life of the people.

I believe that if the ruling political party gives the CPPCC legal guarantees and the chance to canvass public opinion, e.g. run its own newspaper, the CPPCC can accomplish this task in a most exemplary fashion and thus promote socialist democracy and government by law.

For the CPPCC led by a leading member of the governing party to really assist and supervise the party in power without itself taking part in actual politics, rational form of working relationship between the two is first required. Since the CPPCC is not a party in opposition contending with the CPC for power, it will not undertake convert activities directed against the ruling party and the latter will have no call to look upon it as a "hostile party." Similarly, as those units and individuals who participate in the CPPCC have undertaken to abide by certain principles, one of which is that they will "study hard, on a voluntary basis, Marxism-Leninism-Mao Zedong Thought," (another sign of the ruling party respecting their freedom of thought) members of the CPPCC who because of pressure of work cannot find time to study and acquire a thorough understanding of Marxism-Leninism-Mao Zedong Thought should not be looked down upon as ideologically backward.

Furthermore, as those participants in the CPPCC are not members of various state organs, the ruling party will not be able to order them about easily. As CPPCC members did not participate in this conference as aspirants to high office they will not always say all the nice things the ruling party would like to hear. Since the party in power is dedicated to building up the country and serving the people, and the CPPCC is determined in the interests of the people to assist "the other side" to help build up the country in a short time, the best and most rational relationship between them would be one between a "collective leadership working for the good of the people" and a "collective capable minister" assisting the leadership, like that which existed between the first Tang emperor and his prime minister.

(V) *Conclusion: China Should First of All Run Her Own Affairs Well*

In 1975 Premier Zhou En-lai, despite being a very

sick man, delivered the *Report on the Work of the Government* to the Fourth National People's Congress. In this report he put forward the breathtaking proposal of realizing the four modernizations within this century. The leaders of China today have written Zhou's proposal into the Constitution, solemnly declaring to the people of China and the world that "this is what we have promised you we will accomplish." However, in his report, there is something else which Zhou adjures the people of China to do. It is in the sentence in the last paragraph which reads, "We should first of all run China's affairs well." Why do I say this sentence is an earnest adjuration? If readers compare the content of his speech with the measures taken over the past year by the present leaders to eliminate the ugly excesses committed by the Gang of Four the answer is readily found. It was what Zhou had worked and fought for all his life. When he said these words in 1975, he was warning the Gang of Four and their breed not to be so simpleminded and naive, claiming that "ideology" would do away with all ideas of race, national frontiers and other realities and everyone would become dear socialist brothers. If China's affairs had gone on being run by the Gang, China would not have even been able to look after herself still less "strive to make a greater contribution to humanity"!

To bring about the four modernizations within this century the operative word is "well" in the sentence: "We should first run China's affairs well." To run her affairs well, there must not be centralism at the expense of democracy, discipline at the expense of freedom, unity at the expense of individual ease of mind and lively, vigorous political environment. With the Gang of Four muzzling people and banning books and malevolently defaming the country's greatest statesmen, destroying faithful cadres, persecuting fine citizens, advocating anarchy, shouting empty slogans and dogmatic assertions, making the people angry and indignant but unable to give voice to their feelings, and driving everyone into deep despair, the country could only retrogress, rent by dissensions and thrown into chaos. The only way to create a healthy environment for China to run her affairs well is to bring about political modernization under the principle of everyone accepting the leadership of the ruling political party and working together to build socialist democracy and government by law through setting up new things, putting them to the test of practice and then improving them and applying them again and again. If the leaders of the Standing Committee of the NPC and all deputies put paramount importance to exercising political power on behalf of the people, would they not be using the power invested in them by the Constitution to function as a balancing force in regard to the organs exercising Party power and executive power? If the leaders and members of the CPPCC give preeminence to their duty of speaking out on behalf of the people would they not then be doing the work defined in the CPPCC constitution of performing a supervisory function in regard to the organs exercising Party power and executive power? As the organs exercising Party and executive power would have the quasi-parliamentary Standing Committee of the NPC as a counterbalance as well as the supervision of the CPPCC representing popular opinion, would these organs then not provide more leadership and do less of the deciding?

The whole world is watching the people of China to see if they will be able to realize the four modernizations by the year 2000. As I do not wish the people of China to lose faith in the CPC and China to become the laughing-stock of the world, I have again made known my suggestions about things which are essential for bringing out the four modernizations before the end of this century. We must let the world say in the year 2001, on January 1, "The Chinese are a nation who do what they say!" This is why I started this article with "This is what we have promised the people" and end with "We should first run China's affairs well."

Respect for Law — Reflections on a Small Incident at the Customs

Wu Qing

A lot of people have much to complain about the customs at Shumchen. I too want to talk about the Shumchen customs but not to criticize it particularly.

One year I was coming back to Hongkong after a visit to my home village. Passing through customs I was put through routine inspection. I had made many trips either to my home village or to the Canton Fair and had got used to the attitude of the Shumchen customs people. As long as nothing happened to really make me lose my temper I considered it a smooth passage. This time there was a small incident, nothing out of the ordinary, but it gave me food for thought for a long, long time.

I had stayed longer than usual at my home village and so had received a letter from my wife in Hongkong telling me a few things about the children. After reading it I stuck it in a suitcase. At the customs the inspection man picked up the letter when going through the suitcase.

"What's this?" he asked.

"A letter from my wife," I replied after looking to make sure.

"What's in it?"

What's in it? Nothing to hide from others but I didn't try to remember so I was unable to answer right away.

The man was already taking the letter out of the envelope. I thought it very rude of him and so said, "This is a personal letter. But you can read it if you want."

He was already doing it, without a word of apology. He was perfectly at ease, without the least sign of feeling he was doing something he shouldn't. But I felt he had no reason to read my letter. We are used to respecting the rights of the individual and think it's very rude to read other people's personal correspondence without permission. Even if there is a need to do so for some particular reason we would, out of courtesy, ask for permission. Customs people are no exception, I thought.

To my mind, while customs has the duty to inspect, the duties should be clearly defined and should not be overextended at will. No doubt customs inspectors should be highly vigilant, but I rather think it ridiculous for them to think they could discover anything out of the ordinary from a personal letter in a suitcase. Even if they thought they might find something, they should at least be more or less sure that this traveler was a suspicious character and they should go through the proper procedures before they took the traveler as a suspect and interrogated him and searched his belongings.

I'm quite sure that the customs man never considered any of this. To him every traveler was a suspect under surveillance and he was doing a sacred duty in interrogating him and looking through all his belongings.

At the time a lot of questions crossed my mind: Did I have the right to protest? What would be the grounds of my protest? Was he infringing on my personal freedom? Was asking too many questions illegal interrogation? (A really smart customs man would start a courteous and friendly conversation with the traveler he suspects and try and get what he wants while doing so.) Was there any law or decree I could fall back on?

For answers my mind was a blank. I'm sure my relatives and friends who live on the mainland couldn't answer these questions either. I'm sure they have never even thought of such questions. If I raise them they would probably think me naive or even ridiculous.

I thought of the Constitution, which stipulates that citizens have freedom of correspondence. Could this be quoted to refuse letting the man read my personal letter? I didn't know. But at the time the only thing I could think of was the Constitution, it being the only law I knew of. But I said nothing about it. In a peculiar atmosphere that had prevailed for long years, it seemed rather ridiculous even to talk about the Constitution, much less cite it.

The inspection that time did not lead to any trouble or argument. After reading the letter the customs man only asked what local products I'd bought (because my wife wrote something about buying some local products if there were any.) After I told him what I'd bought he let me go.

But I couldn't help thinking: Was he right in reading my letter? Maybe he was. But even if I thought he was wrong, I couldn't sit down and hold a discussion with him. The best way was to find the proper decree or law to help us resolve the difference in views. What questions should I raise? What rights could I base myself on in my argument? I don't know the answers.

What worries me is people simply don't have such concepts in their minds. They simply have no idea of what legality is. To them whoever has the power has the say. Since the customs man was inspecting, it's best to keep quiet.

Customs inspection is, after all, a small matter. A look at a family letter is an even smaller matter. But what about the important matters?

During the Cultural Revolution a great many cadres were treated unlawfully. When a cadre was considered as having done something wrong, he was "hatted" (labeled as some kind of undesirable element) and locked up somewhere. After a long time he was allowed to go home since after all he hadn't done anything wrong. This was a common happening. But it was illegal because first, the man was locked up without legal procedures; second, no decree was ever proclaimed during the Cultural Revolution saying that a person could be treated this way; and third, exposures now show them to be the acts of Lin Biao and Gang of Four followers in violation of fixed policies.

What could one do when faced with such illegal acts?

As far as the person involved was concerned, even if he was carrying a copy of the Constitution with him, it probably wouldn't have done him any good. He would be locked up anyway. Of course when he was missing his family should have the right to demand to know what had happened to him. There should be certain legal channels through which they could contact him and demand that things were done according to law.

I suppose some people will laugh and think me naive. For during the Cultural Revolution there was a time when even local public security departments were "smashed up." So what was the use of thinking about legal procedures then? But at least let us first establish the concept of legal rights and get the majority of people to accept it. Only then can we talk about turning the concept into actual rights.

But if we don't even think the concept is important, then there is no point in fighting to have citizens' rights written into the Constitution and cheering it.

PART TWO

The Chinese Communist Party

and the new New Democracy

Proceeding from Reality

Qi Xin

Reality

To seek truth from facts, proceed from reality, integrate theory with practice, and formulate policies and methods in the light of actual situations — this is being stressed by the Chinese Communist Party these days in opposition to approaching things from concept and theory.

To proceed from reality is a basic tenet of materialism. Yet during the Cultural Revolution a lot of the press articles and policies and measures of the Chinese Communist Party were not based on reality but on Mao quotations which had become the criterion of right and wrong in everything. When people had differences of opinions, each would select quotations to his own advantage, quote them and claim that he was upholding truth. It was all a great battle of quotations. Whoever tried to base arguments on reality would be labeled as "pragmatists," "revisionists" or "opposing Mao Zedong Thought."

Over a long period Mao Zedong had been built up as "absolute authority" on everything. The ten years of the Cultural Revolution had further built up the idea that his words were the criterion of all truth. This is an attitude that cannot be changed overnight.

Beginning from the end of March 1978 the Chinese Communist press no longer printed Mao quotations in bold type. On May 31 *Guangming Daily* aired the view that one should do more than quoting the ready-made formulas of Marxism-Leninism and Mao Zedong Thought. On June 6 the Chinese Communist Party published Deng Xiaoping's speech at the All-Army Political Work Conference in which he dwelt at length on the importance of seeking truth from facts.

He said, "The purpose of holding meetings, giving reports, passing resolutions or doing any kind of work is to solve problems." If in doing all this one does not proceed from reality and seek truth from facts, then "we'll only be making empty talk and cannot solve any problem."

He explained why practice is the one and only test of truth. "Chairman Mao," he said, "said that he seldom quoted from Marx and Lenin in his writings, that he felt uneasy that his words were quoted frequently and over and over by the newspapers. People should learn to write in their own words. This of course does not mean one shouldn't quote from others at all, only that one shouldn't do it all the time. . . . The living soul of Marxism is to make specific analysis of specific conditions. Marxism-Leninism-Mao Zedong Thought will lose vitality if it is not integrated with actual conditions. It is the duty of leading cadres to integrate the instructions of the Central Committee or upper-level organizations with the actual conditions of their own units. They should not function like a receiving department and simply transmit instructions."

Deng went on to say, "We cannot solve any problem by merely copying old documents word for word, much less solving it correctly. If that's all we do, even if we pay lavish lip service to Mao Zedong Thought, we'll actually be going against it. We must clear away the pernicious influence of Lin Biao and the Gang of Four, set things on the right course, unshackle ourselves spiritually and emancipate our minds thoroughly. This is indeed a serious task."

To the writer's mind, "unshackling spiritually" means

people are once again free to proceed from reality instead of having to use Mao quotations as the criterion of everything.

Honesty

When we try to solve actual problems by proceeding from reality, inevitably we will face the difficulties, shortcomings and mistakes that exist in reality. Only when we face them squarely will we be able to overcome them. Contradictions are resolved by exposing them first.

During the Cultural Revolution the Chinese Communist press very rarely reported the specific problems, mistakes and shortcomings in the political and economic life on the Chinese mainland. It very rarely exposed contradictions. If it did, it had to be some overwhelmingly shocking news — the Liu Shaoqi question, the Lin Biao incident, the Gang of Four incident, or the "criticize Deng" movement engineered by the Gang. The impression one gets is that the high-ranking leaders are never wrong. When any of them does make a mistake, his political career is finished. When this happens again and again, people begin to lose faith in the Communist press. People abroad now tend to dismiss the Chinese Communist press and publications as pure "propaganda." By propaganda they don't mean "wide publicity of certain facts or truth" but "untrue or partially true reports serving certain political purposes." In other words, Chinese Communist propaganda is either exaggerated or one-sided. It reports only good news, never bad news.

An article dealing with writing style in the first issue of the recently republished monthly *Chinese Language (Zhongguo Yuwen)* points out that the prevailing style of writing is deeply influenced by Gang of Four formulas, its most outstanding characteristic being to "brag and tell lies or half truths." People who have done something well are described as near perfect. People who have made mistakes or have shortcomings are denounced as thoroughly bad. Problems in work are never mentioned or touched upon vaguely as something that had happened in the past. Achievements are blown up out of all proportion. To stress 'unafraid of hardship' something that had happened on a fine day is changed to a day of wind and snow. To show somebody who did something 'with initiative' even though he had done nothing beforehand, he is described as 'making full preparations.' To emphasize 'enthusiastic support,' discussions that actually took place on the following day are described as 'going on all through the night.'"

Awesome-sounding reasons are given for this kind of half-true propaganda, such as "in making propaganda one must proceed from the viewpoint of class struggle" or "everything should serve politics" or "we cannot expose our weakness to the enemy."

In a word, guided by a "viewpoint of class struggle" honesty can be thrown to the winds. But why be afraid to let the "enemy" know about your problems and shortcomings? Isn't it losing a great advantage to avoid a little trouble when you try to hide from your people truths already known to the enemy?

In recent months the Chinese Communist press has been reporting more shortcomings, exposing more contradictions and printing criticism of things done by the authorities. The June 16 *Guangming Daily* carried an article criticizing the *Second Draft Proposal of Simplified Han Characters* saying that it is immature and has a lot of shortcomings, that opinions were not solicited widely beforehand and to use the simplified words widely as soon as the draft proposal was published is tantamount to a surprise attack.

On the other hand, whether in China or abroad, there are still people who cling to their spiritual shackles and hold that the leader's authority is untouchable, that there are no counter-opinions on the mainland or even if there are, they represent a tiny minority and should not be brought into the open. One can tell from reading the Communist press that there are still a great many cadres who are afraid to make decisions, who only dare act as a "receiving department," who like to sing the praises of others and hear praises about themselves. Obviously not a few among the Chinese Communist leadership have realized that this dishonest style of work must be changed if progress is to be made.

Practicality

Two Chinese Communist political slogans are "discuss the intangibles" and "discuss the tangibles." The former means discussing theory, principles and policies. The latter means discussing practical work. The Chinese Communist Party has always stood for combining these two aspects. But for a long time in the past people dealt only with the intangibles. Many people spent all their time talking and did no practical work. As a result, economic growth and practical work lagged pitifully and theoretical work, as it was not integrated with practice, made no progress either. No significant theoretical work on social science appeared during the Cultural Revolution that has any bearing on the composition, system and development of a socialist society.

Theory is important but it can develop only when integrated with reality, that is, applied to solving practical problems. Lately, quite a number of weighty articles on the theory of socialist social science have appeared in the Communist press. The June 16 *People's Daily* published an article by Xin Bengsi entitled *On the Criterion of Truth.* It explains in theory why practice is the sole criterion of truth and refutes the view that "Marxism is also a criterion of truth." It points out that when we say "Marxism is truth" it does not mean "Marxism is the criterion of truth." "Just as no truth can be proven by itself, Marxism cannot prove itself true but has to be proven true by practice." "Neither can Marxism serve as a criterion of other truths. For example, can a certain Marxist principle prove true the principles of modern natural science? Shouldn't scientific principles be proven true by scientific experiments? . . . To make Marxism a criterion of truth is actually making it a system of cognition that does not have to be tested by practice or developed through practice, a system of cognition that is predetermined, self-explanatory and self-contained. Such a system is not scientific truth, only a mysterious spiritual product of certain 'prophets.'"

Clearly the aim of the article is to refute in theory the attitude of making Mao quotations the criterion of everything so that all speeches, policies and measures hereafter will again be worked out from a materialist approach.

If theoretical discussions are conducted in order to solve actual problems, then theory itself will develop. Discussing theory for its own sake will only lead to retrogression in theory.

Demolishing the Myth of the Infallibility of Mao Zedong

Qi Xin

On its 57th anniversary (July 1, 1978), the Chinese Communist Party published the text of Mao Zedong's talk to some 7,000 senior cadres of the CPC on January 30, 1962. This *Talk at an Enlarged Working Conference Convened by the Central Committee of the CPC* (below simplified as *Talk to 7,000*) had appeared in Red Guard publications during the Cultural Revolution, and was included in a Japanese-language edition of *Long Live Mao Zedong Thought*. It had never appeared in any official mainland China publication before. Next day, July 2, the Party daily *People's Daily* and journal *Red Flag* separately ran editorials underlining the importance the Chinese Communists put on this talk today. *Red Flag* headed its editorial *A Powerful Ideological Weapon for Realising the General Task for the New Period* and the daily gave its editorial the title of *Democratic Centralism Should Be Practised in Earnest.* Both editorials stressed the relevance of the *Talk to 7,000* to contemporary political life in China. Publishing the text of Mao's talk was more than commemorative.

It was significant in that it broke with the established Chinese Communist practice of avoiding all mention of Mao Zedong ever making a mistake, and let Mao demolish the myth of his infallibility with his own words. It also stressed the need for democracy. Ye Jianying said not long after

---

[1] See *Peking Review* * 27 1978, pp. 6–22

the Gang of Four was toppled that for several years "political life inside and outside the Party was very abnormal." Mao's *Talk to 7,000* in 1962 more or less points out why such an abnormal situation could arise. It seems that the Chinese Communists now realise they have a big problem on their hands to get democracy to work in China.

"Did Mao make mistakes?" and "Was there democracy in China?" have been the two most oft asked questions in recent years among Chinese inside and outside the country, and among foreigners interested in China. Confusion over these two questions has caused many to doubt what they believed in the past. It has caused many to fear for the future of China.

How did Mao's 1962 talk touch upon these two questions? And how does this talk made 16 years earlier relate to the present political situation?

Was Mao Ever Wrong?

Did Mao make mistakes? This is a question that simply cannot be asked in mainland China. Even now, after Mao's talk in which he clearly admits to making mistakes has been published, it is very hard to imagine within the near future the official Chinese press discussing what specifically were his mistakes. Ever since the setting up of the People's Republic in 1949, the Chinese Communists, particularly after the Cultural Revolution broke out, have been building up Mao as a great leader who never made a mistake. Everything developed according to his "great strategic plans"! These myths were once resolutely upheld by the Chinese Communists of every echelon. Of course, there were many who did not believe these myths, but in the political atmosphere prevailing then, nobody dared say so. During the Cultural Revolution a friend of mine once raised the question: Chairman Mao said that one should always look at things with a 'one-divides-into-two' attitude.* Shouldn't we also look at

---

* Looking at things from both sides, taking in both merits and shortcomings.

Demolishing the Myth of the Infallibility of Mao 83

Mao Zedong Thought with a 'one-divides-into-two' attitude? For this, my friend was branded a "counter-revolutionary opposed to Mao Zedong Thought."

As everyone knows from his own experience, there is no one who does not make a mistake sometime or other in his life. And as the Cultural Revolution developed, particularly after 1974, many people in mainland China began to have their doubts about these assidously fostered assertions. They could see from everyday life the assertion that Mao never makes a mistake to be plainly a myth. Their doubts increased after the Gang of Four was ousted and many of their misdeeds came to light, especially in reassessing the "Counterattack on the Rightist Wind to Reverse Correct Verdicts", "Criticism of Deng" and "dictatorship of a sinister line in the 17 years following liberation." Abroad, there was even talk about a Gang of Five, and this idea is not entirely unknown in China. Since Mao was the supreme leader, he cannot be entirely blameless for the emergence of the Gang of Four. Still, because his contributions to the Chinese revolution are very great, his prestige among the people is high, and in addition, he has been given a tremendous build-up, so doubts are usually not too openly voiced.

In February 1977 *The Seventies* published the minutes of a forum on *China During the Cultural Revolution*** in which one speaker said that Mao's Thought expressed in the last years of his life had become "petrified." After this article appeared I heard many vehemently deny this was the case. While in Canton in August, 1977 I heard a cadre declare in public, "Chairman Mao has never made a mistake! None whatsoever! There must not be a shadow of doubt about the last years of his life!" From a dialectical materialist viewpoint this declaration itself is pretty petrified.

Yet three months before I heard this dogmatic declaration the Communist Party of China had put out the fifth volume of the *Selected Works of Mao Zedong*. In it, in at

---

** *The Case of the Gang of Four* by the same author

least six places, Mao mentioned that no one can avoid making mistakes, that there was not a single person in the world who did not make mistakes.***This shows that those in highest authority in China were already aware that if the mistakes in the past were to be righted and things were to be done properly words or sentences from Mao should no longer be used as the criterion for distinguishing right from wrong. Later, in evaluating the first 17 years after liberation (1949–1966), on the questions of education, science and technology, literature and the arts, and the policy towards intellectuals, particularly with regard to the rehabilitation of Deng Xiaoping and Huang Kecheng, the Chinese Communists no longer let themselves be restricted by Mao's impulsive opinions or some resolution or document he had once approved. If everything that Mao said was regarded as eternally correct then the vast changes which have taken place on the mainland over the past year could not have occurred and, naturally, there could have been no rehabilitation of Deng Xiaoping.

Ever since May–June, 1978, many articles have appeared in the Chinese Communist press, particularly Deng Xiaoping's June speech at the All-Army Political Work Conference, in which heavy emphasis is placed on proceeding from reality and not from dogma. "Everything must proceed from reality" and not by "copying straight from Marx, Lenin and Chairman Mao and resting content with mechanical copying, transmitting and reproducing" and so on, "doing everything strictly according to books." "Practice alone," Deng declared, "is the criterion of truth," and "not Marxism." On June 24, *Jiefangjun Bao* published a long article by a Special Correspondent under the title of *A Fundamental Principle of Marxism* which was reprinted by *Guangming Daily* the following day. This "fundamental principle" the article discusses is "the integration of theory with practice." "Only practice," it said, "can prove the objective truthfulness

---

****Teng Hsiaoping, a political biography* by the same author for details.

of a political line. The result of practice will show whether this line is conducive to the development of the social productive forces, whether it has brought real gains to socialism and the masses — this is the only arbiter of the correctness or incorrectness of a line."

The article came out strongly against "turning Marxism-Leninism into a religious dogma. . . including the dogma in the form of publishing 'quotations'," and stated that "As to certain particular principles, conclusions and slogans of Marxism-Leninism-Mao Zedong Thought, they will change along with the change of historical conditions." "It is necessary, normal and inevitable to revise certain outdated principles on the basis of Marxism-Leninism-Mao Zedong Thought and in the light of the actual situation." *Guangming Daily* on June 25 in its editorial *Unity of Theory with Practice* discussed the problem of "petrification" of theory and slogans. Quoting Lenin, it said, "Every slogan the Party addresses to the people is bound to become petrified, become a dead letter, yet remain valid for many even when the conditions which rendered it necessary have changed. That is an unavoidable evil, and it is impossible to ensure the correctness of Party policy unless we learn to combat and overcome it". [1]

Five days later the CPC published Mao Zedong's 1962 *Talk to 7,000*. In this talk Mao said: "On June 12 last year (1961), the last day of the Working Conference in Peking convened by the Central Committee of the Communist Party of China, I discussed my own shortcomings and mistakes. I asked comrades to convey what I said to the provinces and localities. I found out later that many localities were not informed. It's as if my mistakes could or should be kept hidden. Comrades, they mustn't be kept hidden! Of all the mistakes made by the Central Committee I am responsible

---

[1] V. I. Lenin, *Valuable Admissions to Pitirim Sorokin*, p. 190 Volume 28, *Collected Works*, Moscow, 1965, Progress Publishers.

for those directly related to me and I have a share of the responsibility for those not directly related to me, because I am its Chairman. It's not that I want other people to slough off their responsibility — there are some other comrades who also bear responsibility — but I am the person who ought to be primarily responsible...""For shortcomings and mistakes in our work in the last few years, the responsibility rests first with the Central Committee and, in the Central Committee, primarily with me."

These two passages of Mao's dispose of the myth that Mao never made a mistake. Note that Mao emphatically repeats that it is he who should primarily be held responsible for the shortcomings and mistakes of the Central Committee. Applying the spirit of his statements to what happened during the Cultural Revolution and his last years, then Mao is directly or indirectly responsible for the errors of the Central Committee. (Attacking a vast number of veteran cadres, nominating Lin Biao to be his successor, and writing this into the Party Constitution, upgrading Wang Hongwen, distorting history to attack by innuendo certain leading cadres, mounting a "Counterattack On the Rightist Wind To Reverse Correct Verdicts", "Criticism of Deng" and the handling of the Tian An Men Incident and the related decisions and so on.) According to what Mao said himself, Mao, as the Chairman of the Central Committee, should be held responsible for these mistakes. Even though people may not speak about them because of his tremendous contribution to the Chinese revolution, the poor state of his health during his last years and the ensuing chaos of the Cultural Revolution which enabled ambitious careerists like the Gang of Four to get into high position, Mao was directly or indirectly responsible.

Mao's Mistakes

In his talk, Mao spoke of his shortcomings and mistakes. What were they? They were not mentioned specifically in his talk in 1962. Neither was the self-criticism he made on June 12, 1961, on the last day of the Working Conference convened by the Central Committee included in the Japanese *Long Live Mao Zedong Thought*. Perhaps, after a suitable lapse of time, when the Chinese Communists begin dealing specifically with the questions and errors of this period, they will bring out the self-criticism. But from the *Talk to 7,000* published this year, it can be seen more or less what exactly Mao's shortcomings and mistakes were during those years.

He pointed out in his talk: "We must . . . sum up the working experience of 12 years, particularly that of the past four years, for there are many questions and consequently many opinions. . . . A few provinces have shown some initiative and let people speak out. The early ones started self-criticism in 1959, the late starters began in 1961."

These words indicate that the conference was mainly convened to sum up the working experience during the four years from 1958 to 1961. The shortcomings and mistakes Mao spoke of were made during these four years. During this period the rift between China and the Soviet Union started, the Great Leap Forward, the General Line for building socialism and the People's Communes were summed up as the "three red banners," the Lushan Meeting of 1959 and the struggle against "Right deviation" took place and were followed by three years of natural disasters and grave economic difficulties.

In Mao's talk he said what led to the formulation of the "three red banners" was that in economic construction prior to 1959, "we copied almost everything from the Soviet Union with very little creativeness on our part. It was absolutely necessary to do so at that time, and yet it was also a weakness — a lack of creativeness and of ability to stand on our feet. Certainly this could not be our long-term policy. Beginning from 1958 we established the clear-cut policy of relying mainly on our own efforts while seeking foreign aid by way of support. At the Second Session of the Party's Eighth National Congress in 1958, we adopted the general line of 'going all out, aiming high and achieving greater, faster, better and more economical results in building socialism.' In the same year the People's Communes were established and the slogan of 'Great Leap Forward' was realised. For a certain period after the general line for socialist construction was proclaimed, we hadn't the time to work out a complete set of specific principles, policies and measures suited to our conditions, nor did the possibility exist for us to do so because our experience was still insufficient. ... This possibility came into being only after a period of time, after we had suffered some setbacks and acquired both positive and negative experience."

This means that at that time the policy of the "three red banners" had to be precipitately rushed out so as to shake off reliance on Soviet technology and stand up on one's own feet as rapidly as possible. The concrete manifestations of the "three red banners" were: the big drive for steel, building high-yield fields and changing the system of ownership by the production teams to ownership by the commune. What was attained by adopting the "three red banners"?

For one, the many large water-control projects were started then, and many of the smaller steel plants and mines operating today were also the products of the policy. In addition, Chinese personnel began taking over many technical aspects of work. All these are positive achievements and can't be denied. But on the other hand, there were also a lot of problems, particularly in communization in the rural areas. Communization was carried out too rapidly and there were not enough specific policies and measures worked out to 'cope with the many problems which arose with the sudden change-over to commune ownership. The commune had to administer the production teams' manpower, their means of production, the distribution of products, the livelihood of the peasants themselves (including food, creches, education, births and deaths, and old age, and sick payments.) The commune coped by levelling income between all production teams, deploying manpower and the means of production of production teams without reimbursement and

Demolishing the Myth of the Infallibility of Mao   89

recalling all state credits provided to the peasants. These measures caused panic among the peasantry. Many chopped down the fruit trees in their yards to use the timber for tools, slaughtered their poultry to save them from being communized without payment, and in some communes the peasants were forced to hand over gratis whatever gold or silver jewelry they had. Even private sewing machines were taken away from their owners to build up the assets and property of the commune. In addition to levelling the rich and the poor, there was too much calling on the peasants to do unpaid labour. All these things undermined peasant initiative.

Inappropriate measures led to huge economic losses, which aggravated the difficulties brought on by three successive years of bad weather. Economic losses were also incurred through the vast investments in man-power and material in steel-making and getting very little up-to-standard steel in return, and the huge concentration of manpower and resources on experimental fields to get "hundreds of thousands of catties of grain per *mu*" leaving the rest of fields untended, instead of making use of all arable land to secure greater returns.

The evaluation of the "three red banners" was the focus of struggle at the Lushan Meeting. It ended with the removal of Peng Dehuai from office and was followed by the struggle against "right deviation", which struck hard at a large number of Party cadres throughout the country when, in fact, many of their views were quite correct. For example, a middle-school headmaster I knew appealed for rational close-planting when the rest of the people were working feverishly to produce high-yields through saturation planting. This friend of mine got an excellent yield from his experimental field whereas the peasants under irrational leadership got very little for their excessive zeal. Yet when the struggle against "right deviation" started, the headmaster came under heavy fire, being accused of damaging the enthusiasm of the peasants" and "opposing Chairman Mao's 'Eight-Point Charter for Agriculture'"(the fifth point in the 'Eight Points' called for rational close-planting.)* The headmaster was criticised throughout the country by his colleagues and he was "disciplined inside the Party" and branded a "Right opportunist element." He was rehabilitated only after Chairman Mao's *Talk to 7,000* in 1962.

In his 1962 talk Mao spoke about insufficient experience in implementing the "three red banners" and self-reliance, about attacking people, slapping labels to put pressure on them, not allowing others to speak out, and mishandling some cases. He said: "As soon as cases which have been mishandled are discovered, after re-examination the people concerned will be rehabilitated and apologies will be made to them, so that they will enjoy ease of mind and lift up their head again."

In a nutshell, at that time the Chinese Communist Party had made mistakes in policies and measures in pushing the "three red banners," and in the subsequent movement against right opportunism it wrongly attacked some people so that many were afraid to speak out and democracy inside and outside the Party was seriously impaired. Mao reviewed these mistakes and said he was responsible and stressed the need to practise democracy so as to unite the people and the Party.

Reasons for Mistakes

The Enlarged Working Conference was called in early 1962 right after the "three red banners," the struggle against

---

* Eight-Point Charter for Agriculture; 1, soil-deep ploughing, soil improvement, general survey of soil and land planning; 2, fertilizer — rational application of fertilizer; 3, water – building water conservancy works and rational use of water; 4, seeds – popularization of good strains; 5, close-planting – rational close-planting; 6, plant protection – the prevention and elimination of plant diseases and pests; 7, management – field management; 8, tools – innovation of farm implements.

Demolishing the Myth of the Infallibility of Mao 91

"right deviation" and three years of economic difficulties. Looking back over the 12 years after the founding of the People's Republic, economic construction in the first eight years to a large extent was along Soviet lines. Although the country still lacked the ability to stand on her own feet there were fewer, or less obvious mistakes. In the following four years when economic construction was carried on self-reliantly, there were mistakes and greater difficulties resulted. When the difficulties were initially overcome, the Chinese Communist Party convened the 1962 conference to sum up their work. Mao Zedong in dealing with the shortcomings and mistakes revealed at this meeting said, "We still lack experience in building socialism."

He recalled his talk to Edgar Snow in 1960. "As you know," he said, "we have a set of principles, policies and measures with regard to politics, military affairs and class struggle; but when it comes to socialist construction, we hadn't any in the past, and we still don't have experience. You may say, 'Haven't you been at it for 11 years?' Well, yes, we have, but we still lack knowledge and experience. Even if we are beginning to acquire a little, it doesn't amount to much." When Snow asked Mao about China's long-term construction plans, Mao replied: "I don't know." At the 1962 Working Conference Mao said again to Party members, "Comrades, it's true that we don't have such long-term plans yet."

What Mao said to Snow was totally at variance with what the Chinese Communists had been saying about Mao's "far-sightedness," "great strategic plans" and his prediction that "communism will come by the year 2001," and such things. Like everyone else, Mao had no long-term plans before experience had been acquired.

Mao also admitted: "In socialist construction, we are still acting blindly to a very large extent. For us the socialist economy is still in many respects unknown realm of necessity. Take me by the way of example. There are many problems which I still don't understand. I know very little about industry and commerce for instance. I know something about agriculture, but this is only relatively speaking — I still don't know much." He added that "I have paid rather more attention to problems related to the relations of production, the system. When it comes to the productive forces, I know very little."

So much for all the ballyhoo about the omniscience and omnipotence of Mao, who besides being a philosopher, statesman, military expert and poet had many other attributes which Mao himself denied, such as his being an economist, and even an authority of sports!

Mao in his 1962 talk analysed from a philosophic plane the reasons for the mistakes. "Our understanding of the objective world necessarily involves a process. In the beginning we do not understand, or do not completely understand, and it is only through repeated practice which leads to achievements and victories, tumbles and setbacks, and through comparison of successes and failure that it is possible to develop complete or relatively complete understanding. When that point is reached, we shall have more initiative, enjoy greater freedom and become somewhat wiser. Freedom is the recognition of necessity and the transformation of the objective world. Only on the basis of the recognition of necessity can people have freedom of action. This is the dialectics of freedom and necessity. Necessity as such is objectively existing law. Before we recognize it our action can never be conscious, it partakes of blindness. Under these conditions we are foolish people. Haven't we done many foolish things during the last few years?"

Insufficient experience and the lack of an adequate understanding of the objective laws of things were the reasons for the mistakes and the "many foolish things." But are these unavoidable in any new undertaking? Was it not possible to make fewer mistakes? In his talk, Mao Zedong dwelt particularly on promoting democracy, letting people speak out, collecting and concentrating the views and wisdom of the masses. "If we give full play to democracy," he said, "we will be able to do our work better and overcome the difficulties we meet all the more quickly. Our cause

Demolishing the Myth of the Infallibility of Mao

will then develop much more smoothly."

The focus of Mao's talk was on giving full play to democracy. He recognises that democracy makes it possible for work to be done better. It means he also recognises that autocracy and refusing to listen to other opinions, the opposite of democracy, is a major cause of mistakes.

About Democracy in Practice

In his talk Mao raised some points about democratic centralism.

He first dwelt upon the method of holding the conference. With the Chinese Communists, the usual method was, as Mao said, hearing a report first, then discussing it and approving it with a show of hands. This was not a democratic method. The discussions were only a way for the participants to show their absolute support for the report. At the 1962 meeting, Mao Zedong proposed holding the conference in another way. Instead of calling the Political Bureau to discuss the draft report and then approving it before presenting to the meeting, Mao proposed getting a few people to draw up a draft and distributing it directly to the 7,000 at the meeting to discuss in groups and state their views. The views were then collected and turned over to a committee which would study them and incorporate them into the draft. The revised draft was then presented to the full meeting for approval. This method, Mao said, would give full play to democracy, pool the wisdom from all quarters and would really get everyone's contribution.

The second point he said in his talk about democratic centralism was the method of using discussions and reasoning and letting people speak out to resolve problems and differences among the people, and not to resort to curses, fists, knives and guns. The initiative of the masses must not be suppressed through not allowing people to speak or refusing to listen to their views and opinions, he said.

Mao also proposed genuine collective leadership and not

one-man autocracy by the first secretary. An important principle he set down was that the minority must be subordinate to the majority. "Take the Standing Committee of the Political Bureau of the Central Committee by way of example," he said, "it often happens that when I say something, regardless of whether it is correct or incorrect, if the others don't agree, I must accede to their opinion because they are the majority." He was against what he called "one-man tyranny," First Secretary despotism. "Isn't there an opera called *'The Tyrant Bids His Lady Farewell?'*" he asked. "If these comrades remain unchanged, the day will come when they too will be 'biding their ladies farewell.'"

Another important point Mao raised concerning democratic centralism was that "the minority must be allowed to reserve their opinions. . . ." "And it is advantageous to allow the minority both inside and outside the Party to do so," Mao said.

Mao held that to create a democratic atmosphere so that people will dare speak out, make criticism, raise dissenting views and opinions, there should be fewer arrests and fewer executions. He advocated "not seizing on other's faults, not putting hats on people (sticking labels) and not wielding the big stick so that people will be free from fear and will dare to speak out." He said, "If we arrest and execute people at will, everyone will fear for himself and nobody will dare to speak. In such an atmosphere there can't be much democracy."

How To Ensure Genuine Democracy?

What Mao said about democratic centralism is all very correct in theory, but one glance at the political reality of Communist China, particularly during the Cultural Revolution, the discrepancy between theory and reality is glaring, in some places practice was the direct opposite of theory.

Take for instance the method of holding meetings. Over the past ten years or so every time we read a report

Demolishing the Myth of the Infallibility of Mao

about the various conferences the Chinese Communists have held, the method employed was not the one Mao advocated, but the method he had condemned as being "not so good." It has consisted of two or three people delivering reports and all the other delegates saying something to endorse the reports. There have been no dissenting views or even amendments, not even a supplementary idea or an explanation. Even the 11th Party Congress and the 5th National People's Congress held after the Gang of Four was purged varied very little from the earlier congresses, as far as we can make out from the press, anyway.

As for using the method of discussions and reasoning to resolve problems and contradictions among the people, it has been the exact reverse since the Cultural Revolution started. In the big-character posters (dazibao) plastered up on walls everywhere and in the big "debates" during the Cultural Revolution, there was very little reasoning, but an over-abundance of curses, fists, knives and guns, arrests, executions, seizing on the imagined faults of others, slapping labels liberally, wielding the big stick and even extorting confessions through torture, and other cruel and bestial methods. No one dared to say what they really thought. The whole country was in the grip of terror. There was absolutely no democracy to speak of.

Prior to the ouster of the Gang of Four the Chinese Communist press had consistently refused to allow a single dissenting view to appear in print. Things today have vastly improved. Every so often the mainland press carries reports about the less luminous side of society in their pages, also Letters to the Editor criticising this and that. The criticisms all come within set limits, mainly about things which the highest authorities have already pointed out for censure. But few are the independent criticisms. For instance, are the Chinese Communists again indulging in a personality cult? Shouldn't there be a fixed term of office for the highest leader? Have Mao and the Cultural Revolution been factually assessed? Were the excesses which have come to light due solely to the Gang of Four, or was it because of the

Cultural Revolution? These are questions many are asking behind closed doors, but which have yet to appear in the mainland press.

As to the other principles about the minority subordinating to majority decision, opposition to one-man autocracy and allowing the minority to reserve their opinions, they simply vanished after the Cultural Revolution began. According to the press communiques, the reports, and resolutions at Chinese Communist conferences were always approved "unanimously."

One does not have to have a very high level of understanding of Marxism-Leninism to realise that there is something not quite proper about writing Lin Biao's succession to Mao into the Party Constitution, and the April 7, 1976 decision removing Deng Xiaoping from all posts inside and outside the Party. Then why were the decisions "unanimously approved?" The April 7 decision states that it was proposed by Chairman Mao and unanimously approved by the Political Bureau. This means that Mao had made the proposal and even those who had objected had not dared to say "No." They were not expected to, so approval was "unanimous." The behaviour of the majority of the Political Bureau members since Mao's death shows that at least in the matter of April 7 decision concerning Deng Xiaoping, the majority had been subordinated to the minority. Nor had the majority been allowed to "reserve their opinions." It couldn't have been "unanimously approved" otherwise.

During the Cultural Revolution, particularly during the last years of Mao's life, there was a strong smell of "one-man or minority autocracy." Otherwise, why was democratic centralism so singularly absent in those years?

The July 2, 1978, editorial of *People's Daily* quoting from Mao's 1966 decision to print and distribute his 1962 *Talk to 7,000* said, "It is quite a problem, this question of genuinely implementing democratic centralism. It will require painstaking education, trials at selected spots and popularization and consistent application before there will be genuine democratic centralism. Otherwise, it will only

Demolishing the Myth of the Infallibility of Mao 97

be empty talk with most comrades." That same year even as Mao Zedong uttered these words a most undemocratic period began on the Chinese mainland. What Mao had said to the 7,000 cadres became empty talk.

Why had this happened? In his 1962 talk and his 1966 decision, Mao had believed it was essentially a question of education. "Some comrades still know nothing about democratic centralism. They should now begin to establish this in their minds," Mao had said, and stressed that there must not be "one-man tyranny." In other words, there can be no democracy if the person with authority does not work in a democratic way. *People's Daily* also said on July 2 that "democratic centralism is fundamentally a question of world outlook. Was it slaves or heroes who made history? The answer involves a fundamental viewpoint — historical materialism or historical idealism. Unless this fundamental viewpoint is clarified there can be no genuine democratic centralism."

I agree with this. But on the other hand, the political realities of Communist China over the years tell us it is far from enough to pin the hopes for genuine democratic centralism in a region, province or nation or in the Party only on educating the people and improving a leader's moral character, his thinking and method of work. This leaves too much to chance. To have real democracy, there must be strict observance of a system of "bidding his lady farewell." That is, there should be organs of check and balance and rules for periodical checks. If leaders are found and proved to have a serious autocratic style of work, then they should be made to "bid their ladies farewell." (Note, what Mao meant by "bidding their ladies farewell" was being "toppled," "demoted" and so on, not literally "bidding adieu to their wives.") If all that can be done is to wait until every First Secretary, every chief man, is properly educated before there is genuine democracy, then democracy will remain a hollow and pious wish.

Another point is that publicity given to leaders at all levels including the supreme leader, must be based on facts, exactly as they are, no more and no less, and both shortcomings and achievements should be publicized. Never give people the impression that so-and-so never makes a mistake! Or that so-and-so's mistakes must never be mentioned! If the build-up leads to this impression then at any meeting there will be no minority subordinating to the majority, but the reverse, perhaps subordinating to one person, because that person never makes a mistake, is always correct and every proposal and every opinion that person advances is correct. This being the case, why would anyone dare disagree with that person?

If Mao's *Talk to 7,000* had been made public in 1962, and perhaps his 1961 self-criticism as well, it would have been extremely difficult for Lin Biao to sell his personality cult and for the Gang of Four to make quotations from Mao into sacred dogma. It would also have been extremely difficult during the last years of Mao's life for a situation to arise in which, as Ye Jianying said, "the political life inside and outside the Party was extremely abnormal."

Can the Chinese Communists provide genuine democracy? This is a question many inside and outside the country are deeply concerned with. Publication of Mao's 1962 *Talk to the 7,000* was a significant start and should do a lot to establish the concept of democracy. If specific counterbalancing organs of power are built into the system and the practice of making out that the leaders never make a mistake is abandoned, then there is every hope of some form of democracy on the Chinese mainland.

The 'Leftist' Ideological Trend

in China

Qi Xin

Political movements and line struggles have surfaced continuously in China since the establishment of the People's Republic in 1949. The focus has been opposition to a rightist line, or the correct line versus a rightist line. For over twenty years there has been no mention of a 'leftist' line, nor has there been any public or genuine movement to oppose a 'leftist' deviation. The history of recent political movement includes the Anti-Rightist Campaign in 1957, the struggle against the rightist opportunism of Peng Dehuai, the movement against rightist deviation after August 1962, the 'Four Clean' Movement to rectify capitalist roaders within the Party at the end of 1964, the struggle against Liu Shaoqi's revisionist line at the start of the Cultural Revolution in 1966, the movement to criticize the 'left in form, right in essence' line of Lin Biao at the end of 1971, the campaign to criticize Confucius in 1974, the movement to 'repulse the rightist deviationist wind' that started in 1975 and the criticism of the 'fake left, real right' line of the Gang of Four which began in October of 1976 and which ended recently. All of these were struggles against rightist tendencies and deviations.

Although Lin Biao and the Gang of Four were widely regarded as having carried out an ultraleft line, Communist Party propaganda has always added 'actual right' or 'real right' labels to the denunciations of them. When the rectification and criticism of Lin Biao began at the end of 1971, people expected that the ultraleftist ideology which he had pushed since the Cultural Revolution began would be thoroughly cleared away. Instead, the direction of the movement was aimed at criticizing Confucius and Lin Biao on the evidence of a few hand-written characters by Lin Biao quoting Confucius's "restrain oneself and restore the rites." This was seized upon as proof of Lin Biao's ultrarightist essence. When Deng Xiaoping was being criticized, it was "the capitalist roaders are still on the capitalist road," but when the Gang of Four fell, they were also criticized as "capitalist roaders on the capitalist road." Lin Biao and Liu Shaoqi obviously followed different tendencies, but both were dubbed rightist. The Gang of Four and Deng Xiaoping clearly represented opposing factions, but both were called 'capitalist roaders.'

A recent article in the *People's Daily* [1] written by the Shanghai Publishing Bureau criticism group criticizing the Gang of Four's ultraleftist features insists that their line was in fact "a rightist line that could not be more rightist." It goes on to say that their ultraleftism was "a manifestation of their rightist line, a strategic method of achieving their rightist goals. . . using fake 'leftism' to cover up real rightism."

What is 'leftist'? What is 'rightist'? What is the connection between the 'fake left, real right' of the Gang of Four and 'leftist' ideology in China? Which should be thoroughly criticized, the ultra-rightist essence of the Gang of Four, or the 'leftist' ideological trend? Since Liberation, has there been such a thing as a 'leftist' ideological trend or 'leftist' line? If so, what has its influence been? These are questions which need to be discussed.

In the vocabulary of the Chinese Communist Party, there are two kinds of left, one without quotations and one with. The former refers to left in the positive sense; that is, progressive or revolutionary politically, as in left-wing writers as progressive, revolutionary writers. The latter includes quotation marks and indicates an overly 'leftist' ideological

---

[1] *People's Daily*, June 28, 1976.

trend, or so-called 'leftist' opportunism in political line. Its characteristics are: thinking which is beyond the actual stage of social development, beyond the level of mass consciousness; subjective and unrealistic demands; adventurousness in orientation, policy and action and overzealousness in dealing with struggle. The mistakes of 'leftist' opportunism arise from petit-bourgeois fanaticism, impetuosity, lack of investigation, failure to link up theory with practice and pay attention to tactics, starting from theory and subjectivism in doing things. In the history of the Chinese Communist Party, Wang Ming's 'leftist' opportunism inflicted tremendous damage on the Chinese revolution.

At the other end of the spectrum is rightist opportunism. The Chinese Communist Party holds that rightist opportunism has the following characteristics: lagging behind the masses's level of consciousness when objective conditions are ripe and the masses are demanding to move forward. Rightist leadership always listens to the advice of backward elements and stays bogged down in conservatism. The rightist line in the history of the Chinese Communist Party was expressed in the emphasis on unity with the Guomindang to the exclusion of struggle. To retreat when an agricultural movement is reaching a peak, to hold back when the conditions are ripe for attack, to surrender when victory is within grasp — these are expressions of a rightist line.

According to the Marxist-Leninist point of view, opportunism, whether it is rightist or 'leftist', is a betrayal of principles in political ideology or line within the Party. It is a reflection of bourgeois thinking in the Party and the results are detrimental to the revolution, so its essence is rightist. What is deemed rightist in Chinese Communist Party vocabulary is the opposite of left (without quotations) and refers to conservatism and reaction in political thinking.

The dialectical theory of knowledge holds that everything has both form and essence. Every phenomenon manifests a certain intrinsic quality, and every intrinsic quality must express itself in phenomena, so there is no form without essence and no essence without form. Essence is buried in the heart of form and we can only get to know it through its form, which can be complex and changeable. Sometimes its outward form may seem at odds with its essence and convey an illusory quality, but this illusory quality merely covers up its essence. In order to recognize and analyse the real essence of a thing, one must begin from a close examination of the form or phenomena. Therefore, while the essence of both 'leftist' and rightist opportunism is rightist, its manifestation and ideology are quite dissimilar. If, in criticizing 'leftist' and rightist opportunism, we ignore the form and merely criticize the essence, then we cannot grasp the differences in their character.

The article by the Shanghai Publishing Bureau mentioned above argued that Lin Biao and the Gang of Four weren't just guilty of a 'leftist' tendency, but they were so rightist that "they couldn't be more right." It contends that those guilty of a 'leftist' tendency "subjectively want revolution" whereas the Gang of Four were "a black gang of old and new counterrevolutionaries that had wormed its way into our Party, wildly trying to overthrow the Party and usurp power and change dynasties, subvert the dictatorship of the proletariat and destroy the socialist system."

This scathing denunciation of the Gang of Four doesn't explain things very persuasively. To say that those who commit 'leftist' errors "subjectively want revolution" – does this imply that those who commit rightist errors subjectively don't want revolution? Subjective intentions and motives are not a very fruitful subject for discussion as there is no proof available for what people really think. The important thing is to look at the results. The ultraleftist line of Lin Biao and the Gang of Four had the actual effect of bringing tremendous losses to the country and suffering to the people. No amount of protestation about how good their intentions were can be excused in light of this reality. It is not necessary to claim what evil intentions they had when they went to Yenan in the forties, or that they were bad from the time they were born. People can change; things can develop. A person can become ambitious to usurp Party and

State power during the process of rising in the ranks. Not to admit this is to fly in the face of dialectics.

As for the ultraleftist trend of thinking among the masses, it cannot be separated from the ideological superstructure created by the Gang of Four through their propaganda. For example, the reluctance of certain cadres to carry out the new system of material bonuses comes from the constant denunciation of 'material incentives' since the start of Cultural Revolution. The thinking that 'left' is better than right which is still prevalent can be directly traced to the ultraleftist line of the past and to the propoganda of the Gang of Four.

What should be criticized isn't the motives of the Gang of Four or solely their rightist essence, but the manifestation of their opportunism in fake leftism, or 'leftist' deviation. The Chinese Communist Party, judging from the Shanghai article, only attacks the rightist essence, but what has had most influence since the Cultural Revolution and needs to be cleared away more than anything is the question of 'leftist' deviation.

Zhou Enlai, in his *Report on the Work of the Government* in August of 1973, pointed out that one political tendency will cover another political tendency. For example, Chen Duxiu's right opportunism of 'all unity, no struggle' covered Wang Ming's 'all struggle, no unity' brand of 'leftist' opportunism. Rectifying Wang Ming's leftist deviation resulted in his rightist deviation, just as opposition to Liu Shaoqi's revisionism covered up Lin Biao's revisionism. This latter was a case of rightist deviation covering for a 'leftist' deviation — Lin Biao's. Both he and the Gang of Four pushed a 'left' opportunist line, only further 'left' than Wang Ming, or an ultraleftist line.

How could an ultraleft line divorced from reality be carried out for so long? The answer is tied to the fact that the Chinese Communist Party has, since Liberation, only opposed rightism and not 'leftism'. This 'leftist' deviation or tendency has existed in the Party for a long time and enabled Lin Biao and the Gang of Four to get into power with ultraleftist slogans to carry out an ultraleftist line. To understand the background for this we have to go back to the Anti-Rightist Campaign of 1957.

The factors at this time which contributed to the development of a 'leftist' ideological trends were: China's international isolation and containment; the heightening of vigilance due to the Hungarian Incident of 1956; Khruschev's secret report to the 20th Soviet Party Congress; and the great aspirations which were fostered by China's success in changing agriculture, handicraft and private enterprises to a socialist orientation. Khruschev's criticism of Stalin, while it paved the way for a revisionist line in the Soviet Union, also let out a democratic breath of fresh air and allowed for a relaxation of political rigidity and tyranny throughout the international Communist movement. The violent incidents which occurred in Hungary and Poland in June and October of 1956 attracted the attention of the Chinese Communist Party, who felt that their political power was consolidated and that it would not be endangered by allowing the masses to speak out and express opinions.

Following the 8th Party Congress at which the 'Hundred Flowers' policy was first announced, an open rectification movement was launched and people invited to express criticisms and opinions. The Party did not expect such a strong reaction as posters and sharp criticisms, demonstrations and protests expressed dissatisfaction with many of the Party's policies, even to the point of negating the Party itself. During this confusing period, ideological and political problems were mixed together, as were contradictions among the people and those between the people and the enemy.

Other factors contributing to the confusion were: 1) a small minority of real rightists tried to create havoc and subvert the state; 2) opinions of the intelligensia which reflected bourgeois and petit-bourgeois thinking were problems of understanding rather than political problems; 3) many Party cadres who were guilty of bureaucratism and subjectivism etc., deserved the criticism they received; 4) the Party miscalculated the result of open rectification and faltered in its leadership, first opening the movement too widely, and then closing it too abruptly. Fearing that the situation would get out of control and turn into a Hungarian type of incident, the Party turned the movement for airing views into a national Anti-Rightist Campaign.

The Anti-Rightist Campaign of 1957 was initiated too suddenly. There was not enough time for policies and orientation to be fully understood by grassroots cadres, and the result was a 'left' deviation which became prominent in many areas:

1) The target of attack was too wide. Rightist became the enemy during the campaign and were lumped with landlords, rich peasants, counter-revolutionaries and bad elements. In 1957 over 400,000 people, mostly intellectuals, were labelled rightists. Thousands more were criticized without being labelled and family members were also adversely affected. When it came to entering the Party, going to school, finding work, joining the army, getting a good salary or promotion, finding a marriage partner etc., most of them were discriminated against. Taking all this into account, some one million people were affected;

2) Turning problems of understanding into political problems. Most intellectuals were patriotic and were willing to work for socialism but found it difficult to work under Party leadership. Many criticisms reflected old thinking and education or the democratic thinking of the West, and at the time it gave the impression that high level intellectuals were trying to undermine the leadership of the workers and peasants. The Party took these problems of understanding as political problems and used criticism, struggle and suppression rather than persuasion and education to solve them. Intellectuals were treated as enemies, an approach that was not in the interests of unity and the winning over of the intelligensia to serve socialism;

3) Criteria for revolutionaries divorced from reality after the Anti-Rightist Campaign. The Party emphasized the need for intellectuals to transform their world view and criticized 'white' experts for solely concentrating on expertise without

taking 'redness' or proletarian politics into account. Yet those who were 'red' but not 'expert' were not criticized. The exhortation to be 'red' – that is, to know Marxism-Leninism, assume the world outlook of the proletariat, master dialectical materialism and wholeheartedly serve the people– became more demanding than the prerequisites for Party membership and asked too much of intellectuals at the time. It was overly 'left'; and

4) The rightist labels were left on too long. Of 400,000 declared rightists, a minority had their labels removed after 3 years or so and had their citizen's rights restored. But most were labelled for over 20 years and only recently had the label removed. Some were young and active in the scientific and cultural field and had a bright future, but after being discriminated against for over 20 years, they have lost their enthusiasm for doing their work and their best years are gone. Nor did the Party admit when it was mistaken in declaring a person a rightist, but insisted that its original decisions were correct, that removing the label was a correct implementation of policy and that the victim should be grateful. People resented this bitterly.

The overly 'left' methods of the Anti-Rightist Campaign alienated and estranged the intelligensia, and had the effect of encouraging them to play it safe, hide their real opinions and protect themselves. This 'leftist' deviation prepared the basis for the attacks on intellectuals during the Cultural Revolution, and the designation of intellectuals as synonymous with 'bourgeois intellectuals' deserving of 'overall dictatorship' was a further development of this ideological trend.

The Adventurism of Communization

Another instance of 'left' deviation was in the transition to people's communes. The Chinese Communist Party had early on set down a preliminary plan for the gradual socialist transformation of agriculture: land reform, mutual-aid teams, elementary cooperatives, advanced cooperatives, then on to a suitable form developing eventually into ownership by the whole people. The feeling then was that by the time ownership by the people was a reality, the country would be on the threshold of communism.

Land reform mainly redistributed land belonging formerly to landlords and rich peasants and gave it to the tillers. The small agricultural economy which resulted was then reorganized into small units of mutual-aid teams, thus initiating cooperative farming. The next step, the combining of several teams into an elementary cooperative, created units similar to today's production teams. When two or more of these were combined, advanced cooperatives which were like today's brigades were born. Generally speaking, a mutual-aid team consisted of several households, an elementary cooperative combined several dozen households and an advanced cooperative several hundred households. Through this process, collective farming was elevated step by step and socialist transformation gradually effected.

At the beginning of the 1950's, the plan was to "achieve basic industrialization and complete the socialist transformation of agriculture, handicraft industry and bourgeois enterprises within 18 years." This transitional period was supposed to include 3 years for recovery and three 5 year plans. Thus, in the fall of 1953 agricultural cooperativization was announced and the second half of 1955 saw a peak in the cooperative movement. By December, 60% of peasant households had joined cooperatives. The leadership estimated that the elementary stage of cooperativization would be completed by the end of 1956 and that another 3 or 4 years would be required to accomplish the formation of advanced cooperatives nationwide. The method of carrying this out was to combine the best of a group of elementary cooperatives together to form advanced cooperatives of over a hundred households in 1956, and then to repeat this again in the following year. These two groups were to make up 25% of the total. This was to be a step by step process according to the schedule. There were no plans afoot for communization.

The characteristics of the Chinese Communist Party's leadership of the cooperative movement were:

1) Extensive ideological preparation. The advantages of cooperativization and its methods, essence, development, direction etc. were explained patiently to the masses. Problems were discussed extensively. The mass line was carried out thoroughly.

2) Mutual-aid teams were common and well-established by the time the cooperative movement was initiated. In some places, peasants were already looking forward to a higher form of cooperation and some had even begun to organize prototypes of elementary cooperatives. The majority of these achieved substantial increases in production after cooperativization. If the Chinese Communist Party had not supported this movement in the second half of 1955, then it would have been guilty of a rightist deviation and conservatism, lagging behind the masses.

3) Paying attention to models, conscientiously summing up experience before taking action. For example, the Wang Guofan cooperative in Zunhua County of Hubei province consisted of 23 households and had only one three-legged mule. It was dubbed a "poor stick" cooperative. Through great effort, they managed, over a 3-year period, to establish a sound economic base for the cooperative. Similarly the Jinxing cooperative in the Taihang Mountains was also a poor region, but after 3 years of cooperativization, it was transformed into a large cooperative of 283 households with a capital accumulation of over 11,000 yuan— an increase of over 10,000 yuan in 3 years. The Chinese Communist Party quickly summed up the experience, set up models for emulation and gave the peasants of the whole country encouragement and confidence in pointing out the way of development.

4) Leading cadres went down to the grass roots to understand the trend and development and set down a suitable policy and orientation. Mao Zedong did a lot of work himself in

research and investigation and editorial work for the book *Socialist Upsurge in China's Countryside*. During this period he showed an ability to discover and resolve contradictions and criticized the rightist tendencies as the most dangerous deviations. This was a correct assessment and enabled the movement to develop and flourish after the rightist tendency was criticized; and

5) Conscientious implementation of the policies of cooperativization. The Party adhered to the policy of looking after the interests of the poor and middle peasants and tried not to harm the interests of peasants in general. Cadres followed the policy of relying on education and the principle of voluntary participation. They allowed the peasants time to consider things carefully. At the same time, they did not underestimate the complex ideological difficulties in transforming the system of ownership for 80% of the population.

In February of 1957, Mao Zedong viewed the situation thus: "As I see it, if we can set up cooperatives in the first five year plan and consolidate them in the next five years, that will be doing very well."[2] After the establishment of cooperatives in 1957, there were still many problems, especially after several natural disasters which affected harvests and reduced incomes. But when peasants began to wonder if it was worthwhile, and even the Minister of Agriculture, Liao Luyan, was discouraged by the situation, Mao encouraged the cadres, saying: "Cooperativization can definitely be successful, but not within one or two years." Yet, little over a year later, without plan or preparation, the Party launched a nationwide communization movement.

It appears that not even the Party itself was prepared for the movement. There was no mention of communization at the Chengdu Conference in March, 1958, or at the Hankou Conference in April, or even at the 2nd Plenary Session of the 8th Party Congress a month later. The period between April and May saw, however, the beginning of communes,

---

[2] *Selected Works of Mao Tsetung*, Vol. 5. p. 380 (Chinese edition)

especially in Henan, where the cooperative movement had gone well and the peasants had spontaneously organized into larger units. This information reached the Central Committee by August, and at the Beidaihe Conference, the leadership decided on communization and issued the decision that "Communization is the road in transition between collective ownership by the whole people" and was "a good way to build socialism." Within 2 months, many places had formed communes, and by the end of 1958, communization was basically achieved throughout the nation.

Once communes were started, industry, agriculture, commerce, education, military, forestry, animal husbandry, side occupations and fishery were politically unified into a prototype communist organization. The commune was to arrange the storage of farm implements, distribute goods and manage the work force. People thought communism was right around the corner. In retrospect it is obvious that this kind of thinking was unrealistic in the extreme.

The start of communization before cooperatives were consolidated created numerous problems. Among these were:
1) The transformation of ownership in socialist society requires a transitional period. It was not like the democratic revolution when an order could be given and land taken from landlords and redistributed to peasants. The transition from small collective ownership to large collective ownership to communal ownership cannot be achieved by adminstrative fiat, but must be done gradually. The successful experience of the cooperative movement was not sufficiently assimilated and as a result the different functions of the production team, brigade and commune regarding use of materials and land and the distribution of goods were blurred. Small collective ownership was negated, rich and poor peasants were levelled and lumped together and lack of experience in large collective management of production led to losses. All these shortcomings incurred the opposition of the peasants.
2) Absolute equalitarianism. There were no income differences between production teams and between individuals. Every-

one was made to eat out of a 'communal pot' in communal dining halls. The socialist principle of 'each according to his labour' in distribution was eliminated. This was an overestimation of the productive forces which did not realize that the communist principle of 'each according to his needs' was impossible at the time.

3) The overcentralization of power weakened ownership of the production team. Commune administrations frequently and arbitrarily took over the property of production teams and redistributed it upwards. They also transferred labour power without compensation. This served as a damper on the enthusiasm of most peasants.

For the above reasons, the communization movement proved itself to be an adventurist, 'leftist' deviation in thinking which had to be modified. Although it has been in existence for some twenty years, only in a few areas is it a step better than advanced cooperatives, namely some factories and enterprises, irrigation projects, power stations and collective organizations. The production team (formerly the elementary cooperative) is still predominant in the three levels of ownership. For example, according to 1975 statistics[3] for suburban communes outside of Shanghai, communal ownership stands at 34.2% and brigade ownership stands at 15.1%, while production teams still owned 50.7%. As for organization of labour power, labour management, distribution of products and so on, the production team is still by and large the basic accounting unit. The move from this to the brigade as the basic accounting unit and then on to the commune as the basic accounting unit will require a long time. In theory, then, the transfer of ownership is more successfully achieved by a step by step transition as in the cooperative movement than by sudden and violent revolutionary means.

The communization movement of 1958 was carried

---

[3] Zhang Chun-qiao, *On Exercising Complete Dictatorship Over The Bourgeoisie*. See *Peking Review*, April, 1975.

out too quickly and too soon. The fact that it created so many problems and had to be modified to what are actually still advanced cooperatives, shows that it was carried out too soon. The cooperative movement produced many advanced models and prototypes, such as the Wang Guofan and Jinxing cooperatives, but 20 years after the beginning of communization, there are still no real models. The most frequently named model, Dazhai, is only a brigade (the former advanced cooperative). Communization overreached the actual stage of development in China at the time.

There were several factors which contributed to the Chinese leadership's adventurism regarding communization. Some of these were: 1) The success of the cooperative movement in 1955 made people overconfident. Instead of doing the same deep investigation, the leadership thought they could go ahead without it; 2) The success of the cooperative movement came about as a result of long opposition to rightist deviation. This covered up a 'leftist' deviation which did not receive enough attention by the leadership; 3) The Anti-Rightist Campaign of 1957 led to the Great Leap Forward, when reports of production and record harvests made the Central Committee think there was a material basis existing when in fact there wasn't. This led them into rushing into 'left' deviationist thinking.

The problems of communization should have been summed up much earlier, but in the past 20 years, the Chinese Communist Party, in only opposing the right and not the 'left,' still hasn't properly evaluated the adventurism of communization. An article in the August, 1978 issue of *Red Flag* by Li Shi entitled *Conscientiously Study Chairman Mao's Theory about People's Communes* criticizes ultra-leftist trends at the beginning of the communization movement, but at the same time defends the Party's denunciation of Peng Dehuai for saying that communes had been 'premature' and 'a mess'. There is a contradiction here: to admit that an ultra-leftist orientation existed implies that it was too adventurist and that the attempt to communize was made Charter for Agriculture." (the fifth point in the 'Eight Points' mature.'

The article argues that, after seeing commune prototypes spontaneously created in various provinces throughout the summer of 1958, Mao convened the Beidaihe Conference where a decision was made to establish people's communes. Within half a year "people's communes were developing vigorously and made tremendous achievements." According to official statistics, within two months over 700 thousand agricultural cooperatives had established 26 thousand people's communes. The article also points out that the transformation to commune ownership should have taken several decades, after the gradual transition from ownership by production team to brigade as the basic accounting unit, then on to commune ownership with the commune as the basic accounting unit. This depended on economic and political conditions; that is, there had to be a strong material base established so that the move would be a profitable one at every level and the people opt for it voluntarily.

But communization in 1958 was carried out virtually overnight. Communal ownership was established within six months rather than over several decades. Economic and political conditions, needless to say, were nonexistent. It was, in a word, 'premature.' The necessity for 'several decades' and suitable 'economic and political conditions' to run communes successfully was only admitted between 1959 and 1962, after ownership and basic accounting was returned from the commune to the production team. What Peng Dehuai criticized in 1959 were the people's communes that were established at the beginning with ownership transferred to the commune (which also became the basic accounting unit), and not the people's communes of 1962 where basic accounting was returned to the production team. The charge of 'premature' was levelled at this earlier form in which ownership was by the whole commune. This was an accurate assessment.

The article admits that 1) economic and political conditions were not ripe for the initial over-enthusiasm for communization; 2) after several months, the Party decided to retreat to the brigade as the basic accounting unit (1959) and controlling unit for ownership; then again after three years drew it further back to the production team. In other words, they went back to the original elementary cooperative as the basic accounting unit — only the name was changed from elementary cooperative to production team. This is still the basic situation today, twenty years later; 3) The system of ownership has not really changed since before communization. Deploying labour power on a wider scale, one of the supposed advantages of communization, could have been done through other means, and perhaps more equitably and fairly. By admitting these points, the article tacitly acknowledges that the original plans for communization were indeed 'a mess.'

The article also exposes the ultraleft theories advanced by Chen Boda, Mao Zedong's one time secretary and cohort of Lin Biao, who claimed that "within one or two years we can make the transition to communism." At the time of communization, however, it wasn't his theory, but Peng Dehuai's, which was attacked as 'right opportunism.' Chen Boda, on the other hand, continued to rise in power and prominence, reaching a peak when he became head of the Cultural Revolution Group and a famous theoretician. His downfall only came in 1970 after he conspired with Lin Biao. Even though in 1958 he was far below Peng Dehuai in position and experience, his ultraleft theories had great influence because of support from Mao himself, who, on December 12, 1958, was quoted as saying that "it should take another 15 to 20 years or a little more to reach communism." If this quote is accurate, then responsibility for the 'left' deviation of the Party at that time must in part at least be attributed to him.

The Great Leap Forward, initiated in the same year as communization, was another expression of the 'left' deviationist ideological trend. Its background lay in the split of thinking between the Soviet and Chinese Parties that had developed since 20th Soviet Party Congress was held in 1956, signs that the Soviet Union wanted to impose its changes in policy internationally and the Chinese realization that Soviet technical and scientific assistance might not be counted on in the future. The international pressure from both the United States and the Soviet Union made the Chinese leadership determined to establish an independent economic system and self-sufficient agriculture to prepare for any eventuality. Industry needed greater steel production to develop and bolster military defence. Internally, the rectification movement among intellectuals and cadres was underway following the Anti-Rightist Campaign. The emphasis on 'red and expert' and the fury of the Anti-Rightist and rectification movements intimidated most intellectuals into compliance, so that they didn't speak out against the many un-scientific and inefficient activities of the Great Leap Forward. Also some people in the leadership perhaps felt that destroying blind faith in intellectuals by exhorting the masses on to great achievements would be a good lesson for all intellectuals. And so the Great Leap Forward was mobilized.

In January and February of 1958, the Party put forward the task of economic reconstruction as one "to catch up with England in steel production and other major industries within 15 years." The general line was: "Go all out, aim high to achieve socialism with greater, faster, better and more economical results" and pushed for the simultaneous development of industry and agriculture, central and regional industries, large and small scale enterprises, native and foreign production techniques and heavy and light industries. It also promoted the mass line and warned against taking the safe, conventional approach, calling on people to "cast off superstition and liberate your thinking" so as to "create miracles on earth." With this propaganda and encouragement, the Great Leap Forward got underway.

As steel was crucial to the development of industry, the Party put forth the slogan 'take steel as the key link.' In 1957, English steel production stood at 22 million tons while Chinese steel production stood at 5.2 million, or about ¼ the English total. Before 1958, Chinese industry, though primitive, was well-planned and made gradual progress. In

1956, Zhou Enlai set the steel production target at 10.5 to 12 million tons for the period between 1956 and 1960. This was already a substantial increase, but was well within the realm of possibility. The slogan 'surpass England in 15 years.' however, threw everything into confusion. In neither planning nor techniques nor production facilities had the Party leadership done enough proper estimates or preparation. Instead they put sole emphasis on subjective consciousness and relied on two unrealistic factors – mobilizing the masses to engage in backyard steel production and to go all out to battle in the military spirit reminiscent of the war years.

In June of 1958, Mao Zedong set forth the first year's target at 10.7 million tons. In August at the Beidaihe Conference, it was raised to 30 million tons. After one year of the Great Leap, the target of 10.7 million tons was reached, a figure twice that of 1957. Some small steel factories were built, some mines opened and a basis for steel production was established. But the cost of this enterprise was tremendous. The gains were that people's consciousness was raised – this is rather abstract and difficult to quantify or pin down -- but the loses in the economic sphere, despite the record of 10.7 million tons, were: 1) The overdeployment of labour to forging steel in the so-called 'people's smelters.' Organizations and offices nationwide, armed forces units, schools, villages, neighbourhoods all built 'backyard furnaces' which used primitive techniques; 2) Tremendous waste of lumber for fuel to replace coke, which was not generally available; 3) Congestion of transport due to lack of planning. As people tried to get iron to their locales, they often had to rely on animal power and manpower to transport it by foot from places far away; 4) The quality of steel produced was generally inferior and much of it was unusable because furnaces were not hot enough to forge a higher grade; 5) The waste of raw material disupted normal production. Steel was given top priority and other areas suffered as a result; 6) The destruction of useful implements such as pots and pans to meet the requirements for steel quotas.

Chairman Mao Zedong revising the Constitution of the People's Republic of China (draft), the first socialist constitution of China, in 1954.

The Chinese Government claimed in 1958 that a Hubei commune had produced a recorded yield of 36,956 jin of rice in an experimenting field of 1.016 mu.

Working a bellows: a peasant on a commune engages in back-yard furnace production of pig iron. The operation of thousands of primitive blast furnaces drained the labor supply, leaving farms shorthanded, and resulted in inferior products. Such failures caused the Government in 1959 to shift the emphasis from huge communes to smaller production brigades.

Mao Zedong and Zhou Enlai surrounded by Red Guards during the Cultural Revolution.

Mao Zedong and his 'comrade-in-arms' Lin Biao at the opening session of 12th meeting of the Eighth Central Committee of Chinese Communist Party.

Mao Zedong reviewing for the first time the "mighty army" of the Cultural Revolution on the Tiananmen Gate rostrum on August 18, 1966.

People from all over Peking came to Tiananmen Square to express their mourning for the late Premier, Zhou Enlai, at the Qing Ming Festival April 5, 1976.

First Session of Fifth National People's Congress of China opens in Peking. On the rostrum are Executive Chairmen of the Presidium of the Session Hua Guofeng, Yeh Jianying, Deng Xiaoping, Li Xiannian, Wang Dongxing and Admae Soong.

Hua Guofeng at the closing session of the Fifth National People's Congress of China.

The new Vice-chairman of the Chinese Communist Party, Chen Yun.

The new Politburo member of the Central Committee of the Chinese Communist Party, Hu Yaobang.

Wall posters at 'democracy wall' in Peking.

The 'Leftist' Ideological Trend in China

A massive operation of this type and this scale was only possible in China at the time. The causes were a lack of experience and technical expertise, a generally low educational level and lack of understanding about modern production as well as the 'left' ideological trend existing in the leadership. Also, without the mobilization of the masses and the national enthusiasm for progress, such a large-scale undertaking would never have gotten off the ground. From an economic perspective, the resulting losses vastly outweighed the gains.

Where the industrial Great Leap Forward focussed on smelting steel, the agricultural version concentrated on high-yield experimental plots. Mao Zedong set down an *Eight Character Constitution* for increasing agricultural production. These eight points were: water conservation, fertilizer, deep ploughing, selective seeding, close planting, careful tending, tool innovation and farm management. He also put emphasis on scientific farming and technical improvement, but left out the opening up of new farmland — a crucial omission considering the scarcity of arable land in proportion to population. These eight points provided the guiding orientation for the Great Leap in agriculture.

Of the eight points, water conservation saw the greatest successes in 1958. Plans for starting irrigation projects extended throughout the country. Most of the large model reservoirs existing today got their start during the Great Leap Forward, and served their areas well during the floods and droughts after 1959. In the Peking district, for example, Mao and other leaders personally took part in working on the Ming Tomb Reservoir. During this period, over 10 large and medium-sized and a hundred or so small reservoirs were built in the vicinity of Peking, as well as numerous transport canals and irrigation canals affecting 70% of the farmland.

Deep ploughing, fertilizing and close planting did not fare so well. Mass mobilization was initiated without technical leadership, and since most people didn't have a minimum scientific knowledge, normal production was disrupted.

118 China's New Democracy

Deep ploughing in some areas was pushed irrespective of conditions – the deeper the better – so that land was ploughed over a metre deep, mixing red clay in with the soil and burying the fertilizer at the bottom, leading to opposite results from those intended. The same excesses occurred with close planting and adding fertilizer. 'The closer the better' became the watchword to fend off the label of conservatism and lack of innovation, and in adding fertilizer some places dumped so much onto the fields that seedlings were suffocated.

At this time, many older and experienced peasants were pushed aside for 'conservative thinking.' Intellectuals who expressed different opinions were labelled 'bourgeois.' Along with cadres who dared to speak out and those who wouldn't participate wholeheartedly they were accused of dampening the enthusiasm of the masses. On the other hand, those who made the boldest claims and resolutions called themselves by such names as 'The May 4th Assault Force Experimental Plot.' Not to be outdone, the leadership would respond with its own 'County Committee Organization Experimental Plot.'

A close friend related to me an example of what occurred during the Great Leap Forward in a county in Guangdong province which attempted to produce the impossible figure of 200 thousand catties of grain per *mu* on the 'County Committee Experimental Plot' of just over 2 *mu*. They assembled over a hundred people to work in this plot, including county level cadres, soldiers, students and workers divided into labour teams determined to work a miracle. The most arduous part of the process was the deep ploughing, where the earth had to be ploughed to a metre depth. To do this, they couldn't use an ordinary plough, but had to use a crane and shovel to excavate the earth inch by inch. After the red clay was dug up and turned over, the top was layered with thousands of pounds of various rich fertilizers. With such deep ploughing and so much fertilizer, it was exceedingly difficult to transplant rice seedlings. A worker who stepped into the paddy immediately found himself waist deep in mire and could move only with the

The 'Leftist' Ideological Trend in China 119

greatest difficulty. To overcome this, the planters went out in small boats and planted over the edge of the boat. It was a slow process, but luckily there was a huge workforce. Of course, to get 200 thousand catties per *mu*, the rice seedlings had to be planted very closely. As a result, before the grain had a chance to sprout the stalks had already withered. The paddy was a sea of withered stalks.

Since such a disastrous defeat could not be countenanced, especially by a 'County Committee Experimental Plot', a decision was quickly made to uproot all the withered plants and bury them, re-level the paddy and transfer the rice plants from 20 surrounding *mu* of land to be replanted in the experimental plot. As these 20 *mu* of rice were only three days from harvesting and were therefore about ready to ripen, they could be very closely planted. But then they were planted so closely that the wind would not pass through and there was a danger that the grain would rot on the stalk. Again, emergency measures were taken and a dozen or so blowing machines were set up on platforms around the plot and turned on the rice around the clock to keep it well aired. When the crop was finally harvested, it weighed in at a thousand catties per *mu*. While this was nowhere near the projected target of 200 thousand catties, it was nevertheless unprecedented. However, taking into consideration the waste of manpower and resources, especially the crops from nearby 20 *mu*, it was an unmitigated disaster.

This target of 200 thousand catties per *mu* was nothing extraordinary. Some groups aimed at 999 thousand catties and publicly proclaimed this target on signboards beside their plots. Those with any understanding of scientific farming who passed by would joke that even with the mud and soil included, it wouldn't come near that figure.

According to Mao's original calculations, 800 catties per *mu* was within the realm of possibility, but at lower levels estimates were more reckless and less prudent, leading to wildly improbable targets. But even if real production could not obviously come close to those abstract totals, production teams nevertheless began reporting harvests as having reached targeted figures. The exaggerated figures were part of a hysteria which most people went along with. Those who reported accurately were criticized and pressured into changing their figures, while those merely reported the inflated target figures as the real ones were praised and complimented. The result was that the production figures sent by provincial and county levels to the Centre were wrong, and the leadership was misled.

After the establishment of people's communes in October of 1958, the distorted harvest figures led many communes which set up communal dining halls to give meals away for free. Within a month there was a crisis when the Centre requested certain grain quantities to be turned over to the state for storage or for export. As the figures reported were far from the truth, production teams could not comply and serious contradictions emerged between the Centre and the regions. In the end, the Centre could not get what it requested and in fact had to transport grain to some areas to alleviate shortages. Shortages eventually became so serious that people in many areas had to go scrounging in the hills scavenging for food. Students stopped classes, workers stopped work, and offices closed while everyone went off to gather wild herbs for the state to distribute to solve the temporary shortages. Even Mao referred to this situation in a talk given in March, 1959 at a meeting in Zhengzhou. Fortunately, national cooperation averted chaos and enabled the country to survive through a difficult time.

The popular view and the official view diverge when it comes to evaluating the Great Leap Forward. The official line has been to affirm it in principle and to minimize discussion of its shortcomings. The popular view is much more negative. Liberated thinking, water conservation projects, steel production and small industries are often cited in the official version as proving the worth of the Great Leap, but people who went through it tend to feel bitterly about the unscientific waste of manpower and material resources. They remember the tense market situation after 1958, when foodstuff and daily necessities were scarce, including such items as cloth, toothpaste, soap, combs, matches, etc. The official explanation for this situation was the three years of natural disasters and the repayment of the debt to the Soviet Union, but this doesn't explain why the disastrous consequences have lasted so long and why even now the standard of supply is not up to the level that it was at in 1958 before the Great Leap.

The inescapable conclusion is that the main reason for the extended economic slump and market shortages was the undermining of agricultural and industrial policies and stable development instigated by communization and the Great Leap Forward. Add to this the fact that the mistakes committed by the Party at the time have never been justly evaluated and that the 'left' ideological deviation has not been criticized, and the result has been the serious dampening of mass enthusiasm. By the time the Cultural Revolution began, this 'leftist' ideological deviation was even more dangerous, and had a correspondingly disastrous effect on the economy.

The Question of Peng Dehuai

The view that communization was 'premature' and 'a mess,' that the backyard furnaces were 'more failure than success,' and that the 'leftist' thinking during communization and the Great Leap Forward was 'an expression of petit-bourgeois fanaticism' was advanced by Peng Dehuai and attacked as 'rightist opportunism.' A final assessment of Peng Dehuai would require access to all the facts — and is something only the Communist Party authorities can undertake. With the limited information and evidence available here, we can only present some individual views on the 'left' ideological trend prominent at the time. Whether Peng Dehuai should be considered as having headed an erroneous political line only the Chinese Communist Party itself can decide.

122　China's New Democracy

What is lacking for a full analysis here are the details of the Lushan Conference in July and August of 1959 which resulted in Peng Dehuai's downfall and the denunciation of him as a 'right opportunist.' Up until this time he had concurrently held positions as Politburo member, vice-Premier of the State Council, vice-Chairman of the Defence Council and Defence Minister. The Chinese leadership has never revealed what happened at the Lushan Conference. We can only glean an outline of events from unofficially published versions of Mao's speeches from before and after the conference.

It appears that the Lushan Conference was convened to sum up the experience and lessons of communization and the Great Leap Forward. The conference opened with leading cadres at every level delivering blistering attacks on policies which they felt had brought them great difficulties. These attacks tended to negate entirely the Great Leap Forward, the General Line and People's Communes. The leadership had not expected criticism to be so intense and even Mao was taken aback. Of the critics, Peng Dehuai was the highest placed and his criticisms were perhaps the sharpest. Aside from speaking during the conference, he also petitioned Mao in writing, expressing the opinions discussed above, namely that communization was 'premature' and 'a mess,' that the Great Leap and the backyard steel smelters were 'more failure than success,' and that the whole undertaking reflected 'petit-bourgeois fanaticism.'

After these criticisms were expressed, a furious debate ensued. Mao counterattacked in a speech on August 16th in which he reportedly said:

I said yesterday morning under the subject 'How a Marxist-Leninist Ought to Approach a Revolutionary Mass Movement' that 'I don't know which genius did it, but someone got hold of some machine guns and mortars and fired a series of bursts here at the Lushan Conference among our rightist friends.' Well, this question was answered for me last night: it wasn't a genius here at Lushan but comrade Liu x x from Peking

The 'Leftist' Ideological Trend in China 123

and his two assistants who so zealously and willfully did it.[4]

Liu x x probably refers to Liu Shaoqi, but whoever it was, in the end Mao found enough support that after a complex struggle he was able to impose his views and suppress Peng Dehuai. The highest level of leadership found enough common ground to declare that "at the present time a new current has surfaced both within and without the Party, a rightist mood, thinking and activity which has grown and gone wildly onto the offensive." Peng Dehuai was named as the leader of these right opportunists.

Although Peng Dehuai was dismissed from office, his specific crimes have never been publicly announced. During the Cultural Revolution he was accused in a pamphlet of having 1) been a right opportunist 2) formed a military club and anti-Party clique made up of himself, Huang Kecheng, Zhang Wentian and Zhou Xiaozhou; and 3) conspired with the Soviet Union. On this last point, he was alleged to have agreed with the Soviet suggestion that the Chinese army follow the Soviet Union's orders. Of the three crimes, the one most criticized was his opposition to the Great Leap Forward and to communization, that is, his 'rightist opportunism.' There has been no specific evidence made public regarding his forming a military club and colluding with the Soviet Union. Even if he had supported closer military cooperation with the Soviet Union, given the friendly relations at the time, this opinion should at the most have been criticized, and not resulted in his dismissal from office.

Without further hard evidence, the case against Peng Dehuai remains a tenuous one. Even if the views expressed by Peng at the Lushan Conference were mistaken, he still voiced them through the proper channels. As for opposing Mao, he did express his opposition directly in a letter and didn't intrigue and conspire, speak falsely or try to stage a coup. If he was dismissed merely for expressing a different opinion, then the decision was not a just one.

Following Peng's dismissal in 1959, a national anti-

---

[4] *Long live Mao Tsetung*, 1969 edition. pp. 307–308.
(Chinese Edition)

rightist campaign was mobilized, and cadres at every level who had criticized the Great Leap Forward and communization were in turn criticized. When I asked about Peng Dehuai's case during a trip to China this year, most of the cadres and friends held to the official evaluation of him, but couldn't support it with any evidence. It appears that the government's continuous propaganda against him has convinced most people that the verdict was correct, even though real evidence is lacking.

The question of Peng Dehuai also involves Wu Han's historical play *'Hai Rui Dismissed from Office.'* Since Yao Wenyuan's critique of the play was the spark that set off the Cultural Revolution, Peng's case is also linked with it. The resemblance between Hai Rui and Peng Dehuai is indeed striking. Hai Rui had petitioned the Emperor Jia Jing and expressed critical opinions for which he was dismissed; Peng Dehuai had written Mao Zedong expressing critical opinions for which he suffered the same fate.

If the Chinese Communist Party's handling of the Peng Dehuai case had been correct and reasonable, people would have accepted it and something like the play *Hai Rui Dismissed from Office* would never have been written. Then even if Wu had intentionally tried to point out a resemblance, there would have been no reaction from the people and the effort would have been wasted. Moreover, the Party itself would not have reacted so defensively. The conclusion is that the handling of the case of Peng Dehuai at the Lushan Conference was not entirely fair and just.

The Anti-Rightist Campaign of 1957 and the anti-Rightist movement of 1959 were two movements which seriously suppressed democratic expression. The former was directed at intellectuals outside the Party and the latter was directed at dissenting opinions within the Party. The former silenced the intellectuals and the latter prevented dissenting opinions from being freely expressed in Party meetings for a long time afterwards and encouraged submission to the highest authorities. Both put a damper on the enthusiasm and morale of cadres and intellectuals, with serious consequences. And the Cultural Revolution, which was even more fiercely directed at cadres and intellectuals, made them even more disheartened.

Huang Kecheng, who was implicated in Peng Dehuai's 'military club' in 1959, has already been restored to his posts. No explanation has been given as to whether he made a self-criticism admitting that he belonged to the 'military club' or why he has been forgiven, but it appears that his mistakes were not serious. The question of Hai Rui, the honest official, and of Zhou Xinfang has already been discussed in the Chinese press and the verdicts against them overturned. So has the verdict against Wu Han. If there isn't enough proof that he was a traitor and conspirator, and if his main error was to attack the Great Leap Forward and communization, then Peng Dehuai's verdict should also be overturned. Communization and the Great Leap Forward reflected a 'left' ideological trend in China at the time, and to call realistic and factual observations 'rightist' is an expression of a 'leftist' orientation that is antidemocratic in the extreme.

'Leftism' and the Cultural Revolution

Qi Xin

The influence of 'leftism' did not end with the Great Leap Forward and communization, but continued to affect Chinese political life throughout the sixties. Although more moderate economic and cultural policies were introduced in 1962, the damage of the late fifties, both material and spiritual, had barely been repaired when Mao and other communist leaders began the ten year Cultural Revolution.

It has become popular in China to blame Lin Biao and the Gang of Four for all of the excesses of the Cultural Revolution. Many articles in the Chinese press and speeches by state leaders suggest that without the 'interference and subversion' of Lin and the Gang, the Cultural Revolution could have achieved its aim without causing such widespread confusion and loss of life. This is quite erroneous. The origins of the Cultural Revolution, both political and ideological, should be traced back to the fall of Peng Dehuai, the Great Leap Forward and the extremism within the Central Committee during that period. But my aim here is not to investigate the historical roots of the Cultural Revolution or make a detailed analysis of its development, but rather to outline the influence of 'leftism' in the CPC during this period and its characteristics.

Why, then, did 'leftism' continue to develop within the CPC following the Great Leap Forward? Internationally, China had become increasingly isolated after the Soviet

128 China's New Democracy

criticism of Stalin and China's split with the eastern bloc. With this break, China lost both her main political and economic allies. Though continuing a long ideological debate with the Soviets, China began to pay less attention to international affairs, believing in her own ideological superiority and the need to nurture her own revolutionary traditions and keep pure the doctrine of Marxism-Leninism. Following the years of 1962-65, when Liu Shaoqi, Deng Xiaoping and other leaders were allowed a free hand to ensure quick economic recovery from the years of natural and man-made 'calamities' that followed the Great Leap Forward, Mao began to pay more attention to China's internal problems and the need to train 'successors to the revolutionary cause' among the younger generation. With the conclusion of the debate with the Soviet bloc, Mao turned all of his efforts to solving China's internal political problems, the most pressing of which he felt to be the rise of a Soviet-style bureaucratic Party leadership, a reduced emphasis on politics and the tendency to negate class struggle. Mao later declared that he had searched for a suitable means to solve these problems for a long time before deciding on a mass political movement that would involve everyone in the whole country— the Great Proletarian Cultural Revolution.

In the years prior to 1966, Mao had occasionally made comments on various problems that he had seen in the government. His remarks on education, culture and medical work were especially critical (see *People's Daily*, 25 May 1967). These comments, mostly aphoristic and contradictory, were later taken as a complete negation of the '17 years' of 1949-66 and made the basis for major policy changes. In fact, these scant remarks remain Mao's only official statements on culture, education and health. His statements on class struggle at Party conferences after 1961, the movement to learn from 'Chairman Mao's good student,' the PLA soldier Lei Feng, the collection and publication of *Quotations of Chairman Mao* by Lin Biao and the 'Four Clean' movement of 1964 aimed at criticizing 'those in power taking the capitalist road in the countryside,' were all signs of the

'Leftism' and the Cultural Revolution 129

ever increasing emphasis placed on the politicization of the masses during the early sixties.

What then were the main characteristics of extreme 'leftism' during the Cultural Revolution? Perhaps the most well-known and obvious mark of 'leftism' was the deification of Mao and the development of a Mao-religion. Of course, Mao could have quickly put a stop to the growth of a personality cult in 1966, and in a letter to Jiang Qing in the same year he even expressed serious doubts about the wisdom of backing Lin Biao's political exploitation of the 'great leader cult.' However, not only did the cult grow beyond all expectations, but within the first few months of the Cultural Revolution, Mao's past works, directives and utterances became the sole standard of truth not only in politics, but also in science, culture, economics and personal relationships. Quotations from Mao were painted on walls and buildings, everyone wore Mao badges as a symbol of their faith, and statues of Mao were erected in squares and at the entrance to all public buildings. Artists and cultural performers were quick to follow and created a 'loyalty dance' to be performed by everyone before meals, and all songs made frequent mention of Mao's name and saintly virtues. Mao's every act, whether it be swimming the Yangzi river or chain smoking, was made the object of adoration and popular emulation. By the end of 1966 and the 'smash the four olds' movement, the CPC traditions of seeking truth from the facts and the leadership keeping in close contact with the people were effectively negated. Political direction was given by a handful of leaders who dogmatically applied the words of a single man in Peking to the complex realities of the Chinese political situation.

The first official document of the Cultural Revolution was the *May 16 Circular* which had been issued by Mao in negation of Peng Zhen's report on the discussion of the play *Hai Rui Dismissed from Office*.[1] The *Circular* pointed out that the discussion on the play was not of scholarly interest

---

[1] see Chi Hsin, *The Case of the Gang of Four*, Cosmos Books, 1978, Hong Kong, p. 154

alone, but had an immediate relevance to the class struggle at the time. It declared that the heart of the discussion was Peng Dehuai's 'rightist opportunism' at the Lushan Conference in 1957, and that the proletarian dictatorship should be carried out in all realms of the superstructure, including culture. Thus such a play as *Hai Rui* should be criticized and its supporters overthrown. This line of argumentation negated the Party's traditional method of reasoning with people who had opposing opinions and not forcing consensus. The words 'the proletariat must carry out dictatorship in all realms of the superstructure' were even written into the 1975 Constitution, thus legalizing the arbitrary rule of dogmatic Party leaders. Since the proletarian dictatorship was given priority in all fields, the leader of the spearhead of the proletariat, Mao Zedong, naturally became the supreme authority in all matters. As a result, the emphasis on 'left' politics that had followed the criticism of Peng Dehuai, became, in the Cultural Revolution, the fanatical and one-sided reliance on political dogma and the authority of one man. Thus Mao's earlier policies and sayings took on a new and awesomely powerful meaning. The slogan calling for 'independence and self-reliance' (duli zizhu, zili gengsheng) which had been a general policy for the development of the Chinese economy, became the basis for a rigid policy of isolationism that refused to have truck with 'bourgeois and revisionist' countries. Mao's call in the early sixties to 'put politics in command' was reinterpreted to mean 'politics is everything' and all specialized fields from economic management to scientific research were attacked as 'bourgeois expertism.' Even Mao's directive to agricultural producers to 'take grain as the key link' was taken to an extreme and resulted in forced emphasis on grain production to the detriment of secondary industry. In fact, the debate in China during 1978 concerning 'practice being the sole criterion of truth' has been primarily aimed at giving a theoretical basis for a more reasonable interpretation of Mao's words.

The erratic policy shifts of the CPC leadership following 1956 had resulted in considerable confusion among middle

'Leftism' and the Cultural Revolution 131

and lower level cadres. It was not unusual for cadres in certain areas to be carrying out central government policies months after they had been officially criticized and replaced in Peking. In the Cultural Revolution tardiness in implementing Mao's policies, international or otherwise, became grounds for severe criticism, imprisonment and even death. Thus, not only were those who had carried out the remedial policies of Liu-Deng during the years 1962-5 attacked, but all those who had carried out policies in the past that could be interpreted as conflicting with Mao's official statements and directives were attacked as well. The result, according to Central Committee estimates, was the overthrow and criticism of some ten to fifty thousand cadres in each province. One of the main reasons for the unbridled 'cadre-hunting' of the Cultural Revolution was the contradictions in the two main documents passed by the CPC during the CR on the question of cadres. The *May 16 Circular* warned against 'Khruchev-type people' who had sneaked into the Party, army and government and who were waiting for an opportunity to take over power and carry out revisionism. Yet this document made no mention of just how many 'Khruschev-type people' were suspected of being in power. In the *Sixteen Points*[2], however, emphasis was placed on overthrowing a small number (no more than five percent) of cadres who had become 'people in power taking the capitalist road.' In this document, cadres were even divided into four categories, only one of which was absolutely bad, and violence in dealing with all political struggles was negated. Unfortunately, although the *Sixteen Points* provided an ideal guideline for the CR, it was outdated within days of being issued, and attacks on cadres, verbal, mental and physical, became a major part of the whole movement.

---

[2] Or the *CPC Decision on the Great Proletarian Cultural Revolution*, see Chi Hsin, *Teng Hsiao-ping: a political biography*, 1978 Hong Kong, pp. 65–75.

Due to the lack of a unified central policy on the Cultural Revolution, criticisms, factional fighting and power struggles escalated uncontrollably. In retrospect, the absence of fixed policies and directions is a characteristic of CPC 'leftism.' The Cultural Revolution was not the first movement to receive high-level and undefined support. The Great Leap Forward was also typified by great enthusiasm on the part of Mao and other leaders, but lacked firm directions and targets. In the Cultural Revolution, following the formation of the Red Guards and the 'snatching of power' from the 'capitalist-roader' leadership in 1966-7, Party and government organizations were destroyed and anarchy prevailed. The *People's Daily* even praised this 'disorder under heaven' as being a good thing, and declared that the enemy had been thrown into confusion while the revolutionaries had been able to take power. Mao declared that disorder was good, while Lin Biao claimed 'the greater the disorder the better.' Lin praised physical violence as good training for the people, even if innocents were killed. The back and forth 'struggling' and 'protecting' of cadres who had been in power prior to 1966 led to a situation where, apart from Mao, Lin, Jiang Qing and a few other top leaders, any and every person who had been in power in the past was criticized. The intense and arbitrary movements that occasioned such a situation continued to rent Chinese society continuously for over ten years, and have only come to an end with the conclusion of the movement to criticize the Gang of Four in late 1978.

With a return to a semblance of order in late 1967, a new aberration resulting from extreme 'leftist' policies appeared: workers being called on to take over the leadership of all schools and cultural bodies. Because of the rabid attacks on all older cadres and the formation of numerous opposing factions, an interim leadership was essential. However, the call for workers to form 'Mao Zedong Thought Propaganda Teams' and to take over leadership, though very revolutionary in concept, was not so easily realized. In the first place, many factories were unwilling to send their most enthusiastic and capable workers to take over schools. This resulted in many of the worker teams consisting of the most unpopular, troublesome and corrupt people in the factories. Secondly, the basic tenet of any Communist Party is that it is the vanguard of the proletariat, and as such should be the body that expresses the political will of the proletariat. To demand that workers take direct leadership was to negate the need for a Communist Party, or at least to attempt to realize some form of communism. Not only was such a hope premature, but Mao's statement that workers should 'lead the work in the schools forever' was unrealistic. Even if the worker leadership stayed in the schools for some years, it was inevitable that it would in turn change into a body of cadres and could no longer be considered as workers. The result of the worker teams and leadership in schools after the reorganization of the Party in 1969-70 was a power split between the workers and the Party organization. This split was used by the Gang of Four to control many universities (Peking University and Tsinghua University being the most well-known examples) and was not ended until the fall of the Gang in 1976. Similarly, army propaganda teams sent to take over various units consisted of people who were little more than well-meaning dogmatists, completely unaware of how they should handle the work they were put in charge of. In fact, rather than providing a stable and reasonable leadership, worker and army propaganda teams facilitated the rule of dogmatism, extremism and factions after 1969.

Another important aspect of the extremism of the Cultural Revolution was the reinterpretation of the relationship between 'public and private.' Liu Shaoqi was attacked for advocating the 'combination of public and private' (*gongsironghe*). In its place new slogans such as 'large public and no private' (*dagong wusi*) and 'struggle against the private and criticize revisionism' (*dousi pixiu*) were popularized. The practical results of this propaganda was the negation of the bonus system in factories and the socialist principle of 'each according to his work.' People were expected to work more but not get paid for it – to fight 'economism,' as it was called. Although some people were willing to work harder for the state and the building of socialism, most lacked such high political awareness. The long-term result of this enforced equality and criticism of 'material bonuses' was a dramatic fall in work attendance, production levels and product quality. Though the media represented the battle against 'petit-bourgeois selfishness' as victorious, the realities of the situation were markedly different. Not satisfied with the constant emphasis on the public sector, Lin Biao declared that people had to repress every selfish thought and 'carry out revolution in the depths of the soul.' All art and literature was created with this pointed political purpose in mind and failed completely to reflect the realities of Chinese society and the aspirations of the common people. It was only in 1971 that Zhou Enlai finally made a statement on the relationship between public and private and tried to correct the extremism of the past. He told the American author William Hinton that what should be encouraged was 'putting the public before the private' (*xiangonghousi*), however, he did not negate the private as had Lin and the Gang. Such a slogan is far more in accord with the needs of a young socialist society.

With all of this talk of 'leftism' and the extremism of the Cultural Revolution, it is inevitable that the question arises: was not Mao in favour of the policies of Lin and the Gang of Four? Or, does Mao make a Gang of Five? In fact, from a simple review of 'leftism' in the Communist Party from 1956–76, it is evident that Mao himself was influenced by extreme 'leftist' thinking and actively supported excessive and unrealistic policies. However, Mao was an idealist and his life's work was aimed at the realization of a communist society, and it is in this that his greatest difference with Lin and the Gang of Four lies. While Mao firmly believed in the ideals of the Communist Party and attempted to speed up the realization of communism, Lin and the Gang of Four were no more than politically ambitious schemers who used

Mao and the Cultural Revolution for their own ends.

A full review and appraisal of the Cultural Revolution and the 'left' extremism that occurred during it would require more than a short article as this. I have merely attempted to point out some of the most striking features of the CR and their ideological connections with the period of Great Leap Forward. It is now time for China to make an appraisal of 'leftism' and its influence in recent Chinese history. Although the Chinese media have already done much to encourage a more realistic approach to the complex political question of the past, it will probably be some time before a balanced and realistic appraisal of the years from 1956 to 1976 can be made.

China 1978 — from a New Power Struggle to the End of Class Struggle?

Qi Xin

China in 1978 saw the three-staged movement to criticize the Gang of Four become the arena for an open conflict between the remaining dogmatists of the Cultural Revolution period and the 'pragmatists' who had returned to power in 1976 following the arrest of the Gang of Four. The third stage of the movement against the Gang aimed at criticizing their political line and influence in philosophy, political economy and scientific socialism. In effect, however, it was used by Deng Xiaoping and his supporters to pave the way for a reevaluation of the last twenty years of political life in China. The achievements of this effort were made obvious during the meetings held by the Central Committee of the Chinese Communist Party in late 1978, where the remaining supporters of 'leftism' and the dogmatism of the Cultural Revolution were removed from power. At this same meeting it was announced that the movement against the Gang was ended and with it large-scale political movements in general. From January, 1979, China's main efforts were turned to economic construction and modernization.

Although originally envisaged as a mass campaign against the imprisoned Gang of Four and their followers, the 'reveal and criticize' movement begun in late 1976 soon uncovered the deep-seated problems of dogmatism, bureaucracy, political corruption, disillusionment with politics and a widespread fear of political involvement. With the return to power of Deng Xiaoping in mid-1977, certain leaders of the Chinese

138 China's New Democracy

Communist Party began to press for a review of the Party's policies and history since 1949 in an attempt to recapture the enthusiasm of the early years of the People's Republic. Party leaders hoped that people in China would be more prepared to work hard and achieve the economic targets set by the state once the threat of political repression and criticism was minimized. In fact, if it was not done then it would be impossible to repair the damage of the economically disastrous decade of 1966–76, and plans for modernization would have remained unrealized. The vehicle for the reassessment of the past and revival of Chinese political life centred on what are known in China as the 'three great debates.' These debates formed the basic theme of all major articles and discussions in China in 1978 and have continued to play an important role in 1979.

The first of these debates, and the one that will become of greater importance as time goes on, was that concerning 'working according to economic laws.' In fact, the divergence in the Party over whether to put politics in charge of economic planning and management or to work according to economic realities began early in the 50's. It was only after twenty years of economic setbacks or, at the best, restricted economic development, that the Communist Party has decided to return to the implementation of policies that accord with economic realities and laws. In 1978 the most prominent public proponent of this policy was Hu Qiaomu, one of the economists involved in the drawing up of the three state programmes on economic development under Deng Xiaoping's leadership in 1975. These were later labelled by the Gang of Four as 'poisonous weeds.'[1] A speech Hu made at a State Council economic and planning meeting in mid-78 was published under the title *Work According to Economic Laws and Hasten the Realization of the Four Modernizations*[2], in which he proposed a completely new

---

[1] See Chi Hsin, *The Case of the Gang of Four*, Cosmos Books, Hong Kong 1978, pp. 201–295.

[2] See *Peking Review*, 45–7 1978

basis for China's economic policies.

Hu's article was so controversial in nature that it was blocked from publication for some time, and was only carried in extracts in the major Chinese papers. But Hu was far from being isolated in proposing new economic policies. The reintroduction of material bonuses (along with the continued use of political or ideological incentives) in factories, the fining or closure of inefficient factories, and the system of promotion or demotion for efficient or incompetent factory management have been part of a general revision of state industrial policies. A number of discussions on agriculture were held throughout the year and a general policy of reducing the state's demands on communes and preventing enforced centralization of economic power in the commune rather than the brigade level of rural organizations was passed. The 'Dazhai model' in agriculture, the object of praise since 1964, was reduced in status, and though the spirit of Dazhai was encouraged, it is no longer seen as a model for the rest of the country. The Third Plenum of the CPC at the end of 1978 passed two new agricultural programmes. *The CCP Decision on Some Questions Concerning the Speeding Up of Agriculture Development (Draft)* and *Regulations on Work in People's Communes (Working Draft)*. [3] Although neither of these documents have been published and are still under study and discussion at the local level, details of agricultural reform released during 1978 indicate that it is probable that the new policy favours individual farmers and commune brigades far more than in the past. Premature attempts to reform the commune system according to the Dazhai model have been abandoned, and former agricultural leaders such as Ji Dengkui and Chen Yonggui have been criticized for their dogmatism. In fact, with the per capita level of grain production still at the 1955 level, and CCP promises of basic agricultural modernization within a year, more realistic agri-

---

[3] Ibid, *52 pp. 6–16

cultural policies are much needed. If individual initiative in agriculture continues to be repressed, then the state plans to reduce investment in agriculture and allow it to pay for itself will be unsuccessful.

China's foreign trade has also been a point of great interest since 1976. After a number of years of both 'window shopping' and mass purchases, the Chinese leadership has come to realize some of the hazards of the wholesale import of foreign technology. The importance of an economic and industrial infrastructure geared to cope with imported technology has been made painfully obvious to China with instances of 'turn-key' factories built by foreign companies and left to the Chinese to run. Some large assembly plants and fertilizer factories have been hamstrung by a lack of electricity and serious accidents due to the lack of technical knowhow on the part of Chinese workers. Considerable waste and loss has occurred in nearly every field of imported technology. The result of this has been a firm central policy on the purchase and use of foreign technology. This policy was outlined by Li Xiannian (Politburo leader and economic manager) in September, 1978. Li emphasized the need to buy only foreign machinery that China is incapable of producing itself. He also declared that the basis of such purchases should be that China should aim at learning at the same time as buying and thus be able to design and manufacture its own machinery in the future as well as improvise and improve on foreign models. In outlining this policy, he criticized both the tendency of some ministries and industries to keep foreign purchases to themselves and the jealousy between various groups within China's industry. Though seemingly theoretically sound, Li's policy will require a period of practical application before its efficacy can be evaluated.

Along with the rise to prominence of Hu Qiaomu in economics in 1978, Chen Yun, a veteran Party leader and economist, was not only brought back to power, but elevated to become the fifth most powerful man in China's ruling body: the Standing Committee of the Politburo. After 1949, Chen Yun played a major role in China's economic planning and was made a Vice-Chairman of the CCP at the Eighth Party Congress in 1956. Following the three disastrous years resulting from the Great Leap Forward, Chen advised economic policies strictly based on economic realities. As a result, he was criticized by Mao Zedong for economism and remained virtually powerless until the beginning of the Cultural Revolution when he was criticized and removed from office. Chen's prominence during 1978 and his rise to the Politburo at the Third Plenum underline the changes in economic policy. His forthright and critical remarks during the Third Plenum opened the forum for a reinvestigation of the Peng Dehuai case and the rehabilitation of Tao Chu and other central leaders attacked during the Cultural Revolution. Chen's wealth of experience and honesty made him a popular choice for the head of the Central Committee Disciplinary Committee empowered to keep a check on central leaders and prevent the widespread corruption and misuse of power so common during the days of the Gang of Four.

The second debate of 1978 concerning 'democracy and legality' was not only of immediate relevance to China in its attempt to establish a viable legal and legislatory system but was also important in preventing the rise of another Lin Biao or Gang of Four.

Though much talked of in the past, democracy, even if it be only democracy within the Communist Party itself, has been much flaunted and little realized in China during the last twenty years. The Peng Dehuai case was the most famous as an infringement of inner-Party democracy. Other leaders such as Tao Zhu, Peng Zhen, Chen Yun and Fu Yibo, to name a few, were victims of the Cultural Revolution during which not only democracy within the Party, but the very Party structure itself was negated. Outside the Party such cases are far more numerous and extreme. The Tian An Men 'incident' of April, 1976, is an instance where people were not permitted to openly express their opinions about certain Central Committee leaders and many were actively penalized for participation in the mass demonstrations. The lack of legal restraints on Party and state leaders, on the other hand, has made it virtually impossible to put a check on ambitious and unscrupulous people in the leadership. The situation of there being 'no law and no heaven' as the Chinese saying goes, gave adequate opportunity to people like the Gang of Four and led to the large scale abuse of the Party and state laws by middle and low level cadres throughout the country during the Cultural Revolution.

The discussion on democracy and legality began soon after the Fifth National People's Congress at the beginning of 1978 and the announcement of the new constitution at the same time. The main Chinese daily paper, the *People's Daily*, began to print articles on law and its meaning, explanations of legal terms, the question of the judiciary and its independence, and the need for the codification and popularization of laws in China. Since then, many universities have reestablished legal faculties, legal proceedings have been made public, and special bodies have been set up to codify the laws. Many cases of victimization, unfair accusations, murder, forced suicide and so on have also been reviewed and the decisions on such cases reversed, while the people who have committed crimes have been brought to trial and sentenced according to the seriousness of their offences. As the period being covered by such reinvestigations is over a decade long, the number of case dealt with has been numerous, and the work involved is likely to continue late into 1979.

The most striking realization of democracy and legality during 1978 was the reestablishment of democracy and openness within the Communist Party itself. The Central Committee Work Meeting and Third Plenum of the Eleventh CPC Congress at the end of 1978 were witness to scenes only equalled in importance by the Zunyi Conference of 1935 when Mao Zedong became leader of the Party and the 7000 Cadre's Meeting of 1962 at which Mao made a self-criticism and the extremist policies of the late 50's were checked. Speeches at the 1978 meetings called for a reevaluation of the past twenty years of the Party's history,

China 1978   143

the rehabilitation of Peng Dehuai, Tao Zhu, Fu Yibo, Yang Shangkun, Peng Zhen and other Party leaders who were victims of the 'leftist' current of 1957—76.

Apart from Peng Dehuai and Tao Zhu being posthumously rehabilitated, other leaders attacked in the early days of the CR were reinstated. The Central Committee's decisions concerning the 'rightist deviationist wind' of late 1975 and all the documents pertaining to it, the criticism of Deng Xiaoping in 1976 and the decision on the Tian An Men 'incident' were all cancelled. This in itself is proof that the Party has realized the fall in its popularity during the last few years, and the need for making a realistic reappraisal of past decisions and, if need be, for reversing incorrect decisions.

Criticism of central leaders such as Wang Dongxing (previously head of Mao's security force and the Central Committee office), Wu De (head of Peking municipality 1967-78), Chen Xilian (head of the Peking military region and involved in the supression of the Tian An Men demonstration), Ji Dengkui and others, though severe, did not lead to the purge of these leaders. Since the Third Plenum, these leaders have all lost effective political power, but nevertheless continue to hold high government posts. This method of dealing with political opponents has been virtually unknown in China for over thirty years and marks an end to the 'government by purge' endemic in China since the founding of the People's Republic.

As part of the reestablishment of democracy within the Party, the Central Committee also set up a hundred-man disciplinary committee headed by the newly appointed Vice-Chairman of the Party, Politburo member, and economist, Chen Yun. This committee has power over the actions of members of the Central Committee and can investigate any official who contravenes the Party or State Constitutions. Prior to the setting up of this committee, special investigatory groups were set up temporarily in order to deal with problems of Party discipline. Such a group was set up to investigate Liu Shaoqi in 1967-8, Lin Biao in 1971 and even the Gang of Four. This method was often used by certain high-level members of the Politburo so that the investigation group would carry out private vendettas rather than work to actually uncover the truth. Thus, the newly established committee is of some importance in providing a semi-independent check on Party leaders. Chen is reported to have only accepted the job as head of the committee when he was given assurances by Hua Guofeng himself that the committee would be empowered to investigate only high official, even the Party Chairman.

On a more broadly-based front, 1978 saw the criticism of the practice of Party leaders demanding blind obedience from the masses. A concept deeply entrenched in Chinese tradition, the use of obedience and the authority of senior officials (*zhangguan yizhi*) to rule has effectively prevented people from expressing their opinions openly and has made democracy an impossibility. Equally frequent criticisms of corruption and officials protecting each other have sufficiently loosened the political atmosphere in China to enable a more regular and relaxed relationship between officials and the people. The unprecedented poster campaign in Peking at the end of 1978, which some have called the Peking spring, is one result of the leadership's attempts to enforce the Constitution and protect the rights of the citizen. With such a basis, it is improbable that Chinese political life will experience such repression as witnessed in 1957 or 1967-76 again in the near future.

After strenuous discussions at the Third Plenum, the Central Committee directed the Judicial Department of the People's Congress to compile a Criminal Code. Other laws, regulations and rules aimed at covering the relationship between individuals, organizations and the State are also being compiled. The drafts of a Civil Code, Criminal Code, Government Organizational Laws and Environmental Laws are also being written. It was expected that some of the state organizational laws would be drawn up, approved and put into practice within the first half of 1979. An indication of a strong break with the past was clear when the *People's Daily* stressed that 'everyone must abide by the law', 'everyone is equal before the law' and that 'no-one can be allowed to put themselves above the law.'

The backdrop of the resolution of problems concerning economic policy, legality and democracy during 1978 was the debate on 'practice being the sole criterion of truth.' The most theoretical of the three great debates', the criterion of truth' debate had by far the greatest effect within the Party itself and perhaps the greatest significance for China since the ideological debates of the early sixties. Though far from being an open and shut case, the 'criterion of truth' debate has eventually won the support of the majority of government leaders, led to the reappraisal of the Party's history since 1949 and become the basis for all forward-looking innovations within politics, economics, culture and law. What are the origins of this debate, who led it and who supported it? The answers to these questions reveal the general shift in policy and power during 1978 and form the basis for understanding the significance of the Third Plenum of the CPC itself.

The problems created by a one-sided emphasis on politics regardless of objective conditions, formalism, the use of Mao and his works as a God or a symbol, and the ritual that developed around him during the Cultural Revolution were obvious in China for many years. Yet, even with the fall of the Gang of Four in 1976, there was no thorough reassessment of the CPC and empty-headed political propaganda, the waste, loss and damage caused by subjective political ideologues and the ignorance of the realities of Chinese society and economy. Perhaps the greatest resistance to this type of reassessment was due to the fear that everything from the past would be negated, and people who had anything to do with the Cultural Revolution would be criticized and removed from office. Thus, for almost a year and a half after the fall of the Gang of Four, no substantial attempt was made to analyse the past and solve the problems left over by the Gang of Four and the extreme 'leftist' trends in the Party that had held sway from 1957.

In fact, Mao Zedong himself was the first one to declare that 'the standard of truth can only be social practice' in his article *On Practice* written in 1937. Although Mao's words later became gospel to everyone in China, and were quoted and used *ad nauseum*, they were rarely put into practice. The more recent discussion of the 'criterion of truth', however, began publicly with a short article in the *People's Daily* on March 26th, 1978. Following the publication of this article entitled *There is Only One Criterion*, the editors of the paper received over twenty letters which favoured Marxism and not practice as being the criterion of truth. As a result of these letters, the *People's Daily* had Qi Fensi (the name of a writing group) write a long article in reply. However, before the article was published, the *Guangming Daily* (China's second largest daily paper) received an article by a Hu Fuming, a teacher in the Department of Philosophy of Nanjing University, entitled *Practice is the Criterion of Truth*. The editor could not choose between the two articles and so he finally sent the article from Nanjing to the theoretical group of the CC Party School which was headed by Hu Yaobang. Hu had been a key figure in 1975 when Deng had put him in charge of work at the Academy of Science in Peking. He was also one of the theoreticians involved in the drawing up of the three 1975 documents on economic development and scientific research later attacked by the Gang of Four. In late 1976, he was made deputy head of the CC Party School and the CC Organization Ministry. During the third campaign against the Gang which began in 1978, he set up a select group of theoreticians in the Party School to study the problems involved. The head of the Academy of Social Sciences, Hu Qiaomu, as well as the editor of *People's Daily*, Hu Jiwei, joined Hu Yaobang and began printing theoretical articles in the *People's Daily* as well as starting a 'letters to the editor' column which opened the paper to the public and provided a forum for readers to express their grievances about various injustices. As a result of their involvement with the debate on truth, the 'three Hus' became known as the leaders of the 'pragmatists' (*shijianpai*).

After reading Hu Fuming's article, Hu Yaochang had him invited to Peking to join in the discussion on the 'criterion of truth.' As a result, they decided to add the words 'the only' to the title of the article making it read *Practice is the Only Criterion of Truth* and thereafter published it under the anonymous name of 'Special Correspondent' on May 11th in the *Guangming Daily*. The *People's Daily* reprinted the article the following day. The public reaction caught the 'three Hus' completely by surprise. Telephone calls, telegrams, and letters flooded the offices of the two papers full of praise for the article. On the other end of things, Li Xin, the man appointed by Wang Dongxing to be in charge of theoretical discussions, vehemently opposed the article and even declared that it was 'theoretically specious, ideologically reactionary and politically anti-Mao.' Comments in the *Guangming Daily* article criticizing 'spiritual fetters' were taken to mean Mao Zedong Thought. The main opponents to the Hus were Zhang Pinghua, Minister of Propaganda and a former close associate of Hua Guofeng from Hunan; the former editor of *People's Daily*, Wu Lengxi; the editor and vice-editor of the CPC's theoritical journal, *Red Flag*, Fu Xiong and Hu Sheng. Opposition also came from people who felt that if practice was the only criterion of truth then things that had not been realized such as the plan for the four modernizations as proposed by the Eleventh Congress of the Communist Party could not be said to be truth until they had been put into practice.

On the 2nd of June, Deng Xiaoping made a speech at the All-Army Political Work Conference[4] in which he sup-

---

[4] See *Peking Review*, *25 1978, pp. 14–21

ported the 'pragmatists' and defined the three main schools involved in the 'criterion of truth' debate. The first were those who supported the principle of theory and practice being united, the second were those who talked about Mao Zedong Thought all the time but had forgotten the basic principle of Mao's Thought. This was the attitude that everything should be based on reality and that theory and practice should be united. The third type of person were dogmatists who were in favour of copying everything that Marx, Lenin and Mao said but could not relate it to the actual situations they were faced with. Following this speech, *People's Daily*, *Guangming Daily* and *Jiefangun Daily* published articles under the name of 'Special Correspondent' supporting the view of the 'pragmatists.' Hu and the others invited the 'whatever' faction (those who declared they must support and do *whatever* Mao had said or done, called *fanshipai* in Chinese) to write articles and defend their position, but they declined. At a seminar organized by the Philosophy Research School of the Academy of Social Sciences, the 'whatever' faction was invited to attend and debate but again they refused. The only action they took was to prevent the *Red Flag* magazine (which they controlled) from publishing articles in support of the 'pragmatists' and trying to prevent other papers from publishing or carrying such articles.

At the above meeting it was decided not to take any action against the 'whatever' faction, but to wait and let time and events prove them incorrect. This method of dealing with political opponents in China has been unknown of for many years and marks a different attitude towards inner-Party debates. Nevertheless, the debate continued and came to head in early September (1978) when Wang Dongxing had the magazine *China Youth* banned because it had an article criticizing Mao Zedong Thought as a religious cult as well as some other articles making mention to the Tian An Men 'incident' (which, at the time, was still officially regarded as a 'counterrevolutionary incident'). In fact, the article on Mao Thought-religion (entitled *Overcome Superstition and Apply Science*) was said to be written by Hu Yaobang and his theoretical group. This incident added to the already intense feelings in Peking resulting from the CC's continued silence on the Tian An Men 'incident' and on the Gang of Four era mayor, Wu De. The result was a rash of posters along a wall on the main street of the city — Chenganjie — near Xidan. These posters, which were mainly put up by young workers and students, demanded that *China Youth* be distributed, that the mayor of the city be investigated and replaced and that the verdict on the Tian An Men 'incident' as a counter-revolutionary incident be reversed. A copy of the contraband *China Youth* was also put on the wall. Within two months this same wall was renamed the 'minzhuqiang' or 'wall of democracy' and became a forum for debate and argument of all kinds.

The effect of the banning of *China Youth* was to take the debate on the 'criterion of truth' to the highest level of the CPC leadership. Hua Guofeng, on hearing of the ban (he had just returned from an official visit to East Europe and Iran), approved the magazine for distribution. His comments at the National Day Reception held in Peking on October the 1st, can be seen as an expression of his attitude on the debate. He said, 'Everyone should liberate their thinking a bit more, be more daring, be more resourceful and move ahead quicker.' This was taken as being tacit approval of the 'pragmatists.' On the 9th November, the day before the opening of the CC Work Meeting, an article by a special correspondent in *People's Daily* called for a break with the habits of the past, advocated the abandoning of dogmas and unrealistic political attitudes and warned against attacking people unfairly.

The practical effects of the 'criterion of truth' debate were numerous. Recalcitraint and conservative leaders in provincial governments and even the Central Committee were replaced. The most prominent of these was Wu De's replacement by Lin Hujia (former head of Shanghai and later Tianjin) in Peking, the replacement of the Minister of Propaganda, Zhang Pinghua and the demotion of Wang Dongxing who was relieved of his leadership of the central security force (the '8341 troop') and his position as head of the Central Committee Office. Propaganda work was also removed from his jurisdiction. Hu Yaobang and Hu Jiwei's rise within the CC and the state government marked a victory for the 'pragmatists' and the elimination of the dogmatic Gang of Four ideology within the upper echelon of the CPC leadership. Chen Yun's rise to number five in the Party leadership also marked the implementation of a new economic policy. With these changes achieved, new policies could be agreed on and carried out with far greater speed, and old, unsolved problems could be resolved with little of the fuss and fervour that previously surrounded such reevaluations.

The debate on the 'criterion of truth' had won a major victory. Practice had proved that many of the Central Committee's policies since 1957 had been extreme or incorrect. It was on the basis of the new understanding reached following the debate on truth that the Third Plenum was able to reexamine and reverse many decisions made over the past twenty years. This in turn has ideologically cleared the way for people in China to turn their attention towards the future and concentrate their energies on economic development rather than let them be frittered away on overplayed political issues.

APPENDICES

i) 1954 CONSTITUTION

OF THE

PEOPLE'S REPUBLIC

OF CHINA*

CONTENTS

PREAMBLE
Chapter One
GENERAL PRINCIPLES
Chapter Two
THE STATE STRUCTURE
    Section I.   The National People's Congress
    Section II. The Chairman of the People's Republic of China
    Section III. The State Council
    Section IV. The Local People's Congresses and Local People's Councils
    Section V. The Organs of Self-Government of National Autonomous Areas
    Section VI. The People's Courts and the People's Procuratorate
Chapter Three
FUNDAMENTAL RIGHTS AND DUTIES OF CITIZENS
Chapter Four
NATIONAL FLAG, NATIONAL EMBLEM, CAPITAL

---

* Based on a translation in A. P. Blaustein, *Fundamental Legal Documents of Communist China* (South Hackensack, N.J.: F. B. Rothman, 1962).

PREAMBLE

In the year 1949, after more than a century of heroic struggle, the Chinese people, led by the Communist Party of China, finally achieved their great victory in the people's revolution against imperialism, feudalism and bureaucrat-capitalism; and so brought to an end a long history of oppression and enslavement and founded the People's Republic of China, a people's democratic dictatorship. The system of people's democracy — new democracy — of the People's Republic of China guarantees that China can in a peaceful way banish exploitation and poverty and build a prosperous and happy socialist society.

From the founding of the People's Republic of China to the attainment of a socialist society is a period of transition. During the transition the fundamental task of the State is, step by step, to bring about the socialist industrialization of the country and, step by step, to accomplish the socialist transformation of agriculture, handicrafts and capitalist industry and commerce. In the last few years our people have successfully carried out a series of large-scale struggles: the reform of the agrarian system, resistance to American aggression and aid to Korea, the suppression of counter-revolutionaries and the rehabilitation of the national economy. As a result, the necessary conditions have been created for planned economic construction and gradual transition to socialism.

The First National People's Congress of the People's Republic of China, at its first session held in Peking, the capital, solemnly adopted the Constitution of the People's Republic of China on 20 September 1954. This Constitution is based on the Common Programme of the Chinese People's Political Consultative Conference of 1949, and is an advance on it. It consolidates the gains of the Chinese People's revolution and the political and economic victories won since the founding of the People's Republic of China; and, moreover, it reflects the basic needs of the State in the period of transition, as well as the general desire of the people as a whole to build a socialist society.

In the course of the great struggle to establish the People's Republic of China, the People of our country forged a broad people's democratic united front, composed of all democratic classes, democratic parties and groups, and popular organizations, and led by the Communist Party of China. This people's democratic united front will continue to play its part in mobilizing and rallying the whole people in common struggle to fulfil the fundamental task of the State during the transition and to oppose enemies within and without.

All nationalities of our country are united in one great family of free and equal nations. This unity of China's nationalities will continue to gain in strength, founded as it is on ever growing friendship and mutual aid among themselves, and on the struggle against imperialism, against public enemies of the people within the nationalities, and against both dominant-nation chauvinism and local nationalism. In the course of economic and cultural development, the State will concern itself with the needs of the different nationalities, and, in the matter of socialist transformation, pay full attention to the special characteristics in the development of each.

China has already built an indestructible friendship with the great Union of Soviet Socialist Republics and the People's Democracies; and the friendship between our people and peace-loving people in all other countries is growing day by day. Such friendship will be constantly strengthened and broadened. China's policy of establishing and extending diplomatic relations with all countries on the principle of equality, mutual benefit and mutual respect for each other's sovereignty and territorial integrity, which has already yielded success, will continue to be carried out. In international affairs our firm and consistent policy is to strive for the noble cause of world peace and the progress of humanity.

CHAPTER ONE
GENERAL PRINCIPLES

Article 1

The People's Republic of China is a people's democratic State led by the working class and based on the alliance of workers and peasants.

Article 2

All power in the People's Republic of China belongs to the people. The organs through which the people exercise power are the National People's Congress and the local people's congresses.

The National People's Congress, the local people's congresses and other organs of State practise democratic centralism.

Article 3

The People's Republic of China is a single multi-national State.

All the nationalities are equal. Discrimination against, or oppression of, any nationality, and acts which undermine the unity of the nationalities are prohibited.

All the nationalities have freedom to use and foster the growth of their spoken and written languages, and to preserve or reform their own customs or ways.

Regional autonomy applies in areas where people of national minorities live in compact communities. National autonomous areas are inalienable parts of the People's Republic of China.

Article 4

The People's Republic of China, by relying on the organs

The 1954 Constitution

of State and the social forces, and by means of socialist industrialization, and socialist transformation, ensures the gradual abolition of systems of exploitation and the building of a socialist society.

Article 5

At present, the following basic forms of ownership of means of production exist in the People's Republic of China: State ownership, that is, ownership by the whole people; co-operative ownership, that is, collective ownership by the working masses; ownership by individual working people; and capitalist ownership.

Article 6

The State sector of the economy is a socialist sector, owned by the whole people. It is the leading force in the national economy and the material basis on which the State carries out socialist transformation. The State ensures priority for the development of the State sector of the economy.

All mineral resources and waters, as well as forests, undeveloped land and other resources which the State owns by law, are the property of the whole people.

Article 7

The co-operative sector of the economy is either socialist, when collectively owned by the working masses, or semi-socialist, when in part collectively owned by the working masses. Partial collective ownership by the working masses is a transitional form by means of which individual peasants, individual handicraftsmen and other individual working people organize themselves in their advance towards collective ownership by the working masses.

The State protects the property of the co-operatives, encourages, guides and helps the development of the co-operative sector of the economy. It regards the promotion of producers' co-operatives as the chief means for the transformation of individual farming and individual handicrafts.

Article 8

The State protects the right of peasants to own land and other means of production according to law.

The State guides and helps individual peasants to increase production and encourages them to organize producers', supply and marketing, and credit co-operatives voluntarily.

The policy of the State towards rich-peasant economy is to restrict and gradually eliminate it.

Article 9

The State protects the right of handicraftsmen and other non-agricultural individual working people to own means of production according to law.

The State guides and helps individual handicraftsmen and other non-agricultural individual working people to improve their enterprise and encourages them to organize producers', and supply and marketing co-operatives voluntarily.

Article 10

The State protects the right of capitalists to own means of production and other capital according to law.

The policy of the State towards capitalist industry and commerce is to use, restrict and transform them. The State makes use of the positive sides of capitalist industry and commerce which are beneficial to national welfare and the people's livelihood, restricts their negative sides which are not beneficial to national welfare and the people's livelihood, encourages and guides their transformation into various forms of State-capitalist economy, gradually replacing capitalist ownership with ownership by the whole people; and this it does by means of control exercised by administrative organs of State, the leadership given by the State sector of the economy, and supervision by the workers.

The State forbids capitalists to engage in unlawful activities which injure the public interests, disrupt the social-economic order, or undermine the economic plan of the State.

Article 11

The State protects the right of citizens to own lawfully-earned incomes, savings, houses and other means of life.

Article 12

The State protects the right of citizens to inherit private property according to law.

Article 13

The State may, in the public interest, buy, requisition or nationalize land and other means of production both in cities and countryside according to provisions of law.

Article 14

The State forbids any person to use his private property to the detriment of the public interest.

Article 15

By economic planning, the State directs the growth and transformation of the national economy to bring about the constant increase of productive forces, in this way enriching the material and cultural life of the people and consolidating the independence and security of the country.

Article 16

Work is a matter of honour for every citizen of the People's Republic of China who is able to work. The State encourages citizens to take an active and creative part in their work.

Article 17

All organs of State must rely on the masses of the people, constantly maintain close contact with them, heed their opinions and accept their supervision.

Article 18

All servants of the State must be loyal to the people's democratic system, observe the Constitution and the law and strive to serve the people.

Article 19

The People's Republic of China safeguards the people's democratic system, suppresses all treasonable and counter-revolutionary activities and punishes all traitors and counter-revolutionaries.

The State deprives feudal landlords and bureaucrat-capitalists of political rights for a specific period of time according to law; at the same time it provides them with a way to earn a living, in order to enable them to reform through work and become citizens who earn their livelihood by their own labour.

Article 20

The armed forces of the People's Republic of China belong to the people; their duty is to safeguard the gains of the people's revolution and the achievements of national construction, and to defend the sovereignty, territorial integrity and security of the country.

CHAPTER TWO
THE STATE STRUCTURE

Section I

The National People's Congress

Article 21

The National People's Congress is the highest organ of State authority in the People's Republic of China.

Article 22

The National People's Congress is the only legislative authority in the country.

Article 23

The National People's Congress is composed of deputies elected by provinces, autonomous regions, municipalities directly under the central authority, the armed forces and Chinese resident abroad.

The number of deputies to the National People's Congress, including those representing national minorities, and the manner of their election, are prescribed by electoral law.

Article 24

The National People's Congress is elected for a term of four years.

Two months before the term of office of the National People's Congress expires, its standing committee must com-

The 1954 Constitution 161

plete the election of deputies to the succeeding National People's Congress. Should exceptional circumstances arise preventing such an election, the term of office of the sitting National People's Congress may be prolonged until the first session of the succeeding National People's Congress.

Article 25

The National People's Congress meets once a year, convened by its standing committee. It may also be convened whenever its standing committee deems this necessary or one-fifth of the deputies so propose.

Article 26

When the National People's Congress meets, it elects a presidium to conduct its sittings.

Article 27

The National People's Congress exercises the following functions and powers:

(1) to amend the Constitution;
(2) to enact laws;
(3) to supervise the enforcement of the Constitution;
(4) to elect the chairman and the vice-chairman of the People's Republic of China;
(5) to decide on the choice of the premier of the State Council upon recommendation by the chairman of the People's Republic of China, and of the component members of the State Council upon recommendation by the premier;
(6) to decide on the choice of the vice-chairman and other members of the Council of National Defence upon recommendation by the chairman of the People's Republic of China;
(7) to elect the president of the Supreme People's Court;
(8) to elect the chief procurator of the Supreme People's

Procuratorate;

(9) to decide on the national economic plans;

(10) to examine and approve the State budget and the financial report;

(11) to ratify the status and boundaries of provinces, autonomous regions, and municipalities directly under the central authority;

(12) to decide on general amnesties;

(13) to decide on questions of war and peace, and

(14) to exercise such other functions and powers as the National People's Congress considers necessary.

Article 28

The National People's Congress has power to remove from office:

(1) the chairman and the vice-chairman of the People's Republic of China;

(2) the premier and vice-premiers, ministers, heads of commissions and the secretary-general of the State Council;

(3) the vice-chairman and other members of the Council of National Defence;

(4) the president of the Supreme People's Court; and

(5) the chief procurator of the Supreme People's Procuratorate.

Article 29

Amendments to the Constitution require a two-thirds majority vote of all the deputies to the National People's Congress.

Laws and other bills require a simple majority vote of all the deputies to the National People's Congress.

Article 30

The standing committee of the National People's Congress is a permanently acting body of the National People's

Congress.

The standing committee is composed of the following members, elected by the National People's Congress:

the chairman;
the vice-chairman;
the secretary-general; and
other members.

Article 31

The standing committee of the National People's Congress exercises the following functions and powers:

(1) to conduct the election of deputies to the National People's Congress;

(2) to convene the National People's Congress;

(3) to interpret the laws;

(4) to adopt decrees;

(5) to supervise the work of the State Council, the Supreme People's Court and the Supreme People's Procuratorate;

(6) to annul decisions and orders of the State Council which contravene the Constitution, laws or decrees;

(7) to revise or annul inappropriate decisions issued by the government authorities of provinces, autonomous regions, and municipalities directly under the central authority;

(8) to decide on the appointment or removal of any vice-premier, minister, head of commission or the secretary-general of the State Council when the National People's Congress is not in session;

(9) to appoint or remove the vice-presidents, judges, and other members of the Judicial Committee of the Supreme People's Court;

(10) to appoint or remove the deputy chief procurators, procurators, and other members of the Procuratorial Committee of the Supreme People's Procuratorate;

(11) to decide on the appointment or recall of plenipotentiary representatives to foreign States;

(12) to decide on the ratification or abrogation of treaties

concluded with foreign States;

(13) to institute military, diplomatic and other special titles and ranks;

(14) to institute and decide on the award of State orders, medals and titles of honour;

(15) to decide on the granting of pardons;

(16) to decide, when the National People's Congress is not in session, on the proclamation of a state of war in the event of armed attack on the country or in fulfilment of international treaty obligations concerning common defence against aggression;

(17) to decide on general or partial mobilization;

(18) to decide on the enforcement of martial law throughout the country or in certain areas; and

(19) to exercise such other functions and powers as are vested in by the National People's Congress.

Article 32

The standing committee of the National People's Congress exercises its functions and powers until a new standing committee is elected by the succeeding National People's Congress.

Article 33

The standing committee of the National People's Congress is responsible to the National People's Congress and reports to it.

The National People's Congress has power to recall members of its standing committee.

Article 34

The National People's Congress establishes a Nationalities Committee, a Bills Committee, a Budget Committee, a Credentials Committee and other necessary committees.

The Nationalities Committee and the Bills Committee

The 1954 Constitution

are under the direction of the standing committee of the National People's Congress when the National People's Congress is not in session.

Article 35

The National People's Congress or its standing committee if the National People's Congress is not in session may, if necessary, appoint commissions of inquiry for the investigation of specific questions.

All organs of State, people's organizations and citizens concerned are obliged to supply necessary information to these commissions when they conduct investigations.

Article 36

Deputies to the National People's Congress have the right to address questions to the State Council, or to the Ministries and Commissions of the State Council, which are under obligation to answer.

Article 37

No deputy to the National People's Congress may be arrested or placed on trial without the consent of the National People's Congress or, when the National People's Congress is not in session, of its standing committee.

Article 38

Deputies to the National People's Congress are subject to the supervision of the units which elect them. These electoral units have power to replace at any time the deputies they elect, according to the procedure prescribed by law.

Section II

The Chairman of the People's Republic of China

Article 39

The chairman of the People's Republic of China is elected by the National People's Congress. Any citizen of the People's Republic of China who has the right to vote and stand for election and has reached the age of 35 is eligible for election as chairman of the People's Republic of China.

The term of office of the chairman of the People's Republic of China is four years.

Article 40

The chairman of the People's Republic of China, in pursuance of decisions of the National People's Congress or the standing committee of the National People's Congress, promulgates laws and decrees; appoints or removes the premier, vice-premiers, ministers, heads of commissions and the secretary-general of the State Council; appoints or removes the vice-chairmen and other members of the Council of National Defence; confers State orders, medals and titles of honour; proclaims general amnesties and grants pardons; proclaims martial law; proclaims a state of war; and orders mobilization.

Article 41

The chairman of the People's Republic of China represents the People's Republic of China in its relations with foreign States, receives foreign diplomatic representatives and, in pursuance of decisions of the standing committee of the National People's Congress, appoints or recalls plenipoten-

The 1954 Constitution 167

tiary representatives to foreign States and ratifies treaties concluded with foreign States.

Article 42

The chairman of the People's Republic of China commands the armed forces of the country, and is chairman of the Council of National Defence.

Article 43

The chairman of the People's Republic of China, whenever necessary, convenes a Supreme State Conference and acts as its chairman.

The vice-chairman of the People's Republic of China, the chairman of the standing committee of the National People's Congress, the premier of the State Council and other persons concerned take part in the Supreme State Conference.

The chairman of the People's Republic of China submits the views of the Supreme State Conference on important affairs of State to the National People's Congress, its standing committee, the State Council, or other bodies concerned for their consideration and decision.

Article 44

The vice-chairman of the People's Republic of China assists the chairman in his work. The vice-chairman may exercise such part of the functions and powers of the chairman as the chairman may entrust to him.

The provisions of Article 39 of the Constitution governing the election and term of office of the chairman of the People's Republic of China apply also to the election and term of office of the vice-chairman of the People's Republic of China.

168 *China's New Democracy*

Article 45

The chairman and the vice-chairman of the People's Republic of China exercise their functions and powers until the new chairman and vice-chairman elected by the succeeding National People's Congress take office.

Article 46

Should the chairman of the People's Republic of China be incapacitated for a prolonged period by reason of health, the functions of chairman shall be exercised by the vice-chairman.

Should the office of chairman of the People's Republic of China fall vacant, the vice-chairman succeeds to the office of chairman.

Section III
The State Council

Article 47

The State Council of the People's Republic of China, that is, the Central People's Government, is the executive organ of the highest state authority; it is the highest administrative organ of state.

Article 48

The State Council is composed of the following members:
the premier;
the vice-premiers;
the ministers;
the head of commissions; and
the secretary-general.

The organization of the State Council is determined

by law.

Article 49

The State Council exercises the following functions and powers:

(1) to formulate administrative measures, issue decisions and orders and verify their execution, in accordance with the Constitution, laws and decrees;

(2) to submit bills to the National People's Congress or its standing committee;

(3) to co-ordinate and lead the work of Ministries and Commissions;

(4) to co-ordinate and lead the work of local administrative organs of State throughout the country;

(5) to revise or annul inappropriate orders and directives issued by Ministers or Heads of Commissions;

(6) to revise or annul inappropriate decisions and orders issued by local administrative organs of State;

(7) to put into effect the national economic plans and provisions of the State budget;

(8) to control foreign and domestic trade;

(9) to direct cultural, educational and public health work;

(10) to administer affairs concerning the nationalities;

(11) to administer affairs concerning Chinese resident abroad;

(12) to protect the interests of the State, to maintain public order and to safeguard the rights of citizens;

(13) to direct the conduct of external affairs;

(14) to guide the building up of the defence forces;

(15) to ratify the status and boundaries of autonomous *chou*, counties, autonomous counties, and municipalities;

(16) to appoint or remove administrative personnel according to provisions of law; and

(17) to exercise such other functions and powers as are vested in it by the National People's Congress or its standing committee.

Article 50

The premier directs the work of the State Council and presides over its meetings.
The vice-premiers assist the premier in his work.

Article 51

The ministers and heads of commissions direct the work of their respective departments. They may issue orders and directives within the jurisdiction of their respective departments and in accordance with laws and decrees, and decisions and orders of the State council.

Article 52

The State Council is responsible to the National People's Congress and reports to it; or, when the National People's Congress is not in session, to its Standing Committee.

Section IV

The Local People's Congresses and Local People's Councils

Article 53

The administrative division of The People's Republic of China is as follows:
(1) The country is divided into provinces, autonomous regions, and municipalities directly under the central authority;
(2) Provinces and autonomous regions are divided into autonomous *chou*, counties, autonomous counties, and municipalities; and

(3) Counties and autonomous counties are divided into *hsiang* , nationality *hsiang* , and towns.

Municipalities directly under the central authority and other large municipalities are divided into districts. Autonomous *chou* are divided into counties, autonomous counties, and municipalities.

Autonomous regions, autonomous *chou* and autonomous counties are all national autonomous areas.

Article 54

People's congresses and poeple's councils are established in provinces, municipalities directly under the central authority, counties, municipalities, municipal districts, *hsiang*, nationality *hsiang*, and towns.

Organs of self-government are established in autonomous regions, autonomous *chou* and autonomous counties. The organization and work of organs of self-government are specified in Section V of Chapter Two of the Constitution.

Article 55

Local people's congresses at all levels are the organs of government authority in their respective localities.

Article 56

Deputies to the people's congresses of provinces, municipalities directly under the central authority, counties, and municipalities divided into districts are elected by the people's congresses of the next lower level; deputies to the people's congresses of municipalities not divided into districts, municipal districts, *hsiang*, nationality *hsiang*, and towns are directly elected by the voters.

The number of deputies to local people's congresses and the manner of their election are prescribed by electoral law.

Article 57

The term of office of the provincial people's congresses is four years. The term of office of the people's congresses of municipalities directly under the central authority, counties, municipalities, municipal districts, *hsiang*, nationality *hsiang*, and towns is two years.

Article 58

The local people's congresses at every level ensure the observance and execution of laws and decrees in their respective administrative areas; draw up plans for local economic and cultural development and for public works; examine and approve local budgets and financial reports; protect public property; maintain public order; safeguard the rights of citizens and the equal rights of national minorities.

Article 59

The local people's congresses elect, and have power to recall, members of the people's councils at corresponding levels.

The people's congresses at county level and above elect, and have power to recall, the presidents of people's courts at corresponding levels.

Article 60

The local people's congresses adopt and issue decisions within the limits of the authority prescribed by law.

The people's congresses of nationality *hsiang* may, within the limits of the authority prescribed by law, take specific measures appropriate to the characteristics of the nationalities concerned.

The local people's congresses have power to revise or annul inappropriate decisions and orders issued by people's councils at corresponding levels.

The people's congresses at county level and above have power to revise or annul inappropriate decisions issued by people's congresses at the next lower level as well as inappropriate decisions and orders issued by people's councils at the next lower level.

Article 61

Deputies to the people's congresses of provinces, municipalities directly under the central authority, counties, and municipalities divided into districts are subject to supervision by the units which elect them; deputies to the people's congresses of municipalities not divided into districts, municipal districts, *hsiang*, nationality *hsiang*, and towns are subject to supervision by their electorates. The electoral units and electorates which elect the deputies to the local people's congresses have power at any time to recall their deputies according to the procedure prescribed by law.

Article 62

Local people's councils, that is, local people's governments, are the executive organs of local people's congresses at corresponding levels, and are the administrative organs of State in their respective localities.

Article 63

A local people's council is composed, according to its level, of the provincial governor and deputy provincial governors; or the mayor and deputy mayors; or the county head and deputy county heads; or the district head and deputy district heads; or the *hsiang* head and deputy *hsiang* heads; or the town head and deputy town heads, as the case may be; together with council members.

The term of office of a local people's council is the

same as that of the people's congress at corresponding level.

The organization of local people's councils is determined by law.

Article 64

The local people's councils administer their respective areas within the limits of the authority prescribed by law.

The local people's councils carry out the decisions by people's congresses at corresponding levels and decisions and orders issued by administrative organs of State at higher levels.

The local people's councils issue decisions and orders within the limits of the authority prescribed by law.

Article 65

The people's councils at county level and above direct the work of all their subordinate departments and of people's councils at lower levels, as well as appoint or remove personnel of organs of State according to provisions of law.

The people's councils at county level and above have power to suspend the carrying out of inappropriate decisions of people's congresses at the next lower level; and to revise or annul inappropriate orders and directives issued by their subordinate departments, and inappropriate decisions and orders issued by people's councils at lower levels.

Article 66

The local people's councils are responsible to the people's congresses at corresponding levels and to the administrative organs of State at the next higher level, and report to them.

The local people's councils throughout the country are administrative organs of State, and are subordinate to and under the co-ordinating direction of the State Council.

The 1954 Constitution 175

Section V

The Organs of Self-Government of National Autonomous Areas

Article 67

The organs of self-government of all autonomous regions, autonomous *chou* and autonomous counties are formed in accordance with the basic principles governing the organization of local organs of State as specified in Section IV of Chapter Two of the Constitution. The form of each organ of self-government may be determined in accordance with the wishes of the majority of the people of the nationality or nationalities enjoying regional autonomy in a given area.

Article 68

In all autonomous regions, autonomous *chou* and autonomous counties where a number of nationalities live together, each nationality is entitled to appropriate representation on the organs of self-government.

Article 69

The organs of self-government of all autonomous regions, autonomous *chou* and autonomous counties exercise the functions and powers of local organs of State as specified in Section IV of Chapter Two of the Constitution.

Article 70

The organs of self-government of all autonomous regions, autonomous *chou* and autonomous counties exercise autonomy within the limits of the authority prescribed by the

Constitution and the law.

The organs of self-government of all autonomous regions, autonomous *chou* and autonomous counties administer their own local finances within the limits of the authority prescribed by law.

The organs of self-governemnt of all autonomous regions, autonomous *chou* and autonomous counties organize their local public security forces in accordance with the military system of the State.

The organs of self-government of all autonomous regions, autonomous *chou* and autonomous counties may draw up statutes governing the exercise of autonomy or separate regulations suited to the political, economic and cultural characteristics of the nationality or nationalities in a given area, which statutes and regulations are subject to endorsement by the standing committee of the National People's Congress.

Article 71

In performing their duties, organs on self-government of all autonomous regions, autonomous *chou* and autonomous counties employ the spoken and written language or languages commonly used in the locality.

Article 72

The highest organs of State should fully safeguard the right of organs of self-government of all autonomous regions, autonomous *chou* and autonomous counties to exercise autonomy, and should assist the various national minorities in their political, economic and cultural development.

Section VI
The People's Courts
and
the People's Procuratorate

Article 73

In the People's Republic of China judicial authority is exercised by the Supreme People's Court, local people's courts and special people's courts.

Article 74

The term of office of the president of the Supreme People's Court and presidents of local people's courts is four years.

The organization of people's courts is determined by law.

Article 75

The system of people's assessors applies, in accordance with law, to judicial proceedings in the people's courts.

Article 76

Cases in the people's courts are heard in public unless otherwise provided for by law. The accused has the right to defence.

Article 77

Citizens of all nationalities have the right to use their own spoken and written languages in court proceedings. The people's courts are to provide interpretation for any party unacquainted with the spoken or written language commonly used in the locality.

In an area where people of national minorities live in compact communities or where a number of nationalities live together, hearings in people's courts are conducted in the language commonly used in the locality, and judgments, notices and all other documents of the people's courts are made public in such language.

Article 78

In administering justice the people's courts are independent, subject only to the law.

Article 79

The Supreme People's Court is the highest judicial organ.
The Supreme People's Court supervises the judicial work of local people's courts and special people's courts; people's courts at higher levels supervise the judicial work of people's courts at lower levels.

Article 80

The Supreme People's Court is responsible to the National People's Congress and reports to it; or, when the National People's Congress is not in session, to its standing committee. Local people's courts are responsible to the local people's congresses at corresponding levels and report to them.

Article 81

The Supreme People's Procuratorate of the People's Republic of China exercises procuratorial authority over all departments of the State Council, all local organs of State, persons working in organs of State, and citizens, to ensure observance of the law. Local organs of the people's procuratorate and special people's procuratorates exercise procuratorial authority within the limits prescribed by law.

Local organs of the people's procuratorate and the special people's procuratorates work under the leadership of the people's procuratorates at higher levels, and all work under the co-ordinating direction of the Supreme People's Procuratorate.

Article 82

The term of office of the Chief Procurator of the Supreme People's Procuratorate is four years.

The organization of people's procuratorates is determinated by law.

Article 83

In the exercise of their authority local organs of the people's procuratorate are independent and are not subject to interference by local organs of State.

Article 84

The Supreme People's Procuratorate is responsible to the National People's Congress and reports to it; or, when the National People's Congress is not in session, to its standing committee.

CHAPTER THREE
FUNDAMENTAL RIGHTS AND DUTIES OF CITIZENS

Article 85

Citizens of the People's Republic of China are equal before the law.

Article 86

Citizens of the People's Republic of China who have reached the age of eighteen have the right to vote and stand for election whatever their nationality, race, sex, occupation, social origin, religious belief, education, property status, or length of residence, except insane persons and persons deprived by law of the right to vote and stand for election.

Women have equal rights with men to vote and stand for election.

Article 87

Citizens of the People's Republic of China enjoy freedom of speech, freedom of the press, freedom of assembly, freedom of association, freedom of procession and freedom of demonstration. The State guarantees to citizens enjoyment of these freedoms by providing the necessary material facilities.

Article 88

Citizens of the People's Republic of China enjoy freedom of religious belief.

Article 89

Freedom of the person of citizens of the People's Republic of China is inviolable. No citizen may be arrested except by decision of a people's court or with the sanction of a people's procuratorate.

Article 90

The homes of citizens of the People's Republic of China are inviolable, and privacy of correspondence is protected by law.

Citizens of the People's Republic of China enjoy freedom of residence and freedom to change their residence.

Article 91

Citizens of the People's Republic of China have the right to work. To guarantee enjoyment of this right, the State, by planned development of the national economy, gradually creates more employment, and better working conditions and wages.

Article 92

Working people in the People's Republic of China have the right to rest and leisure. To guarantee enjoyment of this right, the State prescribes working hours and holidays for workers and office employees; at the same time it gradually expands material facilities to enable working people to rest and build up their health.

Article 93

Working people in the People's Republic of China have the right to material assistance in old age, and in case of illness or disability. To guarantee enjoyment of this right, the

State provides social insurance, social assistance and public health services and gradually expands these facilities.

Article 94

Citizens of the People's Republic of China have the right to education. To guarantee enjoyment of this right, the State establishes and gradually extends the various types of schools and other cultural and educational institutions.

The State pays special attention to the physical and mental development of young people.

Article 95

The People's Republic of China safeguards the freedom of citizens to engage in scientific research, literary and artistic creation and other cultural pursuits. The State encourages and assists creative work in science, education, literature, art and other cultural pursuits.

Article 96

Women in the People's Republic of China enjoy equal rights with men in all spheres of political, economic, cultural, social and domestic life.

The State protects marriage, the family, and the mother and child.

Article 97

Citizens of the People's Republic of China have the right to bring complaints against any person working in organs of State for transgression of law or neglect of duty by making a written or verbal statement to any organ of State at any level. People suffering loss by reason of infringement by persons working in organs of State of their rights as citizens have the right to compensation.

Article 98

The People's Republic of China protects the proper rights and interests of Chinese resident abroad.

Article 99

The People's Republic of China grants the right of asylum to any foreign national persecuted for supporting a just cause, for taking part in the peace movement or for engaging in scientific activity.

Article 100

Citizens of the People's Republic of China must abide by the Constitution and the law, uphold discipline at work, keep public order and respect social ethics.

Article 101

The public property of the People's Republic of China is sacred and inviolable. It is the duty of every citizen to respect and protect public property.

Article 102

It is the duty of citizens of the People's Republic of China to pay taxes according to law.

Article 103

It is the sacred duty of every citizen of the People's Republic of China to defend the homeland.

It is an honourable duty of citizens of the People's Republic of China to perform military service according to law.

CHAPTER FOUR
NATIONAL FLAG, NATIONAL EMBLEM, CAPITAL

Article 104

The national flag of the People's Republic of China is a red flag with five stars.

Article 105

The national emblem of the People's Republic of China is: in the centre, Tien An Men under the light of five stars, framed with ears of grain, and with a cogwheel at the base.

Article 106

The capital of the People's Republic of China is Peking.

ii) 1975 CONSTITUTION

OF THE

PEOPLE'S REPUBLIC

OF CHINA

CONTENTS

PREAMBLE

Chapter One
GENERAL PRINCIPLES

Chapter Two
THE STRUCTURE OF THE STATE

    Section I.   The National People's Congress
    Section II. The State Council
    Section III. The Local People's Congresses and the Legal Revolutionary Committees at Various Levels
    Section IV. The Organs of Self-Government of National Autonomous Areas
    Section V. The Judicial Organs and the Procuratorial Organs

Chapter Three
THE FUNDAMENTAL RIGHTS AND DUTIES OF CITIZENS

Chapter Four
THE NATIONAL FLAG, THE NATIONAL EMBLEM AND THE CAPITAL

PREAMBLE

The founding of the People's Republic of China marked the great victory of the new-democratic revolution and the beginning of the new historical period of socialist revolution and the dictatorship of the proletariat, a victory gained only after the Chinese people had waged a heroic struggle for over a century and, finally, under the leadership of the Communist Party of China, overthrown the reactionary rule of imperialism, feudalism and bureaucrat-capitalism by a people's revolutionary war.

For the last twenty years and more, the people of all nationalities in our country, continuing their triumphant advance under the leadership of the Communist Party of China, have achieved great victories both in socialist revolution and socialist construction and in the Great Proletarian Cultural Revolution, and have consolidated and strengthened the dictatorship of the proletariat.

Socialist society covers a considerably long historical period. Throughout this historical period, there are classes, class contradictions and class struggle, there is the struggle between the socialist road and the capitalist road, there is the danger of capitalist restoration and there is the threat of subversion and aggression by imperialism and social-imperialism. These contradictions can be resolved only by depending on the theory of continued revolution under the dictatorship of the proletariat and on practice under its guidance.

We must adhere to the basic line and policies of the Communist Party of China for the entire historical period of socialism and persist in continued revolution under the dictatorship of the proletariat, so that our great motherland will always advance along the road indicated by Marxism-Leninism-Mao Zedong Thought.

We should consolidate the great unity of the people of all nationalities led by the working class and based on the alliance of workers and peasants, and develop the revolutionary united front. We should correctly distinguish contradictions among the people from those between ourselves and the enemy and correctly handle them. We should carry on the three great revolutionary movements of class struggle, the struggle for production and scientific experiment; we should build socialism independently and with the initiative in our own hands, through self-reliance, hard struggle, diligence and thrift and by going all out, aiming high and achieving greater, faster, better and more economical results; and we should be prepared against war and natural disasters and do everything for the people.

In international affairs, we should uphold proletarian internationalism. China will never be a superpower. We should strengthen our unity with the socialist countries and all oppressed people and oppressed nations, with each supporting the other; strive for peaceful coexistence with countries having different social systems on the basis of the Five Principles of mutual respect for sovereignty and territorial integrity, mutual non-aggression, non-interference in each other's internal affairs, equality and mutual benefit, and peaceful coexistence, and oppose the imperialist and social-imperialist policies of aggression and war and oppose the hegemonism of the superpowers.

The Chinese people are fully confident that, led by the Communist Party of China, they will vanquish enemies at home and abroad and surmount all difficulties to build China into a powerful socialist state of the dictatorship of the proletariat so as to make a greater contribution to humanity.

People of all nationalities in our country, unite to win still greater victories!

CHAPTER ONE

GENERAL PRINCIPLES

Article 1

The People's Republic of China is a socialist state of the dictatorship of the proletariat led by the working class and based on the alliance of workers and peasants.

Article 2

The Communist Party of China is the core of leadership of the whole Chinese people. The working class exercises leadership over the state through its vanguard, the Communist Party of China.

Marxism-Leninism-Mao Zedong Thought is the theoretical basis guiding the thinking of our nation.

Article 3

All power in the People's Republic of China belongs to the people. The organs through which the people exercise power are the people's congresses at all levels, with deputies of workers, peasants and soldiers as their main body.

The people's congresses at all levels and all other organs of state practise democratic centralism.

Deputies to the people's congresses at all levels are elected through democratic consultation. The electoral units and electors have the power to supervise the deputies they elect and to replace them at any time according to provisions of law.

Article 4

The People's Republic of China is a unitary multi-national state. The areas where regional national autonomy is exercised are all inalienable parts of the People's Republic of China.

All the nationalities are equal. Big-nationality chauvinism and local-nationality chauvinism must be opposed.

All the nationalities have the freedom to use their own spoken and written languages.

Article 5

In the People's Republic of China, there are mainly two kinds of ownership of the means of production at the present stage: socialist ownership by the whole people and socialist collective ownership by working people.

The state may allow non-agricultural individual labourers to engage in individual labour involving no exploitation of others, within the limits permitted by law and under unified arrangement by neighbourhood organizations in cities and towns or by production teams in rural people's communes. At the same time, these individual labourers should be guided onto the road of socialist collectivization step by step.

Article 6

The state sector of the economy is the leading force in the national economy.

All mineral resources and waters as well as the forests, undeveloped land and other resources owned by the state are the property of the whole people.

The state may requisition by purchase, take over for use, or nationalize urban and rural land as well as other means of production under conditions prescribed by law.

Article 7

The rural people's commune is an organization which integrates government administration and economic management.

The economic system of collective ownership in the rural poeple's communes at the present stage generally takes the form of three-level ownership with the production team at the basic level, that is, ownership by the commune, the production brigade and the production team, with the last as the basic accounting unit.

Provided that the development and absolute predominance of the collective economy of the people's commune are ensured, people's commune members may farm small plots for their personal needs, engage in limited household side-line production, and in pastoral areas keep a small number of livestock for their personal needs.

Article 8

Socialist public property shall be inviolable. The state shall ensure the consolidation and development of the socialist economy and prohibit any person from undermining the socialist economy and the public interest in any way whatsoever.

Article 9

The state applies the socialist principle: "He who does not work, neither shall he eat" and "from each according to his ability, to each according to his work."

The state protects the citizens' right of ownership to their income from work, their savings, their houses, and other means of livelihood.

Article 10

The state applies the principle of grasping revolution,

promoting production and other work and preparedness against war; promotes the planned and proportionate development of the socialist economy, taking agriculture as the foundation and industry as the leading factor and bringing the initiative of both the central and the local authorities into full play; and improves the people's material and cultural life step by step on the basis of the constant growth of social production and consolidates the independence and security of the country.

Article 11

State organizations and state personnel must earnestly study Marxism-Leninism-Mao Tsetung Thought, firmly put proletarian politics in command, combat bureaucracy, maintain close ties with the masses and wholeheartedly serve the people. Cadres at all levels must participate in collective productive labour.

Every organ of state must apply the principle of efficient and simple administration. Its leading body must be a three-in-one combination of the old, the middle-aged and the young.

Article 12

The proletariat must exercise all-round dictatorship over the bourgeoisie in the superstructure, including all spheres of culture. Culture and education, literature and art, physical education, health work and scientific research work must all serve proletarian politics, serve the workers, peasants and soldiers, and be combined with productive labour.

Article 13

Speaking out freely, airing views fully, holding great debates and writing big-character posters are new forms of carrying on socialist revolution created by the masses of the people. The state shall ensure to the masses the right to use these forms to create a political situation in which there are both centralism and democracy, both discipline and freedom, both unity of will and personal ease of mind and liveliness, and so help consolidate the leadership of the Communist Party of China over the state and consolidate the dictatorship of the proletariat.

Article 14

The state safeguards the socialist system, suppresses all treasonable and counter-revolutionary activities and punishes all traitors and counter-revolutionaries.

The state deprives the landlords, rich peasants, reactionary capitalists and other bad elements of political rights for specified periods of time according to law, and at the same time provides them with the opportunity to earn a living so that they may be reformed through labour and become law-abiding citizens supporting themselves by their own labour.

Article 15

The Chinese People's Liberation Army and the people's militia are the workers' and peasants' own armed forces led by the Communist Party of China; they are the armed forces of the people of all nationalities.

The Chairman of the Central Committee of the Communist Party of China commands the country's armed forces.

The Chinese People's Liberation Army is at all times a fighting force, and simultaneously a working force and a production force.

The task of the armed forces of the People's Republic of China is to safeguard the achievements of the socialist revolution and socialist construction, to defend the sovereignty, territorial integrity and security of the state, and to guard against subversion and aggression by imperialism, social-imperialism and their lackeys.

CHAPTER TWO

THE STRUCTURE OF THE STATE

Section I
The National People's Congress

Article 16

The National People's Congress is the highest organ of state power under the leadership of the Communist Party of China.

The National People's Congress is composed of deputies elected by the provinces, autonomous regions, municipalities directly under the Central Government, and the People's Liberation Army. When necessary, a certain number of patriotic personages may be specially invited to take part as deputies.

The National People's Congress is elected for a term of five years. Its term of office may be extended under special circumstances.

The National People's Congress holds one session each year. When necessary, the session may be advanced or postponed.

Article 17

The functions and powers of the National People's Congress are: to amend the Constitution, make laws, appoint and remove the Premier of the State Council and the members of the State Council on the proposal of the Central Committee of the Communist Party of China, approve the national economic plan, the state budget and the final state accounts, and exercise such other functions and powers as the National

People's Congress deems necessary.

Article 18

The Standing Committee of the National People's Congress is the permanent organ of the National People's Congress. Its functions and powers are: to convene the sessions of the National People's Congress, interpret laws, enact decrees, dispatch and recall plenipotentiary representatives abroad, receive foreign diplomatic envoys, ratify and denounce treaties concluded with foreign states, and exercise such other functions and powers as are vested in it by the National People's Congress.

The Standing Committee of the National People's Congress is composed of the Chairman, the Vice-Chairmen and other members, all of whom are elected and subject to recall by the National People's Congress.

Section II
The State Council

Article 19

The State Council is the Central People's Government. The State Council is responsible and accountable to the National People's Congress and its Standing Committee.

The State Council is composed of the Premier, the Vice-Premiers, the ministers, and the ministers heading commissions.

Article 20

The functions and powers of the State Council are: to formulate administrative measures and issue decisions and orders in accordance with the Constitution, laws and decrees;

exercise unified leadership over the work of ministries and commissions and local organs of state at various levels throughout the country; draft and implement the national economic plan and the state budget; direct state administrative affairs; and exercise such other functions and powers as are vested in it by the National People's Congress or its Standing Committee.

Section III
The Local People's Congress and the Local Revolutionary Committees at Various Levels

Article 21

The local people's congresses at various levels are the local organs of state power.

The people's congresses of provinces and municipalities directly under the Central Governments are elected for a term of five years. The people's congresses of prefectures, cities and counties are elected for a term of three years. The people's congresses of rural people's communes and towns are elected for a term of two years.

Article 22

The local revolutionary committees at various levels are the permanent organs of the local people's congresses and at the same time the local people's government at various levels.

Local revolutionary committees are composed of a chairman, vice-chairmen and other members, who are elected and subject to recall by the people's congress at the corresponding level. Their election or recall shall be submitted for examination and approval to the organ of state at the next higher level.

Local revolutionary committees are responsible and accountable to the people's congress at the corresponding level and to the organ of state at the next higher level.

Article 23

The local people's congresses at various levels and the local revolutionary committees elected by them ensure the execution of laws and decrees in their respective areas; lead the socialist revolution and socialist construction in their respective areas; examine and approve local economic plans, budgets and final accounts; maintain revolutionary order; and safeguard the rights of citizens.

Section IV
The Organs of Self-Government of National Autonomous Areas

Article 24

The autonomous regions, autonomous prefectures and autonomous counties are all national autonomous areas; their organs of self-government are people's congresses and revolutionary committees.

The organs of self-government of national autonomous areas, apart from exercising the functions and powers of local organs of state as specified in Chapter Two, Section III of the Constitution, may exercise autonomy within the limits of their authority as prescribed by law.

The higher organs of state shall fully safeguard the exercise of autonomy by the organs of self-government of national autonomous areas and actively support the minority nationalities in carrying out the socialist revolution and socialist construction.

Section V
The Judicial Organs and the Procuratorial Organs

Article 25

The Supreme People's Court, local people's courts at various levels and special people's courts exercise judicial authority. The people's courts are responsible and accountable to the people's congresses and their permanent organs at the corresponding levels. The presidents of the people's courts are appointed and subject to removal by the permanent organs of the people's congresses at the corresponding levels.

The functions and powers of procuratorial organs are exercised by the organs of public security at various levels.

The mass line must be applied in procuratorial work and in trying cases. In major counter-revolutionary criminal cases the masses should be mobilized for discussion and criticism.

CHAPTER THREE

THE FUNDAMENTAL RIGHTS AND DUTIES OF CITIZENS

Article 26

The fundamental rights and duties of citizens are to support the leadership of the Communist Party of China, support the socialist system and abide by the Constitution and the laws of the People's Republic of China.

It is the lofty duty of every citizen to defend the motherland and resist aggression. It is the honourable obligation of citizens to perform military service according to law.

Article 27

All citizens who have reached the age of eighteen have the right to vote and stand for election, with the exception of persons deprived of these rights by law.

Citizens have the right to work and the right to education. Working people have the right to rest and the right to material assistance in old age and in case of illness or disability.

Citizens have the right to lodge to organs of state at any level written or oral complaints of transgression of law or neglect of duty on the part of any person working in an organ of state. No one shall attempt to hinder or obstruct the making of such complaints or retaliate.

Women enjoy equal rights with men in all respects.

The state protects marriage, the family, and the mother and child.

The state protects the just rights and interests of overseas Chinese.

Article 28

Citizens enjoy freedom of speech, correspondence, the press, assembly, association, procession, demonstration and the freedom to strike, and enjoy freedom to believe in religion and freedom not to believe in religion and to propagate atheism.

The citizens' freedom of person and their homes shall be inviolable. No citizen may be arrested except by decision of a people's court or with the sanction of a public security organ.

Article 29

The People's Republic of China grants the right of residence to any foreign national persecuted for supporting a just cause, for taking part in revolutionary movements or for engaging in scientific activities.

CHAPTER FOUR

THE NATIONAL FLAG, THE NATIONAL EMBLEM AND THE CAPITAL

Article 30

The national flag has five stars on a field of red.

The national emblem: Tien An Men in the centre, illuminated by five stars and encircled by ears of grain and a cogwheel.

The capital is Peking.

iii) 1978 CONSTITUTION OF THE PEOPLE'S REPUBLIC OF CHINA

CONTENTS

PREAMBLE

Chapter One
GENERAL PRINCIPLES

Chapter Two
THE STRUCTURE OF THE STATE

    Section I.   The National People's Congress
    Section II.   The State Council
    Section III.   The Local People's Congresses and the Local Revolutionary Committees at Various Levels
    Section IV.   The Organs of Self-Government of National Autonomous Areas
    Section V.   The People's Courts and the People's Procuratorates

Chapter Three
THE FUNDAMENTAL RIGHTS AND DUTIES OF CITIZENS

Chapter Four
THE NATIONAL FLAG, THE NATIONAL EMBLEM AND THE CAPITAL

PREAMBLE

After more than a century of heroic struggle the Chinese people, led by the Communist Party of China headed by our great leader and teacher Chairman Mao Zedong, finally overthrew the reactionary rule of imperialism, feudalism and bureaucrat-capitalism by means of people's revolutionary war, winning complete victory in the new-democratic revolution, and in 1949 founded the People's Republic of China.

The founding of the People's Republic of China marked the beginning of the historical period of socialism in our country. Since then, under the leadership of Chairman Mao and the Chinese Communist Party, the people of all our nationalities have carried out Chairman Mao's proletarian revolutionary line in the political, economic, cultural and military fields and in foreign affairs and have won great victories in socialist revolution and socialist construction through repeated struggles against enemies both at home and abroad and through the Great Proletarian Cultural Revolution. The dictatorship of the proletariat in our country has been consolidated and strengthened, and China has become a socialist country with the beginnings of prosperity.

Chairman Mao Zedong was the founder of the People's Republic of China. All our victories in revolution and construction have been won under the guidance of Marxism-Leninism-Mao Zedong Thought. The fundamental guarantee that the people of all our nationalities will struggle in unity and carry the proletarian revolution through to the end is always to hold high and staunchly to defend the great banner of Chairman Mao.

The triumphant conclusion of the first Great Proletarian Cultural Revolution has ushered in a new period of development in China's socialist revolution and socialist construction.

In accordance with the basic line of the Chinese Communist Party for the entire historical period of socialism, the general task for the people of the whole country in this new period is: To persevere in continuing the revolution under the dictatorship of the proletariat, carry forward the three great revolutionary movements of class struggle, the struggle for production and scientific experiment, and make China a great and powerful socialist country with modern agriculture, industry, national defence and science and technology by the end of the century.

We must persevere in the struggle of the proletariat against the bourgeoisie and in the struggle for the socialist road against the capitalist road. We must oppose revisionism and prevent the restoration of capitalism. We must be prepared to deal with subversion and aggression against our country by social-imperialism and imperialism.

We should consolidate and expand the revolutionary united front which is led by the working class and based on the worker-peasant alliance, and which unites the large numbers of intellectuals and other working people, patriotic democratic parties, patriotic personages, our compatriots in Taiwan, Hongkong and Macao, and our countrymen residing abroad. We should enhance the great unity of all the nationalities in our country. We should correctly distinguish and handle the contradictions among the people and those between ourselves and the enemy. We should endeavour to create among the people of the whole country a political situation in which there are both centralism and democracy, both discipline and freedom, both unity of will and personal ease of mind and liveliness, so as to help bring all positive factors into play, overcome all difficulties, better consolidate the proletarian dictatorship and build up our country more rapidly.

Taiwan is China's territory. We are determined to liberate Taiwan and accomplish the great cause of unifying our motherland.

In international affairs, we should establish and develop relations with other countries on the basis of the Five Principles of mutual respect for sovereignty and territorial integrity, mutual non-aggression, non-interference in each other's internal affairs, equality and mutual benefit, and peaceful coexistence. Our country will never seek hegemony, or strive to be a superpower. We should uphold proletarian internationalism. In accordance with the theory of the three worlds, we should strengthen our unity with the proletariat and the oppressed people and nations throughout the world, the socialist countries, and the third world countries, and we should unite with all countries subjected to aggression, subversion, interference, control and bullying by the social-imperialist and imperialist superpowers to form the broadest possible international united front against the hegemonism of the superpowers and against a new world war, and strive for the progress and emancipation of humanity.

CHAPTER ONE

GENERAL PRINCIPLES

Article 1

The People's Republic of China is a socialist state of the dictatorship of the proletariat led by the working class and based on the alliance of workers and peasants.

Article 2

The Communist Party of China is the core of leadership of the whole Chinese people. The working class exercises leadership over the state through its vanguard, the Communist Party of China.

The guiding ideology of the People's Republic of China is Marxism-Leninism-Mao Zedong Thought.

Article 3

All power in the People's Republic of China belongs to the people. The organs through which the people exercise state power are the National People's Congress and the local people's congresses at various levels.

The National People's Congress, the local people's congresses at various levels and all other organs of state practise democratic centralism.

Article 4

The People's Republic of China is a unitary multi-national state.

All the nationalities are equal. There should be unity and fraternal love among the nationalities and they should help and learn from each other. Discrimination against, or oppression of, any nationality, and acts which undermine the unity of the nationalities are prohibited. Big-nationality chauvinism and local-nationality chauvinism must be opposed.

All the nationalities have the freedom to use and develop their own spoken and written languages, and to preserve or reform their own customs and ways.

Regional autonomy applies in an area where a minority nationality lives in a compact community. All the national autonomous areas are inalienable parts of the People's Republic of China.

Article 5

There are mainly two kinds of ownership of the means of production in the People's Republic of China at the present stage: socialist ownership by the whole people and socialist collective ownership by the working people.

The state allows non-agricultural individual labourers to engage in individual labour involving no exploitation of others, within the limits permitted by law and under unified arrangement and management by organizations at the basic level in cities and towns or rural areas. At the same time, it guides these individual labourers step by step onto the road of socialist collectivization.

Article 6

The state sector of the economy, that is, the socialist sector owned by the whole people, is the leading force in the national economy.

Mineral resources, waters and those forests, undeveloped lands and other marine and land resources owned by the state are the property of the whole people.

The state may requisition by purchase, take over for use, or nationalize land under conditions prescribed by law.

Article 7

The rural people's commune sector of the economy is a socialist sector collectively owned by the masses of working people. At present, it generally takes the form of three-level ownership, that is, ownership by the commune, the production brigade and the production team, with the production team as the basic accounting unit. A production brigade may become the basic accounting unit when its conditions are ripe.

Provided that the absolute predominance of the collective economy of the people's commune is ensured, commune members may farm small plots of land for personal needs, engage in limited household side-line production, and in pastoral areas they may also keep a limited number of livestock for personal needs.

Article 8

Socialist public property shall be inviolable. The state ensures the consolidation and development of the socialist sector of the economy owned by the whole people and of the socialist sector collectively owned by the masses of working people.

The state prohibits any person from using any means whatsoever to disrupt the economic order of the society, undermine the economic plans of the state, encroach upon or squander state and collective property, or injure the public interest.

Article 9

The state protects the right of citizens to own lawfully earned income, savings, houses and other means of livelihood.

Article 10

The state applies the socialist principles: "He who

does not work, neither shall he eat" and "from each according to his ability, to each according to his work."

Work is an honourable duty for every citizen able to work. The state promotes socialist labour emulation, and, putting proletarian politics in command, it applies the policy of combining moral encouragement with material reward, with the stress on the former, in order to heighten the citizens' socialist enthusiasm and creativeness in work.

Article 11

The state adheres to the general line of going all out, aiming high and achieving greater, faster, better and more economical results in building socialism; it undertakes the planned, proportionate and high-speed development of the national economy, and it continuously develops the productive forces, so as to consolidate the country's independence and security and improve the people's material and cultural life step by step.

In developing the national economy, the state adheres to the principle of building our country independently, with the initiative in our own hands and through self-reliance, hard struggle, diligence and thrift, it adheres to the principle of taking agriculture as the foundation and industry as the leading factor, and it adheres to the principle of bringing the initiative of both the central and local authorities into full play under the unified leadership of the central authorities.

The state protects the environment and natural resources and prevents and eliminates pollution and other hazards to the public.

Article 12

The state devotes major efforts to developing science, expands scientific research, promotes technical innovation and technical revolution and adopts advanced techniques wherever possible in all departments of the national economy.

In scientific and technological work we must follow the practice of combining professional contingents with the masses, and combining learning from others with our own creative efforts.

Article 13

The state devotes major efforts to developing education in order to raise the cultural and scientific level of the whole nation. Education must serve proletarian politics and be combined with productive labour and must enable everyone who receives an education to develop morally, intellectually and physically and become a worker with both socialist consciousness and culture.

Article 14

The state upholds the leading position of Marxism-Leninism-Mao Tsetung Thought in all spheres of ideology and culture. All cultural undertakings must serve the workers, peasants and soldiers and serve socialism.

The state applies the policy of "letting a hundred flowers blossom and a hundred schools of thought contend" so as to promote the development of the arts and sciences and bring about a flourishing socialist culture.

Article 15

All organs of state must constantly maintain close contact with the masses of the people, rely on them, heed their opinions, be concerned for their weal and woe, streamline administration, practise economy, raise efficiency and combat bureaucracy.

The leading personnel of state organs at all levels must conform to the requirements for successors in the proletarian revolutionary cause and their composition must conform to the principle of the three-in-one combination of the old, the middle-aged and the young.

Article 16

The personnel of organs of state must earnestly study Marxism-Leninism-Mao Zedong Thought, wholeheartedly serve the people, endeavour to perfect their professional competence, take an active part in collective productive labour, accept supervision by the masses, be models in observing the Constitution and the law, correctly implement the policies of the state, seek the truth from facts, and must not have recourse to deception or exploit their position and power to seek personal gain.

Article 17

The state adheres to the principle of socialist democracy, and ensures to the people the right to participate in the management of state affairs and of all economic and cultural undertakings, and the right to supervise the organs of state and their personnel.

Article 18

The state safeguards the socialist system, suppresses all treasonable and counter-revolutionary activities, punishes all traitors and counter-revolutionaries, and punishes newborn bourgeois elements and other bad elements.

The state deprives of political rights, as prescribed by law, those landlords, rich peasants amd reactionary capitalists who have not yet been reformed, and at the same time it provides them with the opportunity to earn a living so that they may be reformed through labour and become law-abiding citizens supporting themselves by their own labour.

Article 19

The Chairman of the Central Committee of the Communist Party of China commands the armed forces of the People's Republic of China.

The Chinese People's Liberation Army is the workers' and peasants' own armed force led by the Communist Party of China; it is the pillar of the dictatorship of the proletariat. The state devotes major efforts to the revolutionization and modernization of the Chinese People's Liberation Army, strengthens the building of the militia and adopts a system under which our armed forces are a combination of the field armies, the regional forces and the militia.

The fundamental task of the armed forces of the People's Republic of China is: To safeguard the socialist revolution and socialist construction, to defend the sovereignty, territorial integrity and security of the state, and to guard against subversion and aggression by social-imperialism, imperialism and their lackeys.

CHAPTER TWO

THE STRUCTURE OF THE STATE

Section I

The National People's Congress

Article 20

The National People's Congress is the highest organ of state power.

Article 21

The National People's Congress is composed of deputies elected by the people's congresses of the provinces, autonomous regions, and municipalities directly under the Central Government, and by the People's Liberation Army. The deputies should be elected by secret ballot after democratic consultation.

The National People's Congress is elected for a term of five years. Under special circumstances, its term of office may be extended or succeeding National People's Congress may be convened before its due date.

The National People's Congress holds one session each year. When necessary, the session may be advanced or postponed.

Article 22

The National People's Congress exercises the following functions and powers:
(1) to amend the Constitution;
(2) to make laws;

The 1978 Constitution 213

(3) to supervise the enforcement of the Constitution and the law;

(4) to decide on the choice of the Premier of the State Council upon the recommendation of the Central Committee of the Communist Party of China;

(5) to decide on the choice of other members of the State Council upon the recommendation of the Premier of the State Council;

(6) to elect the President of the Supreme People's Court and the Chief Procurator of the Supreme People's Procurator;

(7) to examine and approve the national economic plan, the state budget and the final state accounts;

(8) to confirm the following administrative divisions: provinces, autonomous regions, and municipalities directly under the Central Government;

(9) to decide on questions of war and peace; and

(10) to exercise such other functions and powers as the National People's Congress deems necessary.

Article 23

The National People's Congress has the power to remove from office the members of the State Council, the President of the Supreme People's Court and the Chief Procurator of the Supreme People's Procuratorate.

Article 24

The Standing Committee of the National People's Congress is the permanent organ of the National People's Congress. It is responsible and accountable to the National People's Congress.

The Standing Committee of the National People's Congress is composed of the following members:
the Chairman;
the Vice-Chairmen;
the Secretary-General; and

other members.

The National People's Congress elects the Standing Committee of the National People's Congress and has the power to recall its members.

Article 25

The Standing Committee of the National People's Congress exercises the following functions and powers:

(1) to conduct the election of deputies to the National People's Congress;

(2) to convene the sessions of the National People's Congress;

(3) to interpret the Constitution and laws and to enact decrees;

(4) to supervise the work of the State Council, the Supreme People's Court and the Supreme People's Procuratorate;

(5) to change and annul inappropriate decisions adopted by the organs of state power of provinces, autonomous regions, and municipalities directly under the Central Government;

(6) to decide on the appointment and removal of individual members of the State Council upon recommendation of the Premier of the State Council when the National People's Congress is not in session;

(7) to appoint and remove Vice-Presidents of the Supreme People's Court and Deputy Chief Procurators of the Supreme People's Procuratorate;

(8) to decide on the appointment and removal of plenipotentiary representatives abroad;

(9) to decide on the ratification and abrogation of treaties concluded with foreign states;

(10) to institute state titles of honour and decide on their conferment;

(11) to decide on the granting of pardons;
(12) to decide on the proclamation of a state of war in the event of armed attack on the country when the National People's Congress is not in session; and
(13) to exercise such other functions and powers as are vested in it by the National People's Congress.

Article 26

The Chairman of the Standing Committee of the National People's Congress presides over the work of the Standing Committee; receives foreign diplomatic envoys; and in accordance with the decisions of the National People's Congress or its Standing Committee promulgates laws and decrees, dispatches and recalls plenipotentiary representatives abroad, ratifies treaties concluded with foreign states and confers state titles of honour.

The Vice-Chairmen of the Standing Committee of the National People's Congress assist the Chairman in his work and may exercise part of the Chairman's functions and powers on his behalf.

Article 27

The National People's Congress and its Standing Committee may establish special committees as deemed necessary.

Article 28

Deputies to the National People's Congress have the right to address inquiries to the State Council, the Supreme People's Court, the Supreme People's Procuratorate, and the ministries and commissions of the State Council, which are all under obligation to answer.

Article 29

Deputies to the National People's Congress are subject to supervision by the units which elect them. These electoral units have the power to replace at any time the deputies they elect, as prescribed by law.

Section II

The State Council

Article 30

The State Council is the Central People's Government and the executive organ of the highest organ of state power; it is the highest organ of state administration.

The State Council is responsible and accountable to the National People's Congress, or, when the National People's Congress is not in session, to its Standing Committee.

Article 31

The State Council is composed of the following members:
 the Premier;
 the Vice-Premiers;
 the ministers; and
 the ministers heading the commissions.

The Premier presides over the work of the State Council and the Vice-Premiers assist the Premier in his work.

Article 32

The State Council exercises the following functions and powers:
(1) to formulate administrative measures, issue deci-

sions and orders and verify their execution, in accordance with the Constitution, laws and decrees;

(2) to submit proposals on laws and other matters to the National People's Congress or its Standing Committee;

(3) to exercise unified leadership over the work of the ministries and commissions and other organizations under it;

(4) to exercise unified leadership over the work of local organs of state administration at various levels throughout the country;

(5) to draw up and put into effect the national economic plan and the state budget;

(6) to protect the interests of the state, maintain public order and safeguard the rights of citizens;

(7) to confirm the following administrative divisions: autonomous prefectures, counties, autonomous counties, and cities;

(8) to appoint and remove administrative personnel according to the provisions of the law; and

(9) to exercise such other functions and powers as are vested in it by the National People's Congress or its Standing Committee.

Section III

The Local People's Congresses and the Local Revolutionary Committees at Various Levels

Article 33

The administrative division of the People's Republic of China is as follows:

(1) The country is divided into provinces, autonomous regions, and municipalities directly under the Central Government;

(2) Provinces and autonomous regions are divided into autonomous prefectures, counties, autonomous counties,

and cities; and

(3) Counties and autonomous counties are divided into people's communes and towns.

Municipalities directly under the Central Government and other large cities are divided into districts and counties. Autonomous prefectures are divided into counties, autonomous counties, and cities.

Autonomous regions, autonomous prefectures and autonomous counties are all national autonomous areas.

Article 34

People's congresses and revolutionary committees are established in provinces, municipalities directly under the Central Government, counties, cities, municipal districts, people's communes and towns.

People's congresses and revolutionary committees of the people's commune are organizations of political power at the grass-root level, and are also leading organs of collective economy.

Revolutionary committees at the provincial level may establish administrative offices as their agencies in prefectures.

Organs of self-government are established in autonomous regions, autonomous prefectures and autonomous counties.

Article 35

Local people's congresses at various levels are local organs of state power.

Deputies to the people's congresses of provinces, municipalities directly under the Central Government, counties, and cities divided into districts are elected by people's congresses at the next lower level by secret ballot after democratic consultation; deputies to the people's congresses of cities not divided into districts, and of municipal districts, people's communes and towns are directly elected by the voters by secret ballot after democratic consultation.

The people's congresses of provinces and municipalities directly under the Central Government are elected for a term of five years. The people's congresses of counties, cities and municipal districts are elected for a term of three years. The people's congresses of people's communes and towns are elected for a term of two years.

Local people's congresses at various levels hold at least one session each year, which is to be convened by revolutionary committees at the corresponding levels.

The units and electorates which elect the deputies to the local people's congresses at various levels have the power to supervise, remove and replace their deputies at any time according to the provisions of the law.

Article 36

Local people's congresses at various levels, in their respective administrative areas, ensure the observance and enforcement of the Constitution, laws and decrees; ensure the implementation of the state plan; make plans for local economic and cultural development and for public utilities; examine and approve local economic plans, budgets and final accounts; protect public property; maintain public order; safeguard the rights of citizens and the equal rights of minority nationalities; and promote the development of socialist revolution and socialist construction.

Local people's congresses may adopt and issue decisions within the limits of their authority as prescribed by law.

Local people's congresses elect, and have the power to recall, members of revolutionary committees at the corresponding levels. People's congresses at county level and above elect, and have the power to recall, the presidents of the people's courts and the chief procurators of the people's procuratorates at the corresponding levels.

Deputies to local people's congresses at various levels have the right to address inquiries to the revolutionary committees, people's courts, people's procuratorates and organs under the revolutionary committees at the corresponding levels, which are all under obligation to answer.

Article 37

Local revolutionary committees at various levels, that is, local people's governments, are the executive organs of local people's congresses at the corresponding levels and they are also local organs of state administration.

A local revolutionary committee is composed of a chairman, vice-chairmen and other members.

Local revolutionary committees carry out the decisions of people's congresses at the corresponding levels as well as the decisions and orders of the organs of state administration at higher levels, direct the administrative work of their respective areas, and issue decisions and orders within the limits of their authority as prescribed by law. Revolutionary committees at county level and above appoint or remove the personnel of organs of state according to the provisions of the law.

Local revolutionary committees are responsible and accountable to people's congresses at the corresponding levels and to the organs of state administration at the next higher level, and work under the unified leadership of the State Council.

Section IV

The Organs of Self-Government of National Autonomous Areas

Article 38

The organs of self-government of autonomous regions, autonomous prefectures and autonomous counties are people's congresses and revolutionary committees.

The election of the people's congresses and revolutionary committees of national autonomous areas, their terms of office, their functions and powers and also the establishment of their agencies should conform to the basic principles governing the organization of local organs of state as specified in Section III, Chapter Two, of the Constitution.

In autonomous areas where a number of nationalities live together, each nationality is entitled to appropriate representation in the organs of self-government.

Article 39

The organs of self-government of national autonomous areas exercise autonomy within the limits of their authority as prescribed by law, in addition to exercising the functions and powers of local organs of state as specified by the Constitution.

The organs of self-government of national autonomous areas may, in the light of the political, economic and cultural characteristics of the nationality or nationalities in a given area, make regulations on the exercise of autonomy and also specific regulations and submit them to the Standing Committee of the National People's Congress for approval.

In performing their functions, the organs of self-government of national autonomous areas employ the spoken and written language or languages commonly used by the nationality or nationalities in the locality.

Article 40

The higher organs of state shall fully safeguard the exercise of autonomy by the organs of self-government of national autonomous areas, take into full consideration the characteristics and needs of the various minority nationalities, make a major effort to train cadres of the minority nationalities, and actively support and assist all the minority nationalities in their socialist revolution and construction and thus advance their socialist economic and cultural development.

Section V

The People's Courts and the People's Procuratorates

Article 41

The Supreme People's Court, local people's courts at various levels and special people's courts exercise judicial authority. The people's courts are formed as prescribed by law.

In accordance with law, the people's courts apply the system whereby representatives of the masses participate as assessors in administering justice. With regard to major counter-revolutionary or criminal cases, the masses should be drawn in for discussion and suggestions.

All cases in the people's courts are heard in public except those involving special circumstances as prescribed by law. The accused has the right to defence.

Article 42

The Supreme People's Court is the highest judicial organ.

The Supreme People's Court supervises the administration of justice by local people's courts at various levels and by special people's courts; people's courts at the higher levels supervise the administration of justice by people's courts at the lower levels.

The Supreme People's Court is responsible and accountable to the National People's Congress and its Standing Committee. Local people's courts at various levels are responsible and accountable to local people's congresses at the corresponding levels.

Article 43

The Supreme People's Procuratorate exercises procuratorial authority to ensure observance of the Constitution and the law by all the departments under the State Council, the local organs of state at various levels, the personnel of organs of state and the citizens. Local people's procuratorates and special people's procuratorates exercise procuratorial authority within the limits prescribed by law. The people's procuratorates are formed as prescribed by law.

The Supreme People's procuratorate supervises the work of local people's procuratorates at various levels and of special people's procuratorates; people's procuratorates at the higher levels supervise the work of those at the lower levels.

The Supreme People's Procuratorate is responsible and accountable to the National People's Congress and its Standing Committee. Local people's procuratorates at various levels are responsible and accountable to people's congresses at the corresponding levels.

CHAPTER THREE

THE FUNDAMENTAL RIGHTS AND DUTIES OF CITIZENS

Article 44

All citizens who have reached the age of eighteen have the right to vote and to stand for election, with the exception of persons deprived of these rights by law.

Article 45

Citizens enjoy freedom of speech, correspondence, the press, assembly, association, procession, demonstration and the freedom to strike, and have the right to "speak out freely, air their views fully, hold great debates and write big-character posters."

Article 46

Citizens enjoy freedom to believe in religion and freedom not to believe in religion and to propagate atheism.

Article 47

The citizens' freedom of person and their homes are inviolable.

No citizen may be arrested except by decision of a people's court or with the sanction of a people's procuratorate, and the arrest must be made by a public security organ.

The 1978 Constitution 225

Article 48

Citizens have the right to work. To ensure that citizens enjoy this right, the state provides employment in accordance with the principle of overall consideration, and, on the basis of increased production, the state gradually increases payment for labour, improves working conditions, strengthens labour protection and expands collective welfare.

Article 49

Working people have the right to rest. To ensure that working people enjoy this right, the state prescribes working hours and systems of vacations and gradually expands material facilities for the working people to rest and recuperate.

Article 50

Working people have the right to material assistance in old age, and in case of illness or disability. To ensure that working people enjoy this right, the state gradually expands social insurance, social assistance, public health services, co-operative medical services, and other services.

The state cares for and ensures the livelihood of disabled revolutionary armymen and the families or revolutionary martyrs.

Article 51

Citizens have the right to education. To ensure that citizen enjoy this right, the state gradually increases the number of schools of various types and of other cultural and educational institutions and popularizes education.

The state pays special attention to the healthy development of young people and children.

Article 52

Citizens have the freedom to engage in scientific research, literary and artistic creation and other cultural activities. The state encourages and assists the creative endeavours of citizens engaged in science, education, literature, art, journalism, publishing, public health, sports and other cultural work.

Article 53

Women enjoy equal rights with men in all spheres of political, economic, cultural, social and family life. Men and women enjoy equal pay for equal work.

Men and women shall marry of their own free will. The state protects marriage, the family, and the mother and child.

The state advocates and encourages family planning.

Article 54

The state protects the just rights and interests of overseas Chinese and their relatives.

Article 55

Citizens have the right to lodge complaints with organs of state at any level against any person working in an organ of state, enterprise or institution for transgression of law or neglect of duty. Citizens have the right to appeal to organs of state at any level against any infringement of their rights. No one shall suppress such complaints and appeals or retaliate against persons making them.

Article 56

Citizens must support the leadership of the Communist Party of China, support the socialist system, safeguard the unification of the motherland and the unity of all nationalities in our country and abide by the Constitution and the law.

Article 57

Citizens must take care of and protect public property, observe labour discipline, observe public order, respect social ethics and safeguard state secrets.

Article 58

It is the lofty duty of every citizen to defend the motherland and resist aggression.

It is the honourable obligation of citizens to perform military service and join the militia according to the law.

Article 59

The People's Republic of China grants the right of residence to any foreign national persecuted for supporting a just cause, for taking part in revolutionary movements or for engaging in scientific work.

CHAPTER FOUR

THE NATIONAL FLAG, THE NATIONAL EMBLEM AND THE CAPITAL

Article 60

The national flag of the People's Republic of China has five stars on a field of red.

The national emblem of the People's Republic of China is: Tien An Men in the centre, illuminated by five stars and encircled by ears of grain and a cogwheel.

The capital of the People's Republic of China is Peking.

iv) 1977 CONSTITUTION OF

THE COMMUNIST PARTY

OF CHINA

1977 CONSTITUTION OF THE COMMUNIST PARTY OF CHINA

GENERAL PROGRAMME

The Communist Party of China is the political party of the proletariat, the highest form of its class organization. It is a vigorous vanguard organization composed of the advanced elements of the proletariat, which leads the proletariat and the revolutionary masses in their fight against the class enemy.

The basic programme of the Communist Party of China for the entire historical period of socialism is to persist in continuing the revolution under the dictatorship of the proletariat, eliminate the bourgeoisie and all other exploiting classes step by step and bring about the triumph of socialism over capitalism. The ultimate aim of the Party is the realization of communism,

Marxism-Leninism-Mao Zedong Thought is the guiding ideology and theoretical basis of the Communist Party of China. The Party persists in combating revisionism, and dogmatism and empiricism. The Party upholds dialectical materialism and historical materialism as its world outlook and opposes the idealist and metaphysical world outlook.

Our great leader and teacher Chairman Mao Zedong was the founder of the Communist Party of China and the greatest Marxist-Leninist of our time. Integrating the universal truth of Marxism-Leninism with the concrete practice of the revolution, Chairman Mao inherited, defended and developed Marxism-Leninism in the struggles against imperialism and the domestic reactionary classes, against Right and "Left" opportunist lines in the Party and against international modern revisionism. He led our Party, our army and our people in winning complete victory in the new-democratic revolution and in founding the People's Republic of China, a state of the dictatorship of the proletariat, through protracted revolutionary struggles and revolutionary wars, and then in achieving tremendous victories in the socialist revolution and socialist construction through fierce and complex struggles between the proletariat and the bourgeoisie, and through the unparalleled Great Proletarian Cultural Revolution. The banner of Chairman Mao is the great banner guiding our Party to victory through united struggle.

Socialist society covers a historical period of considerable length. In this period classes, class contradictions and class struggle, the struggle between the socialist road and the capitalist road and the danger of capitalist restoration invariably continue to exist, and there is the threat of subversion and aggression by imperialism and social-imperialism. The resolution of these contradictions depends solely on the theory and practice of continued revolution under the dictatorship of the proletariat.

China's Great Cultural Revolution was a political revolution carried out under socialism by the proletariat against the bourgeoisie and all other exploiting classes to consolidate the dictatorship of the proletariat and prevent the restoration of capitalism. Political revolutions of this nature will be carried out many times in the future.

The Communist Party of China adheres to its basic line for the entire historical period of socialism. It must correctly distinguish and handle the contradictions among the people and those between ourselves and the enemy, and consolidate and strengthen the dictatorship of the proletariat. The Party must rely on the working class wholeheartedly and rely on the poor and lower-middle peasants, unite with the vast numbers of intellectuals and other working people, mobilize all positive factors and expand the revolutionary united front led by the working class. It must uphold the proletarian nationality policy and strengthen the great unity of the people of all nationalities in China. It must carry on the three great revolutionary movements of class struggle, the struggle for production and scientific experiment, it must adhere to the principle of building our country independently, with the initiative in our own hands, and through self-reliance, diligence and thrift, and to the principle of being prepared against war and natural disasters and doing everything for the people, so as to build socialism by going all out, aiming high and achieving greater, faster, better and more economical results. The Party must lead the people of all nationalities in making China a powerful socialist country with a modern agriculture, industry, national defence and science and technology by the end of the century.

The Communist Party of China upholds proletarian internationalism and opposes great-nation chauvinism; it unites firmly with the genuine Marxist-Leninist Parties and organizations the world over, unites with the proletariat, the oppressed people and nations of the whole world and fights shoulder to shoulder with them to oppose the hegemonism of the two superpowers, the Soviet Union and the United States, to overthrow imperialism, modern revisionism and all reaction, and to wipe the system of exploitation of man by man off the face of the earth, so that all mankind will be emancipated.

The correctness or incorrectness of the ideological and political line decides everything. All Party comrades must implement Chairman Mao's proletarian revolutionary line comprehensively and correctly and adhere to the three basic principles: Practise Marxism, and not revisionism; unite, and don't split; be open and aboveboard, and don't intrigue and conspire. They must have the revolutionary boldness in daring to go against any tide that runs counter to these three basic principles.

The whole Party must adhere to the organizational principle of democratic centralism and practise centralism on the basis of democracy and democracy under centralized guidance. It must give full scope to inner-Party democracy and encourage the initiative and creativeness of all Party members and Party organizations at all levels, and combat bureaucracy, commandism and warlordism. The whole Party must strictly observe Party discipline, safeguard the Party's centralization, strengthen its unity, oppose all splittist and factional activities, oppose the assertion of independence from the Party and oppose anarchism. In relations among comrades in the Party, all members should apply the principle of "Say all you know and say it without reserve" and "Blame not the speaker but be warned by his words," adopt the dialectical method, start from the desire for unity, distinguish between right and wrong through criticism or struggle and arrive at a new unity. The Party must strive to create a political situation in which there are both centralism and democracy, both discipline and freedom, both unity of will and personal ease of mind and liveliness.

The Party must conscientiously follow the proletarian line on cadres, the line of "appointing people on their merit," and oppose the bourgeois line on cadres, the line of "appointing people by favouritism." It must train and bring up in mass struggles millions of successors in the revolutionary cause of the proletariat in accordance with the five requirements put forward by Chairman Mao. Special vigilance must be exercised against careerists, conspirators and double-dealers so as to prevent such bad types from usurping the leadership of the Party and the state at any level and ensure purity of the leadership at all levels.

The whole Party must keep to and carry forward its fine tradition of following the mass line and seeking truth from facts, keep to and carry forward the style of work characterized by integration of theory with practice, close ties with the masses and criticism and self-criticism, the style of modesty, prudence and freedom from arrogance and impetuosity, and the style of plain living and hard struggle; and the whole Party must prevent Party members, especially leading Party cadres, from exploiting their position to seek privileges, and wage a resolute struggle against bourgeois ideology and the bourgeois style of work.

A member of the Communist Party of China should at all times and in all circumstances subordinate his personal interests to the interests of the Party and the people; he should fear no difficulties and sacrifices, work actively for the fulfilment of the programme of the Party and devote his whole life to the struggle for communism.

The Communist Party of China is a great, glorious and correct Party, and it is the core of leadership of the whole Chinese people. The whole Party must always hold high and resolutely defend the great banner of Marxism-Leninism-Mao Zedong Thought and ensure that our Party's cause will continue to advance triumphantly along the Marxist line.

CHAPTER I

MEMBERSHIP

Article 1

Any Chinese worker, poor peasant, lower-middle peasant, revolutionary soldier or any other revolutionary who has reached the age of eighteen and who accepts the Constitution of the Party and is willing to join a Party organization and work actively in it, carry out the Party's decisions, observe Party discipline and pay membership dues may become a member of the Communist Party of China.

Article 2

The Communist Party of China demands that its members should:

(1) Conscientiously study Marxism-Leninism-Mao Zedong Thought, criticized capitalism and revisionism and strive to remould their world outlook;

(2) Serve the people whole-heartedly and pursue no private interests either for themselves or for a small number of people;

(3) Unite with all the people who can be united inside and outside the Party, including those who have wrongly opposed them;

(4) Maintain close ties with the masses and consult with them when matters arise;

(5) Earnestly practise criticism and self-criticism, be bold in correcting their shortcomings and mistakes and dare to struggle against words and deeds that run counter to Party principles;

(6) Uphold the Party's unity, refuse to take part in and moreover oppose any factional organization or activity which splits the Party;

(7) Be truthful and honest to the Party, observe Party

discipline and the laws of the state and strictly guard Party and state secrets; and

(8) Actively fulfil the tasks assigned them by the Party and play an exemplary vanguard role in the three great revolutionary movements of class struggle, the struggle for production and scientific experiment.

Article 3

Applicants for Party membership must go through the procedure for admission individually. An applicant must be recommended by two full Party members, fill in an application form for Party membership and be examined by a Party branch, which must seek opinions extensively inside and outside the Party; he or she may become a probationary member after being accepted by the general membership meeting of the Party branch and being approved by the next higher Party committee.

Before approving the admission of an applicant for Party membership, the higher Party committee must appoint someone specially to talk with the applicant and carefully examine his or her case.

Article 4

The probationary period of a probationary member is one year. The Party organization concerned should make further efforts to educate and observe him or her.

When the probationary period has expired, the Party branch to which the probationary member belongs must promptly discuss whether he or she is qualified for full membership. If qualified, he or she should be given full membership as scheduled; if it is necessary to continue to observe him or her, the probationary period may be extended but no more than one year; if he or she is found to be really unfit for Party membership, his or her status as a probationary member should be annulled. Any decision either to transfer a probationary member to full membership, to prolong the probationary period, or to annul his or her status as a probationary member must be adopted by the general membership meeting of the Party branch and approved by the next higher Party committee.

The probationary period of a probationary member begins from the day when the higher Party committee approves the applicant's admission. The Party standing of a Party member begins from the day when he or she is transferred to full membership.

A probationary member does not have the right to vote and to elect or to be elected enjoyed by a full member.

Article 5

When a Party member violates Party discipline, the Party organization concerned should give the member education and, on the merits of the case, may take any of the following disciplinary measures — a warning, a serious warning, removal from his or her post in the Party, being placed on probation within the Party, and expulsion from the Party.

The period for which the Party member concerned is placed on probation should not exceed two years. During this period, he or she does not have the right to vote and to elect or to be elected. If the Party member concerned has been through the period of probation and has corrected his or her mistake, these rights should be restored; if the member clings to the mistake instead of correcting it, he or she should be expelled from the Party.

Proven renegades, enemy agents, absolutely unrepentant persons in power taking the capitalist road, alien class elements, degenerates and new bourgeois elements must be expelled from the Party and not be re-admitted.

Article 6

Any disciplinary measure taken against a Party member must be decided on by a general meeting of the Party branch to which the member belongs and should be submitted to the next higher Party committee for approval. Under special circumstances, a primary Party committee or a higher Party committee has the power to take disciplinary action against a Party member.

Any decision to remove a member from a local Party committee at any level, to place on probation or to expel the member from the Party must be made by the said Party committee and be submitted to the next higher Party committee for approval.

Corresponding provisions on disciplinary measures against members of the Party committees at all levels in the army units should be laid down by the Military Commission of the Central Committee in accordance with the Party Constitution.

Any decision to take a disciplinary measure against a Member or Alternate Member of the Central Committee must be made by the Central Committee or its Political Bureau.

When a Party organization takes a decision on a disciplinary measure against a member, it must, barring special circumstances, notify the member that he or she should attend the meeting. If the member disagrees with the decision, he or she may ask for a review of the case and has the right to appeal to higher Party committees, up to and including the Central Committee.

Article 7

A Party member whose revolutionary will has degenerated, who fails to function as a Communist and remains unchanged despite repeated education may be persuaded to withdraw from the Party. The case must be decided by the general membership meeting of the Party branch concerned and submitted to the next higher Party committee for approval.

A Party member who fails to take part in Party life, to do the work assigned by the Party and to pay membership dues over six months and without proper reason is regarded as having given up membership.

When a Party member asks to withdraw from the Party or has given up membership, the Party branch concerned should, with the approval of its general membership meeting,

1977 Constitution of the CPC

remove his or her name from the Party rolls and report the case to the next higher Party committee for the record.

CHAPTER II

ORGANIZATIONAL SYSTEM OF

THE PARTY

Article 8

The Party is organized on the principle of democratic centralism.

The whole Party must observe democratic centralist discipline: The individual is subordinate to the organization, the minority is subordinate to the majority, the lower level is subordinate to the higher level, and the entire Party is subordinate to the Central Committee.

Article 9

Delegates to Party congresses and members of Party committees at all levels should be elected by secret ballot after democratic consultation and in accordance with the five requirements for successors in the revolutionary cause of the proletariat and with the principle of combining the old, the middle-aged and the young.

Article 10

The highest leading body of the Party is the National Congress and, when it is not in session, the Central Committee elected by it. The leading bodies of Party organizations at all levels in the localities and in the army units are the Party congresses or general membership meetings at their respective levels and the Party committees elected by them. Party congresses at all levels are convened by Party committees at their respective levels. The convocation of Party congresses at all levels in the localities and in the army units and the composition of the Party committees they elect are subject to approval by the next higher Party committee.

Article 11

Party committees at all levels operate on the principle of combining collective leadership with individual responsibility under a division of labour. They should rely on the political experience and wisdom of the collective; all important issues are to be decided collectively, and at the same time each individual is to be enabled to play his or her due part.

Party committees at all levels should set up their working bodies in accordance with the principles of close ties with the masses and of structural simplicity and efficiency. Party committees at the county level and upwards may send out their representative organs when necessary.

Article 12

Party committees at all levels should report regularly on their work to Party congresses or general membership meetings, constantly listen to the opinions of the masses both inside and outside the Party and put themselves under their supervision.

Party members have the right to criticize Party organizations and working personnel in leading posts at all levels and making proposals to them and also the right to bypass the immediate leadership and present their appeals and complaints to higher levels, up to and including the Central Committee and the Chairman of the Central Committee. It is absolutely impermissible for anyone to suppress criticism or to retaliate. Those guilty of doing so should be investigated and punished.

If a Party member holds different views with regard to the decisions or directives of the Party organizations, he or she is allowed to reserve these views and has the right to bring up the matter for discussion at Party meetings and the right to bypass the immediate leadership and report to higher levels, up to and including the Central Committee and the Chairman of the Central Committee, but the member must resolutely carry out these decisions and directives.

Article 13

The Central Committee of the Party, local Party committees at the county level and upwards and Party committees in the army units at the regimental level and upwards should set up commissions for inspecting discipline.

The commissions for inspecting discipline at all levels are to be elected by the Party committees at the respective levels and, under their leadership, should strengthen Party members' education on discipline, be responsible for checking on the observance of discipline by Party members and Party cadres and struggle against all breaches of Party discipline.

Article 14

State organs, the People's Liberation Army and the militia and revolutionary mass organizations, such as trade unions, the Communist Youth League, poor and lower-middle peasant associations and women's federations, must all accept the absolute leadership of the Party.

Leading Party groups should be set up in state organs and people's organizations. Members of leading Party groups in state organs and people's organizations at the national level are to be appointed by the Central Committee of the Party. Members of leading Party groups in state organs and people's organizations at all levels in the localities are to be appointed by the corresponding Party committees.

CHAPTER III

CENTRAL ORGANIZATIONS OF

THE PARTY

Article 15

The National Congress of the Party should be convened every five years. Under special circumstances, it may be convened before its due date or postponed.

Article 16

The plenary session of the Central Committee of the Party elects the Political Bureau of the Central Committee, the Standing Committee of the Political Bureau of the Central Committee and the Chairman and Vice-Chairmen of the Central Committee.

The plenary session of the Central Committee of the Party is convened by the Political Bureau of the Central Committee.

When the Central Committee is not in plenary session, the Political Bureau of the Central Committee and its Standing Committee exercise the functions and powers of the Central Committee.

CHAPTER IV

PARTY ORGANIZATIONS IN THE LOCALITIES AND THE ARMY UNITS

Article 17

Local Party congresses at the county level and upwards and Party congresses in the army units at the regimental level and upwards should be convened every three years. Under special circumstances, they may be convened before their due date or postponed, subject to approval by the next higher Party committees.

Local Party committees at the county level and upwards and Party committees in the army units at the regimental level and upwards elect their standing committees, secretaries and deputy secretaries.

CHAPTER V

PRIMARY ORGANIZATIONS OF THE PARTY

Article 18

Party branches, general Party branches or primary Party committees should be set up in factories, mines and other enterprises, people's communes, offices, schools, shops, neighbourhoods, companies of the People's Liberation Army and other primary units in accordance with the need of the revolutionary struggle and the size of their Party membership, subject to approval by the next higher Party committees.

Committees of Party branches should be elected annually, committees of general Party branches and primary Party committees should be elected every two years. Under special circumstances, the election may take place before its due date or be postponed, subject to approval by the next higher Party committees.

Article 19

The primary organizations of the Party should play the role of a fighting bastion. Their main tasks are:

(1) To lead Party members and people outside the Party in studying Marxism-Leninism-Mao Zedong Thought conscientiously, educate them in the ideological and political line and in the Party's fine tradition and give them basic knowledge about the Party;

(2) To lead and unite the broad masses of the people in adhering to the socialist road, in criticizing capitalism and revisionism, in correctly distinguishing and handling the contradictions among the people and those between ourselves

and the enemy and in waging a resolute struggle against the class enemy;

(3) To propagate and carry out the line, policies and decisions of the Party, and fulfil every task assigned by the Party and the state;

(4) To maintain close ties with the masses, constantly listen to their opinions and demands and faithfully report these to higher Party organizations and be concerned about their political, economic and cultural life;

(5) To promote inner-Party democracy, practise criticism and self-criticism, expose and get rid of shortcomings and mistakes in work, and wage struggles against violations of the law and breaches of discipline, against corruption and waste, and against bureaucracy and all other undesirable tendencies; and

(6) To admit new Party members, enforce Party discipline, and consolidate the Party organizations, getting rid of the stale and taking in the fresh, so as to purify the Party's ranks and constantly enhance the Party's fighting power.

TALK AT AN ENLARGED WORKING CONFERENCE CONVENED BY THE CENTRAL COMMITTEE OF THE COMMUNIST PARTY OF CHINA

January 30, 1962

MAO ZEDONG

Comrades! I'm now going to put forward a few ideas. Altogether I'll deal with six points, focusing on the question of democratic centralism while also touching on other questions.

The first point: The way the present conference is being held.

More than 7,000 people have come to this Enlarged Central Working Conference. At the outset, several comrades prepared a draft report. Before the draft could be discussed by the Political Bureau of the Central Committee, I suggested to them that rather than first holding a meeting of the Political Bureau to discuss it, we should immediately issue it to the comrades attending the conference for their comments and opinions. Comrades, there are among you people from various fields and localities — from provincial, prefectural and county Party committees, from the Party committees of various enterprises and from central departments. Most of you are closer to the lower levels and should know the situation and problems better than us comrades on the Standing Committee, the Political Bureau and the Secretariat of the Central Committee. Besides, since you occupy different posts, you can raise questions from different angles. That is why we should ask for your opinions. As expected, after the draft report was issued to you, it brought about lively discussion. While agreeing with the basic policy of the

Central Committee, you also put forward many ideas. Later, a drafting committee of 21 was set up, which included responsible members from regional bureaus of the Central Committee. After eight days of discussion it produced the second draft of the report. It should be said that this second draft is the Central Committee's concentration of a discussion by over 7,000 people. Without your ideas it could not have been written. Both the first and second parts have undergone very substantial revision in the second draft, and for this you should be given the credit. I hear that you have all commented on the second draft quite favourably and consider it to be fairly good. If we hadn't used this method but had run the conference in the usual manner — that is, hearing a report first, then discussing it and approving it with a show of hands — we wouldn't have done as well.

This is a question of how to hold meetings. Distribute the draft, invite comments from those present and make amendments accordingly before giving a report. When making a report, one shouldn't just read it out, but should offer some supplementary ideas and explanations. By following this method we can promote democracy more fully, pool wisdom from all quarters and compare different points of view, and our meetings will become more lively. It has been advisable to use this method for the present conference which is being held to sum up the working experience of 12 years, and particularly that of the past four years, for there are many questions and consequently many opinions. But can all conferences adopt this method? No, not all. To use this method we must have plenty of time. It may sometimes be used at sessions of our people's congress. Comrades from provincial, prefectural and county Party committees, when you call meetings in future, you too can adopt this method if conditions permit. Of course, you are busy and cannot usually spend a lot of time on conferences. But there's no harm in having a try when you find the conditions right.

What sort of method is this? It's the method of democratic centralism, the method of the mass line: first democracy, then centralism; from the masses, to the masses; integration of the leadership with the masses. This is the first point I wanted to discuss.

The second point: The question of democratic centralism.

It seems that some of our comrades still don't understand democratic centralism as described by Marx and Lenin. Some of these comrades are already veteran revolutionaries, of the 1938 mould or some other mould – anyway, they've been members of the Communist Party for several decades and still don't understand this question. They are afraid of the masses, afraid of the masses speaking out, afraid of mass criticism. What possible reason is there for Marxist-Leninists to be afraid of the masses? While they avoid mentioning their own mistakes, these comrades are likewise afraid of having their mistakes mentioned by the masses. The more they're afraid, the more they're going to be haunted by ghosts. In my opinion, one shouldn't be afraid. What is there to be afraid of? Our attitude is, uphold the truth and readily correct mistakes. The question of what is right or wrong, what is correct or incorrect, in our work falls under contradictions among the people. Contradictions among the people can't be resolved by curses or fists, still less by knives or guns. They can be resolved only by discussion and reasoning, criticism and self-criticism. In a word, they can be resolved only by the democratic method, by letting the masses speak out.

There should be full democracy both inside and outside the Party, that is, democratic centralism should be practised in earnest in both spheres. Problems should be brought out into the open frankly and the masses allowed to speak out, speak out even if we are going to be abused. The worst that can come out of this abuse is that we will be toppled and thus be unable to continue in our current jobs – demotion to lower organizations or transfer to other localities. What's so impossible about that? Why should a person go only up and not down? Why should one work only in one place and not be transferred to another? I think that, whether they are justified or not, both demotion and transfer have advantages. They help to temper people's revolutionary will, enable them to investigate and study many new situations, and acquire more useful knowledge. I myself had experience in this respect and benefited a great deal from it. If you don't believe my point, you may give it a try. Sima Qian said: "When King Wen was detained, he produced the *Book of Changes*; when Confucius was in distress, he compiled the *Spring and Autumn Annals*. Qu Yuan was exiled and so composed the *Li Sao*. Zuoqiu Ming lost his sight and the *Guo Yu* followed. Sun Zi was mutilated before he wrote his book on military science. Lu Bu-wei was transferred to the Shu region and so the world inherited his *Lu Lan*. Han Fei was imprisoned in the Kingdom of Chin and he wrote 'Shuo Nan' and 'Gu Fen,' two chapters of his great work. Of the 300 poems in the *Book of Odes* most were written by sages to vent their pent-up indignation." In modern times, people have had doubts about whether in fact King Wen produced the *Book of Changes* or Confucius compiled the *Spring and Autumn Annals*, and we can leave these examples aside and let the specialists solve these problems. But Sima Qian believed these things to be true. And it is a fact that King Wen was detained and that Confucius was in distress. Except for the one about Zuoqiu Ming's going blind, the events related by Sima Qian all refer to the incorrect handling of people by their superiors in ancient times. There were cases where we too handled some cadres incorrectly, and no matter whether their handling was completely incorrect or only partially so, after re-examination they should be rehabilitated according to the merits of each case. But, generally speaking, such incorrect treatment – demotion or transfer – tempers their revolutionary will and enables them to absorb much new knowledge from the masses. Here

The Talk to the 7000   251

I must make it clear that I am not advocating indicrimininate, incorrect treatment of our cadres, our comrades, or anybody else, in the way the ancients detained King Wen, harassed Confucius, exiled Qu Yuan and removed Sun Zi's knee-caps. I am not advocating this way of doing things, I am opposed to it. What I mean is that at every stage of human history there have always been such cases of mishandling. In class societies such cases are numerous. In a socialist society such things cannot be entirely avoided either. They are unavoidable whether in periods of leadership with a correct or with an incorrect line. There is one distinction, however. Under a correct line, as soon as cases which have been mishandled are discovered, after re-examination the people concerned will be rehabilitated and apologies will be made to them, so that they will enjoy ease of mind and lift up their heads again. But under an incorrect line, this becomes impossible, and the mistakes can be corrected at a suitable occasion only by those who represent the correct line through the method of democratic centralism. As for those who have actually made mistakes and who, after criticism by comrades and review at a higher level, have been correctly demoted or transferred, it goes without saying that such demotion or transfer will help them to correct their mistakes and acquire new knowledge.

At present, there are some comrades who are very afraid of the masses initiating discussion and putting forward ideas which differ from those of the leading organs or the leaders. Whenever a problem is being discussed, they suppress the initiative of the masses and don't allow them to speak out. This attitude is abominable. Democratic centralism is written into our Party Constitution and state Constitution, but they don't apply it. Comrades, we are revolutionaries. If we have really made mistakes, mistakes which are harmful to the cause of the Party and the people, we should seek the opinions of the masses and of comrades and criticize ourselves. Such self-criticism should sometimes be repeated several times over. If once is not enough and people are not satisfied, it should be done a second time; if they are still not satisfied, then it should be done a third time; it should go on until nobody has any more criticisms. Some provincial Party committees have done just this. A few provinces have shown some initiative and let people speak out. The early ones started self-criticism in 1959, the late starters began in 1961. Some provinces, such as Honan, Kansu and Chinghai, were forced to carry out self-criticism. Some people say there are other provinces which seem to be starting self-criticism only now. But no matter whether they carry out self-criticism on their own initiative or are forced to do so, no matter whether they do so early or late, provided they look squarely at their mistakes and are willing to admit and correct them and let the masses criticize them — provided they adopt this attitude, we should always welcome it.

Criticism and self-criticism is a method; it is the method of resolving contradictions among the people and indeed the only method. There is no other method. But if we don't have full democracy and don't truly practise democratic centralism, this method of criticism and self-criticism cannot be applied.

Don't we have many difficulties right now? It is impossible to overcome these difficulties unless we rely on the masses and arouse the enthusiasm of the masses and the cadres. But if you don't explain the situation to the masses and the cadres, open your hearts to them and let them voice their opinions, if they are still afraid of you and don't dare speak, it will be impossible to arouse their enthusiasm. I said in 1957 that we should create "a political situation in which we have both centralism and democracy, both discipline and freedom, both unity of will and personal ease of mind and liveliness." We should create such a political situation both inside and outside the Party. Otherwise it will be impossible to arouse the enthusiasm of the masses. We cannot overcome difficulties without democracy. Of course, it's even more impossible to do so without centralism. But if there's no democracy there won't be any centralism.

Without democracy there can't be correct centralism because centralism can't be established when people have divergent views and don't have unity of understanding. What is meant by centralism? First, there must be concentration of correct ideas. Unity of understanding, of policy, plan, command and action is attained on the basis of concentrating correct ideas. This is unity through centralism. But if all those concerned are still not clear about the problems, if their opinions are still unexpressed or their anger is still not vented, how can you achieve this unity through centralism? Without democracy, it is impossible to sum up experience correctly. Without democracy, without ideas coming from the masses, it is impossible to formulate good lines, principles, policies or methods. As far as the formulation of lines, principles, policies and methods is concerned, our leading organs merely play the role of a processing plant. Everyone knows that a factory cannot do any processing without raw material. It cannot produce good finished products unless the raw material is sufficient in quantity and suitable in quality. If there is no democracy, if there is no knowledge of what is going on down below and no clear idea about it, if there is no adequate canvassing of the opinions of all concerned and no communication between higher and lower levels, and if instead issues are decided solely by the leading organs of the higher levels on the strength of one-sided or inaccurate material, then such decisions can hardly avoid being subjective and it will be impossible to achieve unity in understanding and action or achieve true centralism. Isn't the main topic of our present conference opposition to decentralism and the strengthening of centralism and unity? If we fail to promote democracy in full measure, then will this centralism, this unity, be genuine or sham? Will it be real or empty? Will it be correct or incorrect? Of course it will only be sham, empty and incorrect.

Our centralism is centralism built on the foundation of democracy. Proletarian centralism is centralism with a broad democratic base. The Party committees at all levels are the organs which exercise centralized leadership. But leadership by the Party committee means collective leadership, not arbitrary decision by the first secretary alone. Within Party committees, democratic centralism alone should be practised. The relationship between the first secretary and the other secretaries and committee members is one of the minority being subordinate to the majority. Take the Standing Committee or the Political Bureau of the Central Committee by way of example. It often happens that when I say something, regardless of whether it is correct or incorrect, if the others don't agree, I must accede to their opinion because they are the majority. I am told that there are now some provincial, prefectural and county Party committees where all matters are decided by the first secretary alone. This is quite wrong. How can we justify the idea that what one person says goes? I am referring to important matters here, not to the routine work coming after decisions. If a matter is important, it must be discussed collectively, different opinions must be heeded, and the complexities of the situation and the dissenting opinions must be analysed seriously. Thought must be given to the various possibilities and estimates made of the various aspects of a situation, what is good and what bad, what is easy and what difficult, what is possible and what impossible. This should be done as carefully and thoroughly as possible. To act otherwise is just one-man tyranny. Those first secretaries should be called tyrants and not "squad leaders" practising democratic centralism. Once upon a time there was a certain Xiang Yu who was called the tyrant of Western Chu. He hated listening to opinions which differed from his own. One Fan Zeng offered him advice, but Xiang Yu didn't listen to what he had to say. There was another man named Liu Bang, the founder of the Han Dynasty, who was better at accepting ideas different from his own. An intellectual called Li Yiji went to see Liu Bang. When he was first announced, it was as a scholar of the Confucian school. Liu Bang said there was a war on and he couldn't see scholars. Li Yiji flared up and said to the gate-keeper; "You get in there again and say that I'm a drinking man from Gaoyang, not a scholar." The gate-keeper did as he was told. "All right, ask him in." When Li Yiji entered, Liu Bang was washing his feet but he quickly got up to welcome him. Still angry because Liu Bang had refused to see a scholar, Li Yiji gave him a dressing down. He said, "Look here, do you want to conquer the world or don't you? Why do you take an elder so lightly?" Li Yiji was then over 60 and Liu Bang was younger, so Li called himself an "elder." At this, Liu Bang apologized and promptly accepted Li Yiji's plan of seizing the county of Chenliu. This incident can be found in the biographies of Li Yiji and Lu Jia in the *Historical Records*. In the feudal period, Liu Bang was described by historians as a hero "who was generous and open-minded and who readily listened to advice." Liu Bang and Xiang Yu fought for many years. In the end Liu Bang won and Xiang Yu was defeated. This was no accident. Today some of our first secretaries can't even match the feudal Liu Bang but have a bit of Xiang Yu in them. If these comrades don't change, they'll ultimately be overthrown. Isn't there an opera called *The Tyrant Bids His Lady Farewell*? If these comrades remain unchanged, the day will come when they too will be "bidding their ladies farewell." Why do I have to put the matter so strongly? It's because I hope that by speaking a bit sarcastically, I can prick some comrades and get them to give this some hard thought. It will be best if they can't sleep for a night or two. If they can sleep, then I'll be the unhappy one because they still haven't felt any pain.

Some of our comrades can't bear to hear any opinion contrary to their own and can't tolerate any criticism. That is very wrong. During this conference, the group meeting of one province started off in a very lively manner, but as soon as the secretary of the provincial Party committee went to sit in, a hush fell and nobody said a word. Comrade provincial Party secretary, why do you go and sit there? Why don't you stay in your own room and think things over and let the others talk freely? Since such an atmosphere had been brought about and people don't dare speak in your presence, then you should absent yourself. Whoever makes mistakes must criticize himself, and we must let others speak up, let others criticize. On June 12 last year, the last day of the working conference in Peking convened by the Central Committee of the Communist Party of China, I discussed my own shortcomings and mistakes. I asked the comrades to convey what I said to the provinces and localities. I found out later that many localities were not informed. It's as if my mistakes could or should be kept hidden. Comrades, they mustn't be kept hidden! Of all the mistakes made by the Central Committee I am responsible for those directly related to me and I have a share of the responsibility for those not directly related to me, because I am its Chairman. It's not that I want other people to slough off their responsibility — there are some other comrades who also bear responsibility — but I am the person who ought to be primarily responsible. The secretaries of our provincial, prefectural and county Party committees, right down to the secretaries of Party committees of districts, enterprises and communes, being first secretaries, should bear responsibility for shortcomings and mistakes in work. Shirking responsibility, fearing to shoulder it and forbidding people to speak out as if one were a tiger whose backside no one dares touch — ten out of ten who adopt this attitude will fail. People will always speak out sooner or later. You think that people really won't dare to touch the backsides of tigers like you? They bloody well will!

Unless we fully promote people's democracy and inner-Party democracy and unless we fully implement proletarian democracy, it will be impossible for China to have true proletarian centralism. Without a high degree of democracy it is impossible to have a high degree of centralism, and without a high degree of centralism it is impossible to establish a socialist economy. And what will happen to our country if we fail to establish a socialist economy? It will turn into a revisionist state, indeed a bourgeois state, and the dictatorship of the proletariat will turn into a dictatorship of the bourgeoisie, and a reactionary, fascist dictatorship at that. This is a question which very much deserves our vigilance and I hope our comrades will give it a good deal of thought.

Without democratic centralism, the dictatorship of the proletariat cannot be consolidated. To practise democracy among the people and to exercise dictatorship over the enemies of the people — these two aspects are not to be separated. When they are combined, we have proletarian dictatorship, or what may be called people's democratic dictatorship. Our slogan is: "A people's democratic dictatorship led by the proletariat and based on the alliance of the workers and peasants." How does the proletariat exercise leadership? It leads through the Communist Party. The Communist Party is the vanguard of the proletariat. The proletariat unites with all classes and strata who favour, support and participate in socialist revolution and socialist construction, and exercises dictatorship over the reactionary classes or rather their remnants. In our country where the system of exploitation of man by man has already been destroyed and the economic base of the landlord class and the bourgeoisie done away with, the reactionary classes are no longer as formidable as in the past. For example, they are no longer as formidable as in 1949 when the People's Republic was founded, or as in 1957 when the bourgeois Rightists frenziedly attacked us. Therefore, we speak of them as the remnants of the reactionary classes. But in no case should we underestimate these remnants. We must carry on our struggle against them. The reactionary classes which have been overthrown still seek a comeback. And in socialist society new bourgeois elements continue to emerge. Classes and class struggle exist throughout the socialist stage. This struggle is long and complex and at times even very acute. Our instruments of dictatorship must be strengthened, not weakened.

Our public security system is in the hands of comrades who follow the correct line. But it is possible that security departments in one place or another are in the hands of bad people. And there are also a few comrades doing public security work who don't rely on the masses or on the Party. In ferreting out counter-revolutionaries, they don't follow the line of working through the masses under the leadership of the Party committees, but rely solely on secret work, on so-called professional work. Professional work is necessary; investigation and interrogation are absolutely necessary in dealing with counter-revolutionaries. But the most important thing is to follow the mass line under the leadership of the Party committee. It is especially necessary to rely on the masses and the Party in exercising dictatorship over the reactionary classes as a whole. Dictatorship over the reactionary classes does not mean the physical elimination of all reactionary class elements; the aim is to remould them, to remould them by suitable methods, to make them into new men. Without broad democracy for the people, it is impossible for the dictatorship of the proletariat to be consolidated or for political power to be stable. Without democracy, without arousing the masses and without supervision by the masses, it is impossible to exercise effective dictatorship over the reactionaries and bad elements or to remould them effectively; they will continue to make trouble and may stage a comeback. We must be vigilant on this question, and I hope comrades will give it a good deal of thought too.

The third point: Which classes should we unite with and which classes should we repress? This is a question of basic stand.

The working class should unite with the peasantry, the urban petty-bourgeoisie and the patriotic national bourgeoisie, and first and foremost, with the peasantry. Intellectuals such as scientists, engineers and technicians, professors, teachers, writers, artists, actors, medical workers and journalists do not constitute a class; they are attached either to the bourgeoisie or to the proletariat. Are we to unite only with those intellectuals who are revolutionary? No. So long as intellectuals are patriotic, we shall unite with them and help them do their work well. Workers, peasants, urban petty-bourgeois elements, patriotic intellectuals, patriotic capitalists and other patriotic democrats together comprise more than 95 per cent of the population. Under our people's democratic dictatorship, they all belong to the category of the people. And among the people we must practise democracy.

Those whom the people's democratic dictatorship should repress are landlords, rich peasants, counter-revolutionaries, bad elements and anti-Communist Rightists. The counter-revolutionaries, bad elements and anti-Communist Rightists represent the landlord class and the reactionary bourgeoisie. These classes and bad people comprise about 4 or 5 per cent of the population. It is they whom we must compel to undergo remoulding. It is they who are the object of the people's democratic dictatorship.

With whom do we stand? With the masses who comprise over 95 per cent of the population? Or with the landlords, rich peasants, counter-revolutionaries, bad elements and Rightists who comprise 4 or 5 per cent of the population? We must side with the people and never with their enemies. For a Marxist-Leninist this is a question of basic stand.

Just as this holds true within our country, it also holds true internationally. Sooner or later, the people of all countries, the masses comprising more than 90 per cent of the world's population, will want revolution and support Marxism-Leninism. They won't support revisionism; though some people may support it for a while, they will eventually cast it aside. They are bound to awaken gradually, they are bound to oppose imperialism and reaction, and they are bound to oppose revisionism. A true Marxist-Leninist must stand firmly on the side of the masses who comprise over 90 per cent of the world's population.

The fourth point: Understanding the objective world.

Man's understanding of the objective world, his leap from the realm of necessity to the realm of freedom, involves a process. Take, for instance, the question of how to carry out the democratic revolution in China. From its founding in 1921 to its Seventh Congress in 1945, 24 years elapsed before our Party reached complete unity of understanding on this question. During this period we underwent a Party-wide rectification movement which lasted three and a half years, from spring of 1942 to the summer of 1945. It was a thoroughgoing movement and the method of democracy was adopted, that is to say, no matter who had made mistakes, it was all right provided he acknowledged and corrected them. What is more, everybody helped him to acknowledge and correct them. This was called "learning from past mistakes to avoid future ones and curing the sickness to save the patient" or "starting from the desire for unity, distinguishing right from wrong through criticism or struggle, and arriving at a new unity on a new basis." It was at that time that the formula "unity—criticism—unity" came into being. The rectification movement helped the comrades of the whole Party to reach unity of understanding. It was in that period, and especially after the rectification movement, that the problems of how the democratic revolution ought to be conducted and how the general line of the Party and its specific policies ought to be formulated were completely solved.

In the period between the founding of the Party and the War of Resistance Against Japan, we had the Northern Expedition and the ten years of the Agrarian Revolutionary War. We won two victories and met with two defeats. The Northern Expedition was victorious, but in 1927 the revolution suffered a defeat. Spectacular successes were achieved in the Agrarian Revolutionary War and the Red Army grew to a strength of 300,000. But later we again suffered reverses and our army of 300,000 was reduced to only some 20,000 in the Long March. After it reached northern Shensi, it took in some recruits but still fell short of 30,000, that is, less than one-tenth of the original 300,000. After all, which was stronger, the army of 300,000 or the army of less than 30,000? The army of less than 30,000, because having sustained those heavy reverses and gone through those extreme hardships, we had become tempered and experienced and had rectified the erroneous line and restored the correct line. In the report to this conference, it is said that we have become stronger, not weaker, because our line was correct and our achievements were primary in the past four years and because we have become experienced through making mistakes in our practical work and suffering from them. This is exactly how things stand. In the period of the democratic revolution, we came to understand this objective world of China only after we had experienced victory, then defeat, victory again, then defeat again, only after we had twice drawn comparisons. On the eve and in the course of the War of Resistance Against Japan, I wrote a number of essays, such as *Problems of Strategy in China's Revolutionary War, On Protracted War, On New Democracy* and *Introducing "The Communist,"* and I drafted a number of documents on policy and strategy for the Central Committee. All of them sum up revolutionary experience. These essays and documents could only be written at that time and not before, because until then we hadn't been through storm and stress and couldn't compare our two victories and two defeats, and therefore we weren't adequately experienced and couldn't fully understand the laws governing the Chinese revolution.

Generally speaking, it was the Chinese, and not the comrades of the Communist International handling Chinese problems, who succeeded in gaining an understanding of this objective world of China. These comrades in the Communist International didn't understand Chinese society, the Chinese nation, and the Chinese revolution — or we can say that they didn't understand them well. For a long time we ourselves failed to have a clear understanding of China as an objective world, not to mention the foreign comrades!

It was not until the period of the War of Resistance Against Japan that we formulated a general line for the Party and a whole set of specific policies that suited the prevailing conditions. It was only then that we came to understand the Chinese democratic revolution, this realm of necessity, and that we gained freedom. By that time, we had already been making revolution for some 20 years. Through all those years there was a considerable degree of blindness in our revolutionary work. If anyone claims that any comrade — for instance, any comrade of the Central Committee, or for that matter I myself — completely understood the laws governing the Chinese revolution right from the start, then he is a braggart and you must on no account believe him. It just wasn't so. In the past, and especially in the early years, all we had was a passion for revolution, but when it came to how to make revolution, what the targets were, which targets should come first and which later, and which had to wait until the next stage, we didn't have clear or at least wholly clear ideas for a fairly long time. In giving a historical account of how we Chinese Communists got to know, with much difficulty yet successfully, the laws governing the Chinese revolution in the period of democratic revolution, I hope to guide comrades to understand one thing: that getting to know the laws governing the building of socialism necessarily involves a process. We must take practice as the starting-point and move from having no experience to having some experience, from having little experience to having more experience, from the building of socialism, this still unknown realm of necessity, to the realm of freedom, a leap in cognition — the attainment of freedom through the gradual overcoming of our blindness and the gradual understanding of the objective laws.

The Talk to the 7000 263

We still lack experience in the building of socialism. I've discussed this problem with delegations of fraternal Parties from several countries. I told them that we had no experience in building a socialist economy.

I have also discussed this problem with some journalists from capitalist countries, among them an American called Edgar Snow. He had long wanted to come to China, and in 1960 we let him. I had a talk with him. I said, "As you know, we have a set of experiences, a set of principles, policies and measures with regard to politics, military affairs and class struggle; but when it comes to socialist construction, we hadn't done any in the past, and we still don't have experience. You may say, 'Haven't you been at it for 11 years?' Well yes, we have, but we still lack knowledge and experience. Even if we are beginning to acquire a little, it doesn't amount to much." Snow wanted me to say something about China's long-term construction plans. I said, "I don't know," and he said, "You're being too cautious." I replied, "It's not a question of being cautious. I really don't know, we just don't have the experience." Comrades, it's true that we don't know, we still lack experience and really don't have such long-term plans yet. Nineteen-sixty was the very year we ran into a lot of difficulties. In 1961 I spoke of these things again during a discussion with Montgomery. He said, "In another 50 years you'll be terrific." What he meant was that after 50 years we would become powerful and would be "aggressive" towards others, but not before that. He had already expressed this view to me when in China in 1960. I said, "We are Marxist-Leninists, ours is a socialist state, not a capitalist state, and therefore we won't perpetrate aggression against others whether in 100 years or 10,000 years. As for the construction of a powerful socialist economy in China, 50 years won't be enough, it will take 100 years or even more. In your own country the development of capitalism has taken several hundred years. We won't count the 16th century, since the Middle Ages weren't over yet. But from the 17th century to the present is already more than 360 years. In our country, the building of a powerful socialist economy will take more than 100 years, I reckon." What period was the 17th century? It was the end of the Ming and the beginning of the Ching Dynasty. Another century was to elapse before we came to the first half of the 18th century, or the Qian Long period of the Qing Dynasty, the period when the author of *The Dream of the Red Chamber*, Cao Xueqin, lived, a period which gave birth to fictional characters like Jia Baoyu, who was dissatisfied with the feudal system. In the Qian Long period, the buds of capitalist relations of production already existed in China, but it remained a feudal society. Such is the social background of the emergence of the multitude of fictional characters in the Daguan Garden. Before this, in the 17th century, capitalism was already developing in a number of European countries. It has taken over 300 years for the capitalist productive forces to develop to their present state. Socialism is vastly superior to capitalism and our economy will develop faster than those of the capitalist countries. But China has a large population, had little to start with and is economically backward, so that in my opinion it will be impossible for her to effect a tremendous expansion of the productive forces to catch up with and overtake the world's most advanced capitalist countries in less than 100 years. Perhaps it will actually take only a few decades — say, 50 years — as some people envisage. If it does turn out that way, we'll thank heaven and earth and it will be wonderful! But I would advise comrades to anticipate more difficulties and so to envisage a somewhat longer period.

It took more than 300 years to build up a powerful capitalist economy; what would be wrong with building a powerful socialist economy in our country in about 50 to 100 years? The next 50 to 100 years or so, beginning from now, will be a great era of radical change in the social system throughout the world, an earth-shaking era without equal in any previous historical period. Living in such an era, we must be prepared to engage in tremendous struggles which in form will have many features different from those of struggles in the past. In this undertaking, we must integrate in the best possible way the universal truth of Marxism-Leninism with the concrete realities of China's socialist construction and with those of the world revolution now and in the future and, through practice, gradually get to know the objective laws of struggle. We must be prepared to suffer many failures and setbacks resulting from our blindness, and thereby gain experience and win final victory. When we see things in this light, there are many advantages in envisaging a longer period of time, whereas harm might result from envisaging a shorter period.

In socialist construction, we are still acting blindly to a very large extent. For us the socialist economy is in many respects a still unknown realm of necessity. Take me by way of example. There are many problems in the work of economic construction which I still don't understand. I know very little about industry and commerce for instance. I know something about agriculture, but this is only relatively speaking — I still don't know much. To know more about agriculture one should understand soils, botany, crop cultivation, agro-chemistry, farm machinery and so on. One should also understand the different branches of agriculture, such as grain, cotton, edible oil, hemp, silk, tea, sugar, vegetables, tobacco, fruit, medicinal herbs and miscellaneous products. There are animal husbandry and forestry too. I myself am a believer in the theory of the Soviet soil scientist V. R. Williams. In his work on soil Williams advocated combining farming, forestry and animal husbandry. I think we must have this three-way combination, or agriculture will suffer. I would advise comrades to make a serious study of all these problems of agriculture production when you have some respite from work. I too would like to study them a little more. Up to now, however, my knowledge of these matters has been very scanty. I have paid rather more attention to problems relating to the relations of production, to the system. When it comes to the productive forces, I know very little. As for our Party as a whole, our knowledge of socialist construction is very inadequate. In the forthcoming period we should accumulate experience and study hard, and in the course of practice gradually deepen our understanding and become clearer on the laws of socialist construction. We must put in a lot of hard work and investigate and study it in earnest. We must go down to selected spots at the grass roots, to the production brigades and production teams, and to the factories and shops. We used to do rather well in making investigation and study, but after we entered the cities we didn't do it seriously. In 1961 we pushed it once again, and now the situation has changed somewhat. But it has not yet become common practice among the leading cadres — especially senior cadres — in some places, departments and enterprises. Some provincial Party secretaries have still not gone down to stay at selected spots. If the provincial Party secretaries don't go, how can they ask prefectural Party secretaries and county Party secretaries to do so? This is bad and must be changed.

Twelve years have passed since the founding of the People's Republic of China. These 12 years can be divided into a first period of eight years and a second period of four years. Nineteen-fifty to the end of 1957 constitute the first eight years, 1958 to the present is the second four years. In this conference of ours, we have made a first attempt at summing up the experience of our past work, mainly that of the last four years. This summing-up is reflected in the report to the conference. We have already formulated, or are formulating, or shall formulate, specific policies in various fields. Already formulated are such draft regulations as the 60 articles on rural people's communes, the 70 articles on industrial enterprises, the 60 articles on higher education and the 14 articles on scientific research, all of which have already come into force or are being carried out on a trial basis. They will be revised in future, some perhaps drastically. Among those which are already in the process of formulation are the regulations on commercial work. Among those which will be formulated in future are the regulations on middle-school and primary-school education. We should also formulate some regulations on the work of our Party and government organs and mass organizations. The army has already formulated some regulations. In short, we should do a good job in summing up our experience in industry, agriculture, commerce and culture and education, and in the army, the government and the Party, and work out a complete set of principles, policies and measures so that our work in these seven sectors will progress along the correct path.

It is not enough to have a general line. In addition, under its guidance we must have a complete set of specific principles, policies and measures which are suited to our conditions in industry, agriculture, commerce, culture and education, the army, the government and the Party. Only then can we persuade the masses and the cadres, using these as teaching materials to educate them so that they can have unity of understanding and of action. And only then can we achieve victory in revolution and construction. Otherwise it is impossible. On this point, we had a deep understanding even as far back as the War of Resistance Against Japan. At that time we did function in this way, so that the cadres and the masses achieved unity in their understanding of the complete set of specific principles, policies and measures for the period of democratic revolution and therefore achieved unity in action, which led to victory in that revolution. This is something we all know. During the period of socialist revolution and socialist construction, our revolutionary tasks in the first eight years were: in the countryside, to complete the reform of the feudal land system and then to achieve the co-operative transformation of agriculture, and in the cities, to achieve the socialist transformation of capitalist industry and commerce. In economic construction, our tasks were to rehabilitate the economy and carry out the First Five-Year Plan. Both in revolution and in construction we had a general line which was suited to the objective conditions and which was wholly convincing, as well as a complete set of principles, policies and measures under the guidance of the general line. Hence we could educate the cadres and the masses and unify their understanding, and the tasks were performed fairly well. This is also something we all know. But as things stood in those days, we had to copy the Soviet Union since we had no experience of our own in economic construction. In the field of heavy industry especially, we copied almost everything from the Soviet Union with very little creativeness on our part. It was absolutely necessary to do so at that time, and yet it was also a weakness — a lack of creativeness and of ability to stand on our own feet. Certainly this could not be our long-term policy. Beginning from 1958 we established the clear-cut policy of relying mainly on our own efforts while seeking foreign aid by way of support. At the Second Session of the Party's Eighth National Congress in 1958, we adopted the general line of "going all out, aiming high and achieving greater, faster, better and more economical results in building socialism." In the same year the people's communes were established and the slogan of a "great leap forward" was raised. For a certain period after the general line for socialist construction was proclaimed, we hadn't the time to work out a complete set of specific principles, policies and measures suited to our conditions, nor did the possibility exist for us to do so because our experience was still insufficient. Under these circumstances, a complete set of teaching materials wasn't available to the cadres and the masses, who couldn't get any systematic education on policy and therefore couldn't conceivably have genuine unity in understanding and action. This possibility came into being only after a period of time, after we had suffered some setbacks and acquired both positive and negative experience. Now matters are better. We do have these things or are working them out. Thus we can better carry on socialist revolution and socialist construction. In order to work out a complete set of specific principles, policies and measures under the guidance of the general line, we must employ the methods of drawing on the masses and of making systematic, thorough investigation and study. And we must examine the successful and unsuccessful experience in our work historically. Only thus can we discover laws which are inherent in objective things and which are not subjectively concocted out of people's imaginations, and only thus can we formulate regulations which are suited to our conditions. This is a very important matter and I ask the comrades here to please pay attention to it.

Of the seven sectors — industry, agriculture, commerce, culture and education, the army, the government and the Party — it is the Party that exercises overall leadership. The Party must give leadership to industry, agriculture, commerce, culture and education, the army and the government. Generally speaking, our Party is good. Our Party is mainly composed of workers and poor peasants. The great majority of our cadres are good, and they are all working hard. But we must also realize that there are still some problems and we mustn't imagine that everything is just fine with our Party. At present we have over 17 million Party members, nearly 80 per cent of whom joined the Party after the founding of the People's Republic, that is, in the 50s. Those who joined the Party before our People's Republic was founded constitute only 20 per cent. Of this 20 per cent, those who joined before 1930, that is, in the 20s, totalled 800-odd people according to an estimate several years ago. Some have died in the last couple of years, so perhaps there are only 700-odd left. Among both old and new Party members — especially among the new members — there are some who are impure in character or work style. They are individualists, bureaucrats, subjectivists, or even degenerate elements. There are also some people who are Communists in name but do not represent the working class, on the contrary, they represent the bourgeoisie. All is not pure inside the Party. We must be aware of this fact, or we shall suffer.

This is my fourth point. In short, our understanding of the objective world necessarily involves a process. In the beginning we do not understand, or do not completely understand, and it is only through repeated practice which leads to achievements and victories, tumbles and setbacks, and through the comparison of successes and failures that it is possible to have gradually developed complete or relatively complete understanding. When that point is reached, we shall have more initiative, enjoy greater freedom and become somewhat wiser. Freedom is the recognition of necessity and the transformation of the objective world. Only on the basis of the recognition of necessity can people have freedom of action. This is the dialectics of freedom and necessity. Necessity as such is objectively existing law. Before we recognize it our action can never be conscious, it partakes of blindness. Under these conditions we are foolish people. Haven't we done many foolish things during the last few years?

The fifth point: The international communist movement. On this question I am only going to say a few words.

Whether in China or in other countries of the world, when all is said and done, over 90 per cent of the population will eventually support Marxism-Leninism. There are still many people in the world who have not awakened because of the deceptions of the social-democrats, revisionists, imperialists and reactionaries. But sooner or later they will gradually awaken and support Marxism-Leninism. The truth of Marxism-Leninism is irresistible. Sooner or later the masses of the people will rise in revolution. Sooner or later the world revolution will triumph. Sooner or later those who forbid others to make revolution, such as the characters in Lu Hsun's book — Squire Zhao, Squire Qian and the bogus foreign devil who bar Ah Q from revolution — will be defeated.

The Soviet Union was the first socialist state and the Communist Party of the Soviet Union was created by Lenin. Although the leadership of the Soviet Party and state has now been usurped by revisionists, I would advise comrades to remain firm in the conviction that the masses of the Soviet people and of Soviet Party members and cadres are good, that they desire revolution and that revisionist rule will not last long. Whatever the time — now or in the future, in our generation or in the generations to come — we should learn from the Soviet Union and study its experience. If we don't learn from the Soviet Union, we'll make mistakes. People may ask, since the Soviet Union is under the rule of the revisionists, should we still learn from it? What we should study is the good people and good things of the Soviet Union, the good experience of the Soviet Party, the good experience of Soviet workers and peasants and of those intellectuals who have close ties with the labouring people. As for the bad people and bad things of the Soviet Union and the Soviet revisionists, we should treat them as teachers by negative example and draw lessons from them.

We should always uphold the principle of proletariat internationalist unity. We always maintain that the socialist countries and the world communist movement must unite firmly on the basis of Marxism-Leninism.

The revisionists of the world never stop abusing us. Our attitude is, let them do as they wish. We will duly reply when necessary. Our Party has become accustomed to being abused. Leaving aside those who attacked us in the past, what about the present? Abroad, the imperialists abuse us, the reactionary nationalists abuse us, the reactionaries of various countries abuse us, and the revisionists abuse us; at home, Jiang Jieshi abuses us, and likewise the landlords, rich peasants, counter-revolutionaries, bad elements and Rightists. This has been the case for a long time and we're already used to it. But are we isolated? I for one don't feel isolated. Over 7,000 people are present here. How can more than 7,000 people be isolated? Our country has over 600 million people. Our people are united. How can more than 600 million people be isolated? The masses of the people of all countries are already standing, or are going to stand, together with us. Is it possible for us to be isolated?

The sixth and last point: We must unite the whole Party and the whole people.

We must unite the advanced elements and the activists inside and outside the Party, and unite the middle elements in order to bring along those who lag behind. In this way, we can unite the whole Party and the whole people. Only by relying on such unity can we do our work well, overcome difficulties and build up China. To unite the whole Party and the whole people does not mean that we do not have our own position. Some people say that the Communist Party is a "party of the whole people," but we do not view things in this way. Our Party is the political party of the proletariat, its vanguard, a fighting force armed with Marxism-Leninism. We are on the side of the masses who comprise over 95 per cent of the total population. In no case do we stand on the side of the landlords, rich peasants, counter-revolutionaries, bad elements and Rightists who make up 4 to 5 per cent of the population. The same is true in the international sphere; we advocate unity with all Marxist-Leninist, with all revolutionary people, with the people in general. In no case do we want unity with the anti-Communist and anti-popular imperialists and reactionaries. Whenever possible we'll establish diplomatic relations with them too and strive for peaceful coexistence with them on the basis of the Five Principles. But this is in a category different from our unity with the people of all countries.

If unity is to prevail throughout the Party and the nation, we must give full play to democracy and let people speak up. This holds both inside and outside the Party. Comrades from the provincial, prefectural and county Party committees, when you return, you must let people speak out. All comrades, absent or present, must act in this way. All leading members of the Party must promote inner-Party democracy and let people speak out. What are the limits? One is that Party discipline must be observed, the minority being subordinate to the majority and the entire membership to the Central Committee. Another limit is that no secret faction must be organized. We are not afraid of open opponents, we are only afraid of secret opponents. Such people do not speak the truth to your face, what they say is only lies and deceit. They don't express their real intention. As long as a person doesn't violate discipline and doesn't engage in secret factional activities, we should allow him to speak out and shouldn't punish him if he says wrong things. If people say wrong things, they can be criticized, but we should convince them with reason. What if they are still not convinced? They can be allowed to reserve their opinions. As long as they abide by the resolutions and the decisions taken by the majority, the minority can reserve their opinions. It is advantageous to allow the minority both inside and outside the Party to do so. If they are allowed to reserve their incorrect opinions for the time being, they can correct them in future. Quite often the ideas of the minority turn to be correct. Such cases are common in history. In the beginning, truth is not in the hands of the majority of people, but in those of a minority. Marx and Engels held the truth in their hands, but in the beginning they were in the minority. For a long period Lenin was also in the minority. We've had similar experience in our own Party. When our Party was ruled by Chen Duxiu and also when the "Left" opportunist lines prevailed, truth was not in the hands of the majority in the leading organs but on the contrary in the hands of the minority. Historically, the doctrines of natural scientists such as Copernicus, Galileo and Darwin were not recognized by the majority of people for a very long time, but on the contrary were considered incorrect. In their time they were in the minority. When our Party was founded in 1921, we only had a few dozen members; we were also in the minority, but those few dozen people represented the truth and represented China's destiny.

There is also the question of arrests and executions on which I want to say something. At present, only a dozen or so years after victory in the revolution, as long as elements of the overthrown reactionary classes have not been reformed and, what is more, as long as some of them are still plotting restoration, a few must be arrested and executed; otherwise the people's anger cannot be placated and the people's dictatorship consolidated. But we must not arrest people lightly, and especially we must not execute people lightly. Some bad people, some bad elements and degenerate elements who have infiltrated into our ranks, ride on the backs of the people, piss and shit on them, behaving in a vicious and unrestrained way, and seriously violate laws and discipline. They are petty Jiang Jieshi. We must have a way of dealing with this type of people. The worst among them who have committed heinous crimes have to be arrested and some executed. For if we don't arrest or execute any of them, we won't be able to placate the people's anger. This is what we mean when we say, "We can't avoid arrests, and we can't avoid executions." But we absolutely must not arrest too many or execute too many. As for those whose arrest is optional or whose execution is optional, we must definitely not arrest or execute them. There was a fellow called Pan Hannian who once served as vice-mayor of Shanghai. Previously he had secretly capitulated to the Kuomintang and had become a member of the C. C. Clique. He is now in jail, and we haven't executed him. If we kill one fellow like Pan Hannian, thereby relaxing the restraints on execution, then all those like him would have to be executed. There was another fellow called Wang Shiwei who was a secret Kuomintang agent. While in Yanan, he wrote an article entitled

The Talk to the 7000

"The Wild Lily," in which he attacked the revolution and vilified the Communist Party. He was later arrested and killed. The execution was carried out by the security organs themselves while they were on the march; the decision was not made by the Central Committee. We have often made criticisms on this incident and we hold that he shouldn't have been killed. True, he was a secret agent, he wrote articles to attack us and simply refused to mend his ways. Still we could have just spared him and let him do labour. It wasn't good to kill him. We should arrest and execute as few people as possible. If we arrest and execute people at will, everybody will fear for himself and nobody will dare to speak. In such an atmosphere there can't be much democracy.

Neither should we put hats on people indiscriminately. Some comrades are addicted to using hats to put pressure on people. The moment they start speaking, hats start flying around everywhere and people are so frightened they daren't speak. Of course hats there will always be. Aren't there many hats in the report to the conference? Isn't "decentralism" a hat? But we mustn't put hats on people at will, calling this one a decentralism and that one a decentralist, until everybody is a decentralist. It would be better for the people concerned to put on the hats themselves — and moreover the right hats — rather than have them put on by others. If people put on hats themselves and wear them for a while, they should be removed when everybody agrees that they no longer fit. This will create a good democratic atmosphere. We advocate not seizing on other's faults, not putting hats on people and not wielding the big stick, so that people will be free from fear and will dare to speak out.

Good will and a helpful attitude should be shown towards those who have made mistakes and those who do not allow people to speak out. We mustn't create the kind of atmosphere in which people feel that they can't afford to make any mistakes or that once they have made mistakes, the consequences will be terrible and they will never be able to raise their heads again. As long as a person who has made mistakes really wants to mend his ways and has made a genuine self-criticism, we should express our welcome. We must not make too high demands on a person when he makes a self-criticism the first or second time. It doesn't matter if his self-criticism is not thorough yet. We should let him think again and give him well-intentioned help. A man needs help from others. We must help an erring comrade to realize his mistakes. If people sincerely make self-criticism and are willing to correct mistakes, we should forgive them and adopt a lenient policy towards them. As long as their achievements are still primary and they are reasonably competent, let them continue in their posts.

In my speech I have criticized certain phenomena and criticized certain comrades, but I haven't named them, I haven't pointed out who this one or that one actually is. You know what I mean. For shortcomings and mistakes in our work in the last few years, the responsibility rests first with the Central Committee and, in the Central Committee, primarily with me; second, the responsibility rests with the Party committees of the provinces, municipalities and autonomous regions; third, with the prefectural Party committees; fourth, with the county Party committees; and fifth, with the Party committees of enterprises and people's communes. In short, everyone has his share of responsibility.

Comrades, when you return, you must revitalize democratic centralism. The comrades of the county Party committees should lead the commune Party committees in revitalizing democratic centralism. First of all, collective leadership must be built or strengthened. You must no longer practise the methods of leadership which prolongs the fixed "division of spheres of work and exclusive responsibility." Under that method the secretaries and members of Party committees each work on their own, and there can be no real collective discussion on real collective leadership. It is necessary to promote democracy, encourage others to make criticisms and listen to their criticisms. We must be able to face criticism. We must take the initiative and carry out self-criticism first. We must examine whatever needs examining for one or at most two hours, getting it all out lock, stock and barrel — that'll be the lot. If others consider it insufficient, let them go on. And if what they say is right, we'll accept their criticism. In the matter of letting people speak out, should we be active or passive? Of course it's better to be active. But what if we're already in a passive position? If we were undemocratic in the past and so find ourselves in this passive position now, it doesn't matter. Let everybody criticize us. Let them pour out their grievances all day, and instead of going to the theatre in the evening too. Please come and criticize me day and night. Then I'll sit down and think about it coolly, forgoing sleep for two or three nights. After thinking it through and understanding it, I'll write a sincere self-criticism. Isn't that the way? In short, if you let others speak out, the heavens won't fall and you won't be toppled. And if you don't? Then the day will inevitably come when you are toppled.

So much for my speech today. The central point I have discussed is the question of how to realize democratic centralism and how to promote democracy inside and outside the Party. I recommend that comrades consider this question carefully. Some comrades still lack the democratic centralist way of thinking. Now is the time they should begin to acquire this way of thinking and begin to understand this question. If we give full play to democracy, we can mobilize the enthusiasm of the broad masses inside and outside the Party and unite the broad masses who comprise more than 95 per cent of the whole population. When we have achieved this, we will be able to do our work better and better and overcome the difficulties we meet all the more quickly. Our cause will then develop much more smoothly.

COMMUNIQUE OF THE THIRD PLENARY SESSION OF THE 11TH CENTRAL COMMITTEE OF THE COMMUNIST PARTY OF CHINA

(Adopted on December 22, 1978)

The plenary session unanimously endorsed the policy decision put forward by Comrade Hua Guofeng on behalf of the Political Bureau of the Central Committee on shifting the emphasis of our Party's work and the attention of the people of the whole country to socialist modernization.

The session thoroughly discussed questions in agriculture and held that the whole Party should concentrate its main energy and efforts on advancing agriculture as fast as possible. It agreed to distribute to the provinces, municipalities and autonomous regions for discussion and trial use the Decisions of the Central Committee of the Communist Party of China on Some Questions Concerning the Acceleration of Agricultural Development (Draft) and the Regulations on the Work in the Rural People's Communes (Draft for Trial Use). It discussed arrangements for the national economic plans for 1979 and 1980 and approved them in principle.

The session seriously discussed some major political events which occurred during the Great Cultural Revolution and certain historical questions left over from an earlier period. It decided to cancel the erroneous documents issued by the Central Committee in regard to the movement "to oppose the Right-deviationist wind to reverse correct verdicts" and the Tian An Men events and also examined and corrected the erroneous conclusions which had been adopted on Peng De-huai, Tao Zhu, Po Yipo, Yang Shangkun and other comrades.

The plenary session elected Comrade Chen Yun an additional Vice-Chairman of the Central Committee, elected Comrades Deng Yingchao, Hu Yaobang and Wang Zhen additional Members of the Political Bureau of the Central Committee, and elected a 100-member Central Commission for Inspecting Discipline headed by Comrade Chen Yun.

The session highly evaluated the discussion of whether practice is the sole criterion for testing truth, noting that this is of far-reaching historic significance in encouraging comrades of the whole Party and the people of the whole country to emancipate their minds and follow the correct ideological line.

The session emphatically pointed out: Comrade Mao Zedong was a great Marxist. The lofty task of the Party Central Committee on the theoretical front is to lead and educate the whole Party and the people of the whole country to recognize Comrade Mao Zedong's great feats in a historical and scientific perspective, comprehensively and correctly grasp the scientific system of Mao Zedong Thought and integrate the universal principles of Marxism-Leninism-Mao Zedong Thought with the concrete practice of socialist modernization and develop it under the new historical conditions.

Basing itself on the experience and lessons drawn from the history of our Party, the plenary session decided to improve the practice of democratic centralism within the Party, to amplify the Party rules and regulations and to enforce strict discipline in the Party. The Party members' right to make criticisms within the Party concerning the leadership at higher levels, up to Members of the Standing Committee of the Political Bureau of the Central Committee, must be guaranteed and any practice that does not conform to the Party's democratic centralism and the principle of collective leadership should be resolutely corrected.

The 11th Central Committee of the Communist Party of China held its third plenary session in Peking between December 18 and 22, 1978. It was attended by 169 Members and 112 Alternate Members of the Central Committee. Hua Guofeng, Chairman of the C.P.C. Central Committee, and Ye Jianying, Deng Xiaoping, Li Xiannien, Chen Yun and Wang Dongxing, Vice-Chairmen, were present. Comrade Hua Guofeng presided over the session and made important speeches.

A central working conference held prior to the session made full preparations for it.

The plenary session decided that, since the work of the Central Committee following its second plenary session had proceeded smoothly and the large-scale nationwide mass movement to expose and criticize Lin Biao and the "Gang of Four" had in the main been completed victoriously, the stress of the Party's work should shift to socialist modernization as of 1979. The plenary session discussed the international situation and the handling of foreign affairs, reaching the view that the foreign policy of the Party and the government was correct and successful. The plenary session also discussed the question of how to speed the growth of agricultural production and arrangements for the national economic plans for 1979 and 1980 and adopted relevant documents in principle. The plenary session examined and solved a number of important questions left over from history and the question of the contributions and faults, the correctness and incorrectness of some important leaders. In order to meet the needs of socialist modernization, the plenary session decided to strengthen democracy in Party life and in the political life of the state, put forward in explicit terms the Party's ideological line, strengthen the Party's leading organs and set up a Central Commission for Inspecting Discipline. The plenary session elected Comrade Chen Yun an additional Member of the Political Bureau of the Central Committee, Member of the Standing Committee of the Political Bureau of the Central Committee and Vice-Chairman of the Central Committee, and elected Comrades Deng Ying-chao, Hu Yaobang and Wang Zhen additional Members of the Political Bureau of the Central Committee. In view of the changed situation in Party life since the 11th National Congress of the Party and current urgent needs in Party work, the plenary session decided, in a provisional measure, to add nine Members to the Central Committee — Comrades Huang Kecheng, Song Ren Qiong, Hu Qiaomu, Xi Zhongxun, Wang Renzhong, Huang Huoqing, Chen Zaidao, Han Guang and Zhou Hui — subject to future confirmation by the 12th National Congress of the Party. The plenary session elected Comrade Chen Yun First Secretary of the Central Commission for Inspecting Discipline. Comrade Deng Ying-chao Second Secretary, Comrade Hu Yaopang Third Secretary, Comrade Huang Kecheng Permanent Secretary, and Wang Haoshou and other comrades Deputy Secretaries. Permanent members and members of the commission were also elected.

The plenary session holds that this session and the earlier central working conference are of great importance in our Party's history. Throughout the two meetings, the participants emancipated their thinking on the basis of Marxism-Leninism-Mao Zedong Thought and spoke freely. They fully revived and brought into full play inner-Party democracy and the Party's fine styles of seeking truth from facts, the mass line, and criticism and self-criticism, and enhanced their unity. The meetings truly brought about "a political situation in which we have both centralism and democracy, both discipline and freedom, both unity of will and personal ease of mind and liveliness," as Comrade Mao Zedong advocated. The plenary session decided to spread this atmosphere throughout the Party and the army and among the people of all nationalities in our country.

(1)

The plenary session expresses satisfaction with the work of the Central Committee in the past ten months since the second plenary session. There has been great victory in the momentous nationwide political revolution to expose and repudiate Lin Biao and the "Gang of Four"; there has been additional restoration and growth of the national economy; there is political stability and unity throughout the country; and significant progress has been made with regard to our foreign policy. All this provides good conditions for the whole Party to shift the emphasis of its work to socialist modernization.

The session points out that our country has achieved new and important successes in developing the international united front against hegemonism and in developing friendly relations with countries in all parts of the world. The visits made by our state leaders this year to Korea, Romania, Yugoslavia, Kampuchea, Iran, Burma, Nepal, the Philippines, Bangladesh, Japan, Thailand, Malaysia and Singapore and many other countries in Asia, Africa, Latin America and Europe, the conclusion of the China-Japan Peace and Friendship Treaty and the completion of the negotiations for the normalization of relations between China and the United States are important contributions to peace in Asia and the world as a whole. But the grave danger of war still exists. We must strengthen our national defence, and be prepared to repulse at any moment aggressors from any direction.

The plenary session holds that the normalization of relations between China and the United States further places before us the prospect of the return of our sacred territory Taiwan to the embrace of our motherland and the accomplishment of the great cause of reunification. The plenary session expresses welcome to Taiwan compatriots, compatriots in Hongkong and Macao and overseas Chinese, as patriots belonging to one family, to continue making joint and positive contributions to the reunification and construction of their motherland.

In the early years after the founding of the People's Republic, especially after the socialist transformation was in the main completed, Comrade Mao Zedong instructed the whole Party time and again to shift the focus of our work to the field of the economy and technical revolution. Under the leadership of Comrade Mao Zedong and Comrade Zhou Enlai, our Party did a great deal for socialist modernization and scored important achievements. But the work was later interrupted and sabotaged by Lin Biao and the "Gang of Four." Besides, we had some shortcomings and mistakes in our leading work because we lacked experience in socialist construction, and this also hampered the transition in the focus of our Party's work. Since nationwide mass movement to expose and criticize Lin Biao and the "Gang of Four" has fundamentally come to a successful conclusion, though in a small number of places and departments the movement is less developed, still needs some time to catch up and so cannot end simultaneously, on the whole there is every condition needed for that transition. Therefore the plenary session unanimously endorsed the policy decision put forward by Comrade Hua Guofeng on behalf of the Political Bureau of the Central Committee that, to meet the developments at home and abroad, now is an appropriate time to take the decision to close the large-scale nationwide mass movement to expose and criticize Lin Biao and the "Gang of Four" and to shift the emphasis of our Party's work and the attention of the people of the whole country to socialist modernization.

Communique of the Third Plenary Session 285

This is of major significance for fulfilment of the three-year and eight-year programmes for the development of the national economy and the outline for 23 years, for the modernization of agriculture, industry, national defence and science and technology and for the consideration of the dictatorship of the proletariat in our country. The general task put forward by our Party for the new period reflects the demands of history and the people's aspirations and represents their fundamental interests. Whether or not we can carry this general task to completion, speed socialist modernization and on the basis of a rapid growth in production improve the people's living standards significantly and strengthen national defence — this is a major issue which is of paramount concern to all our people and of great significance to the cause of world peace and progress. Carrying out the four modernizations requires great growth in the productive forces, which in turn requires diverse changes in those aspects of the relations of production and the superstructure not in harmony with the growth of the productive forces, and requires changes in all methods of management, actions and thinking which stand in the way of such growth. Socialist modernization is therefore a profound and extensive revolution. There is still in our country today a small handful of counter-revolutionary elements and criminals who hate our socialist modernization and try to undermine it. We must not relax our class struggle against them, nor can we weaken the dictatorship of the proletariat. But as Comrade Mao Zedong pointed out, the large-scale turbulent class struggles of a mass character have in the main come to an end. Class struggle in socialist society should be carried out on the principle of strictly differentiating the two different types of contradictions and correctly handling them in accordance with the procedures prescribed by the Constitution and the law. It is impermissible to confuse the two different types of contradictions and damage the political stability and unity required for socialist modernization. The plenary session calls on the whole Party, the whole army and the people of all our nationalities to work with one heart and one mind, enhance political stability and unity, mobilize themselves immediately to go all out, pool their wisdom and efforts and carry out the new Long March to make China a modern, powerful socialist country before the end of this century.

(2)

In preparing for the great task of socialist modernization, the session reviewed the experience and lessons of economic construction since the founding of the People's Republic. The session holds that the fundamental policy put forth in the report *On the Ten Major Relationships* which Comrade Mao Zedong made in 1956, summing up China's experience in economic construction, is an objective reflection of economic law and also an important guarantee for the political stability of society. This report still is significant for guidance today. It has been shown in practice that whenever we maintain the society's necessary political stability and work according to objective economic law, our national economy advances steadily and at a high speed; otherwise, our national economy develops slowly or even stagnates and falls back. While we have achieved political stability and unity and are restoring and adhering to the economic policies that proved effective over a long time, we are now, in the light of the new historical conditions and practical experience, adopting a number of major new economic measures, conscientiously transforming the system and methods of economic management, actively expanding economic co-operation on terms of quality and mutual benefit with other countries on the basis of self-reliance, striving to adopt the world's advanced technologies and equipment and greatly strengthening scientific and educational work to meet the needs of modernization. Therefore, there can be no doubt that our country's economic construction is bound to advance rapidly and steadily once again.

The plenary session discussed arrangements for the national economic plans for 1979 and 1980 and approved them in principle, and proposed that the State Council submit them after revisions to the Second Session of the National People's Congress to be held next year for discussion and adoption. The session feels that these arrangements are both forward-looking and feasible. The session points out that the restoration and development of our national economy since the downfall of the "Gang of Four" has been very rapid, and that there have been marked increases in total industrial and agricultural output value and revenue in 1978. But it has to be noted that due to sabotage by Lin Biao and the "Gang of Four" over a long period there are still quite a few problems in the national economy, some major imbalances have not been completely changed and some disorder in production, construction, circulation and distribution has not been fully eliminated. A series of problems left hanging for years as regards the people's livelihood in town and country must be appropriately solved. We must conscientiously solve these problems step by step in the next few years and effectively achieve a comprehensive balance, so as to lay a solid foundation for rapid development. We must make concentrated efforts within the limits of our capabilities to carry out capital construction actively and steadily and not rush things, wasting manpower and material.

The session points out that one of the serious shortcomings in the structure of economic management in our country is the over-concentration of authority, and it is necessary boldly to shift it under guidance from the leadership to lower levels so that the local authorities and industrial and agricultural enterprises will have greater power of decision in management under the guidance of unified state planning; big efforts should be made to simplify bodies at various levels charged with economic administration and transfer most of their functions to such enterprises as specialized companies or complexes; it is necessary to act firmly in line with economic law, attach importance to the role of the law of value, consciously combine ideological and political work with economic methods and give full play to the enthusiasm of cadres and workers for production; it is necessary, under the centralized leadership of the Party, to tackle conscientiously the failure to make a distinction between the Party, the government and the enterprise and to put a stop to the substitution of Party for government and the substitution of government for enterprise administration, to institute a division of responsibilities among different levels, types of work and individuals, increase the authority and responsibility of administrative bodies and managerial personnel, reduce the number of meetings and amount of paper work to raise work efficiency, and conscientiously adopt the practices of examination, reward and punishment, promotion and demotion. These measures will bring into full play the initiative, enthusiasm and creativeness of four levels, the central departments, the local authorities, the enterprises and the workers, and invigorate all branches and links of the socialist economy.

The session discussed in detail questions in agriculture, and agreed to distribute to the provinces, municipalities and autonomous regions for discussion and trial use the Decisions of the Central Committee of the Communist Party of China on Some Questions Concerning the Acceleration of Agriculture Development (Draft) and the Regulations on the Work in the Rural People's Communes (Draft for Trial Use).

The plenary session holds that the whole Party should concentrate its main energy and efforts on advancing agriculture as fast as possible because agriculture, the foundation of the national economy, has been seriously damaged in recent years and remains very weak on the whole. The rapid development of the national economy as a whole and the steady improvement in the living standards of the people of the whole country depends on the vigorous restoration and speeding up of farm production, on resolutely and fully implementing the policy of simultaneous development of farming, forestry, animal husbandry, side-occupations and fisheries, the policy of taking grain as the key link and ensuring an all-round development, the policy of adaptation to local conditions and appropriate concentration of certain crops in certain areas, and gradual modernization of farm work. This requires first of all releasing the socialist enthusiasm of our country's several hundred million peasants, paying full attention to their material well-being economically and giving effective protection to their democratic rights politically. Taking this as the guideline, the plenary session set forth a series of policies and economic measures aimed at raising present agricultural production. The most important are as follows: The right of ownership by the people's communes, production brigades and production teams and their power of decision must be protected effectively by the laws of the state; it is not permitted to commandeer the manpower, funds, products and material of any production team; the economic organizations at various levels of the people's commune must conscientiously implement the socialist principle of "to each according to his work," work out payment in accordance with the amount and quality of work done, and overcome equalitarianism; small plots of land for private use by commune members, their domestic side-occupations, and village fairs are necessary adjuncts of the socialist economy, and must not be interfered with; the people's communes must resolutely implement the system of three levels of ownership with the production team as the basic accounting unit, and this should remain unchanged. Organizations at various levels of the people's commune must firmly carry out democratic management and election of cadres and make public their accounts. The session holds that, for a fairly long period to come, the national figures for the agricultural tax and the state purchase of grain will continue to be based on the five-year quotas 1971–75 and that grain purchase must never be excessive. To reduce the disparity in prices between industrial and agricultural products, the plenary session suggests that the State Council make a decision to raise the grain purchase price by 20 per cent, starting in 1979 when the summer grain is marketed, and the price for the amount purchased above the quota by an additional 50 per cent, and also raise the purchase price for cotton, oil-bearing and sugar crops, animal by-products, aquatic and forestry products and other farm and sideline products step by step, depending on the concrete conditions. The factory price and the market price of farm machinery, chemical fertilizer, insecticides, plastics and other manufactured goods for farm use will be cut by 10 to 15 per cent in 1979 and 1980 on the basis of reduced cost of production, and these benefits will in general be passed on to the peasants. After the purchase price of farm products is raised, the urban workers must be guranteed against a fall in their living standards. The market price of all food grain will remain unchanged, and the selling price of other farm products needed for daily life must also be kept stable; if some prices have to be raised, appropriate subsidies will be given to the consumers. The plenary session also discussed the strengthening of education in agricultural science, the drafting of regional programmes for developing agriculture, forestry and animal husbandry, the establishment of modern farming, forestry, livestock-breeding and fishing centres, the active expansion of rural industry and side-occupations run by people's communes and production brigades and other important questions, and decided upon relevant measures.

The plenary session points out that it is imperative to improve the livelihood of the people in town and country step by step on the basis of the growth of production. The bureaucratic attitude of paying no attention at all to urgent problems in the people's livelihood must be resolutely opposed. On the other hand, since our economy is still very backward at present, it is impossible to improve the people's livelihood very rapidly and it is essential to keep the people informed on the relevant state of affairs and to intensify education in the revolutionary ideas of self-reliance and hard struggle among the youth and other sectors of the people, and leading comrades at all levels must make themselves exemplars in this regard.

(3)

The session had a serious discussion on some major political events which occurred during the Great Cultural Revolution and certain historical questions left over from an earlier period. It holds that satisfactory settlement of these questions is very necessary for consolidating stability and unity, facilitating the shift in the focus of the work of the whole Party and getting the whole Party, the whole army and the people of all our nationalities to unite as one and to look forward so as to mobilize all positive factors to work for the four modernizations.

The session points out that in 1975, in the period when Comrade Deng Xiaoping was entrusted by Comrade Mao Zedong with the responsibility of presiding over the work of the Central Committee, there were great achievements in all fields of work, with which the whole Party, the whole army and the people throughout the country were satisfied. In accordance with Comrade Mao Zedong's instructions, Comrade Deng Xiaoping and other leading comrades of the Central Committee waged tit-for-tat struggles against interference and sabotage by the "Gang of Four." The Gang arbitrarily described the political line and the achievements of 1975 as a "Right-deviationist wind to reverse correct verdicts." This reversal of history must be reversed again. The session points out that the Tian An Men events of April 5, 1976, were entirely revolutionary actions. The great revolutionary mass movement, which unfolded around the Tian An Men events and in which millions upon millions of people in all parts of the country expresses deep mourning for Comrade Zhou Enlai and indignantly condemned the "Gang of Four," provided the mass base for our Party's success in smashing the "Gang of Four." The plenary session decided to cancel the erroneous documents issued by the Central

Committee in regard to the movement "to oppose the Right-deviationist wind to reverse correct verdicts" and the Tien An Men events.

The session examined and corrected the erroneous conclusions which had been adopted on Peng Dehuai, Tao Zhu, Bo Yibo, Yang Shangkun and other comrades, and affirmed their contributions to the Party and the people. It points out that historical questions must be settled in accordance with the principles consistently advocated by Comrade Mao Zedong, that is, seeking truth from facts and correcting mistakes whenever discovered. Only by firmly rejecting false charges, correcting wrong sentences and rehabilitating the victims of frame-ups can the unity of the Party and the people be consolidated and the high prestige of the Party and Comrade Mao Zedong upheld. This task must be fulfilled resolutely without any relaxation after the mass movement to expose and criticize the "Gang of Four" ends. The session unanimously agrees that the adoption of these steps is in itself an example of grasping the scientific system of Mao Zedong Thought comprehensively and accurately and holding high the banner of Chairman Mao.

The session holds that the past practice of setting up special-case groups to examine cadres without Party and mass supervision had great disadvantages and must be abolished once and for all.

The session held a serious discussion on the question of democracy and the legal system. It holds that socialist modernization requires centralized leadership and strict implementation of various rules and regulations and observance of labour discipline. Bourgeois factionalism and anarchism must be firmly opposed. But the correct concentration of ideas is possible only when there is full democracy. Since for a period in the past democratic centralism was not carried out in the true sense, centralism being divorced from democracy and there being too little democracy, it is necessary to lay particular emphasis on democracy at present, and on the dialectical relationship between democracy and centralism, so as to make the mass line the foundation of the Party's centralized leadership and the effective direction of the organizations of production. In ideological and political life among the ranks of the people, only democracy is permissible and not suppression or persecution. It is essential to reiterate the "principle of three nots": not seizing on other's faults, not putting labels on people and not using the big stick. Leadership at all levels should be good at concentrating the correct ideas of the masses and making appropriate explanation and persuasion in dealing with incorrect ideas. The constitutional rights of citizens must be resolutely protected and no one has the right to infringe upon them.

In order to safeguard people's democracy, it is imperative to strengthen the socialist legal system so that democracy is systematized and written into law in such a way as to ensure the stability, continuity and full authority of this democratic system and these laws; there must be laws for people to follow, these laws must be observed, their enforcement must be strict and law breakers must be dealt with. From now on, legislative work should have an important place on the agenda of the National People's Congress and its Standing Committee. Procuratorial and judicial organizations must maintain their independence as is appropriate; they must faithfully abide by the laws, rules and regulations, serve the people's interests, keep to the facts; guarantee the equality of all people before the people's laws and deny anyone the privilege of being above the law.

(4)

The session had a thoroughgoing discussion on continuing to inherit and bring into full play the Marxist style of study advocated by Comrade Mao Zedong, that is, upholding a materialist ideological line. The session unanimously agrees that only if comrades of the whole Party and the people of the whole country, under the guidance of Marxism-Leninism-Mao Zedong Thought, emancipate their thinking, dedicate themselves to the study of new circumstances, things and questions, and uphold the principle of seeking truth from facts, of proceeding from reality and of linking theory with practice can our Party smoothly shift the focus of its work, correctly work out the concrete path, policies, methods and measures for carrying out the four modernizations and correctly transform those aspects of the relations of production and the superstructure that do not correspond with the swiftly developing productive forces.

In the past two years, through the deepening struggle to expose and criticize Lin Biao and the "Gang of Four," many issues of right and wrong in ideology and theory which they turned upside down have been straightened out. However, quite a number of comrades still do not dare to raise questions or deal with them in a straight-forward way. This situation came into being under specific historical conditions. The plenary session calls on comrades of the whole Party and the people of the whole country to continue to free themselves from the mental shackles imposed by Lin Biao and the "Gang of Four" and, at the same time, resolutely overcome the bureaucracy caused by the over-concentration of authority, the failure to reward or punish as deserved and the influence of petty producer mentality so as to help the people emancipate their minds and "start up the machinery."

The session highly evaluated the discussion of whether practice is the sole criterion for testing truth, noting that this is of far-reaching historic significance in encouraging comrades of the whole Party and the people of the whole country to emancipate their thinking and follow the correct ideological line. For a party, a country or a nation, if everything had to be done according to books and thinking became ossified, progress would become impossible, life itself would stop and the Party and country would perish.

The session emphatically points out that the great feats performed by Comrade Mao Zedong in protracted revolutionary struggle are indelible. Without his outstanding leadership and without Mao Zedong Thought, it is most likely that the Chinese revolution would not have been victorious up to the present. The Chinese people would still be living under the reactionary rule of imperialism, feudalism and bureaucrat-capitalism and our Party would still be struggling in the dark. Comrade Mao Zedong was a great Marxist. He always adopted the scientific attitude of "one divides into two" towards everyone, including himself. It would not be Marxist to demand that a revolutionary leader be free of all shortcomings and errors. It also would not conform to Comrade Mao Zedong's consistent evaluation of himself. The lofty task of the Party Central Committee on the theoretical front is to lead and educate the whole Party and the people of the whole country to recognize Comrade Mao Zedong's great feats in a historical and scientific perspective, comprehensively and correctly grasp the scientific system of Mao Zedong Thought and integrate the universal principles of Marxism-Leninism-Mao Zedong Thought with the concrete practice of socialist modernization and develop it under the new historical conditions.

The session holds that the Great Cultural Revolution should also be viewed historically, scientifically and in a down-to-earth way. Comrade Mao Zedong initiated this great revolution primarily in the light of the fact that the Soviet Union had turned revisionist and for the purpose of opposing revisionism and preventing its occurrence. As for the shortcomings and mistakes in the actual course of the revolution, they should be summed up at the appropriate time as experience and lessons so as to unify the views of the whole Party and the people of the whole country. However, there should be no haste about this. Shelving this problem will not prevent us from solving all other problems left over from past history in a down-to-earth manner, nor will it affect our concentration of efforts to speed up the four modernizations, the greatest historic task of the time.

(5)

Basing itself on the experience and lessons drawn from the history of our Party, the plenary session decided to improve the practice of democratic centralism within the Party, to amplify the Party rules and regulations and to enforce strict discipline in the Party.

At the session Comrade Hua Guofeng laid stress on the importance of collective leadership in the Party Central Committee and Party committees at all levels. He proposed that newspapers and publications throughout the country and works of literature and art give more praise to the worker-peasant-soldier masses, the Party and the revolutionaries of the older generation and give less publicity to any individual. The plenary session fully agreed with Comrade Hua Guofeng's proposal and evaluated it highly, regarding it as an important sign of improvement in democratic life within the Party. The plenary session reiterated Comrade Mao Zedong's consistent view that people in the Party should call each other "comrade" and not address each other by their official titles. No personal view by a Party member in a position of responsibility, including leading comrades of the Central Committee, is to be called an "instruction." The session points out that the Party members' right to raise criticism within the Party concerning the leadership at higher levels, up to Members of the Standing Committee of the Political Bureau of the Central Committee, must be guaranteed and any practice that does not conform to the Party's democratic centralism and the principle of collective leadership should be resolutely corrected.

The session holds that just as a country has its laws, the Party should have its rules and regulations. Observance of Party discipline by all Party members and Party cadres is a minimum requirement for restoring normal political life in the Party and the state. Leading Party cadres at all levels should take the lead in strictly observing Party discipline. Disciplinary measures should be taken against all violators of Party discipline with no exception, so that there is a clear distinction between merits and faults, awards and punishments, so that honesty prevails and bad tendencies are eliminated.

The plenary session elected a 100-member Central Commission for Inspecting Discipline, headed by Comrade Chen Yun. This is an important measure to guarantee implementation of the Party's political line. The fundamental task of the commission is to enforce Party rules and regulations and develop a good Party style.

The plenary session points out that the efforts made in the two years since the smashing of the "Gang of Four" have immensely strengthened unity and heightened the political consciousness of the whole Party, the whole army and the people of all China's nationalities. Comrade Hua Guofeng's call to "solve the problems while stabilizing the situation" and "further emancipate our minds, be more courageous and resourceful and step up the pace" has found a warm response in the hearts of the people. So long as the whole Party applies itself to the study of Marxism-Leninism-Mao Zedong Thought and the know-how needed for socialist modernization, continues to seek truth from facts and uphold the mass line, makes bold innovations and at the same time maintains an attitude of modesty and prudence, makes thorough investigation, gives careful direction and fights no battle ill-prepared or lacking assurance of victory, it can definitely speed up the realization of its general task for the new period, and no difficulty can stop the victorious advance of the Party and the people.

Next year will be the 30th anniversary of the founding of the great People's Republic of China. The Third Plenary Session of the 11th Central Committee issues the following call to all comrades in the Party, to commanders and fighters throughout the army, to workers, peasants and intellectuals of all nationalities throughout the country, to people in all political parties and to non-party democratic patriots: The best contribution to the 30th anniversary of the founding of our People's Republic will be to shift the emphasis of our work to socialist modernization and to achieve the expected success next year. Let us rally even more closely under the banner of Mao Zedong Thought, rally round the Party Central Committee headed by Comrade Hua Guofeng. and advance courageously to make a fundamental change in the backward state of our country so that it becomes a great, modern, socialist power.